Liberation Theologies
in the United States

Liberation Theologies in the United States

An Introduction

EDITED BY

Stacey M. Floyd-Thomas
and Anthony B. Pinn

NEW YORK UNIVERSITY PRESS
New York and London

NEW YORK UNIVERSITY PRESS
New York and London
www.nyupress.org

© 2010 by New York University

Library of Congress Cataloging-in-Publication Data

Liberation theologies in the United States : an introduction /
edited by Stacey M. Floyd-Thomas and Anthony B. Pinn.
p. cm.
Includes bibliographical references and index.
ISBN-13: 978-0-8147-2764-5 (cl : alk. paper)
ISBN-10: 0-8147-2764-6 (cl : alk. paper)
ISBN-13: 978-0-8147-2765-2 (pbk.   )
ISBN-10: 0-8147-2765-4 (pbk.   )
1. Liberation theology—United States. 2. United States—Church history—20th century.
3. United States—Church history—21st century. 4. Theology, Doctrinal—United States.
I. Floyd-Thomas, Stacey M., 1969- II.
Pinn, Anthony B.
BT83.57.L48155   2010
230'.04640973—dc22   2009038450

New York University Press books

Manufactured in the United States of America
c 10 9 8 7 6 5 4 3 2 1
p 10 9 8 7 6 5 4 3 2 1

*To
our forebears,
our faith communities, and
our fellow freedom fighters.*

Contents

Acknowledgments

This project required the support and assistance of many people, without whom this volume you now hold would still be nothing more than a few thoughts jotted down and stored in a file named "Liberation Theology BK." While we cannot in this confined space thank all who have played a role in bringing this book to you, we mention a few. The volume editors thank Jennifer Hammer, our editor at New York University Press, for shepherding this project through its various phases.

We also acknowledge and thank our fellow liberationists who, by example, have been an ongoing source of courage, collegiality, insight, strength, and wisdom. Thank you to James Cone, Katie Cannon, Peter Paris, M. Shawn Copeland, J. Deotis Roberts, Miguel De La Torre, Ada María Isasi-Díaz, Kwok Pui Lan, Kelly Brown Douglas, Linda Thomas, Sharon Welch, Mayra Rivera, Cheryl Kirk-Duggan, Cheryl Townsend Gilkes, and Guston Espinoza.

Our classes at Macalaster College, Virginia Tech University, Brite Divinity School, Rice University, and Vanderbilt Divinity School have given us the opportunity to work through the precepts of liberation theology in dialogue with concerned and interested parties. It is in the living laboratory of the classroom that we were able to work through the type of praxis required by liberation theology. We thank our students for their serious engagement of the material. It is their energy and commitment that inspired us to continue work on this project during some of the more difficult moments. In addition, we thank our diligent and astute research assistants, Chris M. Driscoll and Jacob Robinson, for their tireless work in the management of this text and the student assistance of Shauna St. Clair. Each of them is a budding liberationist in his and her own right, and we are grateful for their assistance with several stages of work on this volume.

In addition, we thank our families, especially the life and legacy of Anne H. Pinn, Mary Elizabeth and Sidney Underwood, Charles Floyd, Jerome Floyd, and Greg Floyd. And the presence of love poured out from Lillian

Floyd, Janet Floyd, Desrine Thomas, Sidney and Augusta Underwood, Raymond Pinn, Joyce Pinn, and Linda Bryant.

Our family circle has been extended to include the following friends, and we thank them for their support, solidarity, and encouragement: Ramón Rentas, Freddie D. Haynes III, Debra Peek-Haynes, Mark Toulouse, Eli Valentin, Caroline Levander, Renita Weems, Martin Espinosa, Forrest E. Harris, Herbert Marbury, Brad and Lazetta Braxton, Elaine Robinson, Alexander Byrd, Edward Cox, W. David Nelson, Teresa Fry Brown, and Duane and Taunja Belgrave.

Finally, we express our gratitude and thanks to Juan Floyd-Thomas.

Introduction

From the initial movement of European explorers forward, the creation of what became the United States entailed the destruction and rearrangement of cultures and worldviews. The United States has always been a contested terrain, forged through often violent and destructive sociopolitical arrangements. Markers of "difference" such as race and gender are embedded in the formation and development of this country. One cannot forget, however, that much of the struggle relating to this development took place within the framework of religious belief and commitment that informed, justified, and shaped the self-understanding of the nation.

In the nascent United States, religion and religious discourse would function not only as a safeguard of the status quo but also as a justifier of oppression. Yet while religious discourse buttressed oppressive activities such as the destruction of native populations and the enslavement of Africans, oppressed communities also made use of religion to critique and challenge this abuse. As demonstrated by the chapters in this volume, one of the most forceful presentations of this latter use of religion and religious thought takes the form of liberation theologies. Liberation theologies emerged in the late 20th century, concerned with the transformation of social existence (i.e., liberation) as a religious quest. They are contextual, tied to the experiences and needs of concrete communities. They are political in nature and religious in commitment. For most people in the United States, Latin American liberation theology is typically the first form of liberation theology of which they become aware. While the importance and influence of Latin American liberation theology cannot be ignored, within the U.S. context, liberation theology was first presented in the form of Black theology. It was James Cone's *Black Theology and Black Power* and *A Black Theology of Liberation* that set the initial tone for liberation theology in the United States as a systematic theology.[1]

What is often said of theology in general is certainly true of liberation theologies as well: theology is a second-order enterprise. That is, theology can be understood as a reflection on "faith-based" commitments and activities.

For the theologies outlined in this volume, this reflection entails attention to religious organization and practices, as well as sensitivity and response to political activism initiated within various communities of the oppressed. Theologians committed to the forms of liberation theology described in this book have developed their work as an attempt to respond religiously to the sociopolitical push for equality and full citizenship. It is this history of struggle, of effort to reenvision life in ways that promote justice and freedom, that on some level runs through the history of African Americans, Native Americans, Latino/as, Asian Americans, and other oppressed groups in the United States.

Historian Ronald Takaki with great skill and insight reflects on the historical and political links among the various racial groups that comprise the United States, lending meaning to the phrase "multicultural America." "America," Takaki remarks, "has been racially diverse since our very beginning on the Virginia shore, and this reality is increasingly becoming visible and ubiquitous."[2] This shared historical reality and context has fostered a shared question: What does it mean to live with justice and in freedom?

While the communities represented in this book have long histories of struggle against injustice that reach back to the start of the Modern period and its various developments—colonization, the African slave trade, and so on—much of the context for the liberation theologies developed within these communities is lodged in the political activism of the 20th century. In fact, the 20th century produced the "perfect storm" of political protest, and these developments were not lost on the religiously and theologically minded.

Political Movement: Contexts for Liberation Theologies

The civil rights movement harnessed the energy and insights regarding religion and justice developed over the course of centuries within African American communities. Martin Luther King Jr. and others associated with this movement echoed the interests and commitments of African American religionists of an earlier age, such as David Walker, Maria Stewart, and others. Beginning in the 1950s as a protest against discrimination, much of the civil rights movement, drawing from the social gospel movement, framed its activities with a Christianity-centered demand for transformation. While some raised questions concerning whether religion could actually be used for such "secular" purposes, some academics such as James Cone, Pauli Murray, and J. Deotis Roberts demanded such a connection and gave attention to theological explanation of the call for justice as a mark of proper religiosity.

These thinkers, however, were forced to not simply wrestle with civil rights within the context of the King-identified movement. They were also confronted by those disillusioned with the civil rights movement, those who called for "Black power" as the proper alternative. The latter did not negate the possibility of violence as a legitimate response to injustice, and they demanded a critique of Christianity as opposed to the assumption that it held liberative merit. In response, theologians and other religionists committed to both social transformation and their Christian faith worked to concretely link the two by arguing for the revolutionary nature of the Christian gospel as exemplified by the social critique offered by Jesus Christ. They would articulate this perspective within the context of what they called "Black theology."

In part inspired by Black power, and wrestling with concerns with oppressive U.S. policies, Hispanics organized in the 1960s in response to proposed restrictions on immigration. First associated with the somewhat militant activism of Mexican Americans, "Brown power" marked an effort to carve out healthy life options and robust rights for Hispanic Americans. Organizations such as the Mexican-American Political Association and the Crusade for Justice worked to secure political power as a means by which to change the dynamics of life for Hispanic Americans by increasing job opportunities, improving public education, and fostering the construction of acceptable housing options. The Brown Berets in Los Angeles made use of an aesthetic and agenda similar to that of the Black Panther Party and its expression of Black power.[3] And just as Black power and its push for restoration of Black culture informed the development of Black studies programs, organizations for the advancement of Hispanics also nurtured the development of university programs related to Hispanic culture.[4] Finally, one cannot forget the efforts of César Chávez to organize Mexican American laborers, which played a major and undeniable role in U.S. agriculture.

Although first noted in terms of Mexican Americans, Hispanic sociopolitical activism also came to include efforts within Puerto Rican communities. The connection between Puerto Rico and the mainland United States resulted in a rather tense relationship between issues of race/racism and class. For many Puerto Ricans, the demands of African Americans related to race-based discrimination did not fully capture their connection to the United States, and the dilemma of migrant workers from Mexico did not mirror the economic woes of Puerto Ricans. Nonetheless, as of the 1960s, Puerto Ricans began to organize around issues of education and political power. The status of Puerto Rico as a commonwealth gave the island little power within

U.S. politics and, as a result, served as a source of protest and activism. To address this situation, some Puerto Rican activists called for the island's independence from the United States (e.g., "Free Puerto Rico Now") as the only way to secure a cultural-political identity not dwarfed and dominated by the wants and needs of a colonizing United States. It is within the context of identity formation and political debate marking the efforts of Mexican Americans, Puerto Ricans, and other Hispanics that Latino and Latina theologies have developed as religious responses to existential crises.

During the same time, the civil rights movement addressed the demands of African Americans, and activities such as those of the American Indian Movement marked the 20th-century incarnation of a long and sustained critique of the oppression of American Indians and drew insights from other protest movements in the United States and abroad.[5] Broken deals and the disregard of other political promises met organized resistance against efforts to assimilate American Indians. According to historian James Olson, the transformations of the mid-20th century and the brewing protest altered characteristics of these efforts in that American Indians organizing for their own welfare (e.g., the National Congress of American Indians) replaced liberal whites working on behalf of American Indians. The protest generated during this period of the 1940s and 1950s was given an even greater radical edge during the 1960s and 1970s through developments such as the "Red power movement."[6] This movement, associated with what was called the "new tribalism," involved an effort to create new approaches to the preservation of Indian rights and access to land.[7] In some instances, efforts resembled those of the civil rights movement in that an attempt was made to secure unhindered voting rights. This endeavor was certainly the concern of the American Indian Movement for Equal Rights during the height of its activism in the 1970s and early 1980s. Aggressive activity resulted in the Red power movement gaining victories with respect to issues such as treaty rights (e.g., fishing and hunting rights) and the return of land taken from American Indians over the centuries. Through this work, a strong and independent Indian identity reemerged.[8]

Attention to American Indian activities must include mention of the American Indian Movement (AIM), founded in the late 1960s in Minnesota. Expanding well beyond its place of origin, AIM worked to address what it considered unreasonable police activity in Indian areas, and it organized activities through which to demand greater sovereignty for tribes and the end of state laws that restricted Indian hunting and fishing rights. It is fair to say that the importance of spirituality was not lost on the activists. For example, concern for the integrity of American Indian life and identity, and the role of traditional spirituality in the fostering of this integrity, as well as the need to recognize and critique the destructive dimensions of Christianity, would inform the development of what some call Native American theology.

Beginning in the 1800s, Asians migrated to the United States in search of economic opportunity and political "freedom" based on tales of potential wealth available in California to those willing to work hard.[9] These early numbers were typically Chinese; Japan did not approve migration of its citizens until the end of the 19th and the beginning of the 20th century.[10] Koreans were also brought to the United States as a source of labor in the 20th century. In all, a somewhat diverse Asian American population would develop over the course of two centuries. As was the case with other racial groups, however, Asians would discover a less than welcoming environment expressed during the 19th century in limited opportunities, restrictions on migration, and harsh treatment; in the 20th century, this was played out most graphically in the internment camps of World War II. Struggle for opportunity and full participation in the life of the country developed early. But as with the other communities discussed in this volume, this struggle for opportunity took on a particular character during the late 20th century. The overlap and synergy between late-20th-century struggles of social transformation continue in the Asian American context, where the Black liberation ideology informed their movement and its demand for power and justice. What is interesting, however, is that 1968 marked a major downturn for the African American civil rights struggle, yet it frames what some argue is the first instance of organized protest on the part of Asian Americans. That year the Third World Liberation Front, which included Asian Americans, demanded the inclusion of ethnic studies at San Francisco State University.[11]

The energy and determination of the Asian Americans participating in the strike that sought to instill ethnic studies in the university was mirrored in the community organizations and other activism strategies initiated by Asian Americans elsewhere in the United States. Although activism would hit a rough patch during the 1970s and 1980s, this slowdown did not mark the end of organized struggle for social transformation. According to Asian American studies scholar Glenn Omatsu, the work toward a better life continued in that

Japanese Americans joined together to win redress and reparations. Filipino Americans rallied in solidarity with the "People Power" movement in the Philippines to topple the powerful Marcos dictatorship. Chinese

Americans created new political alignments and mobilized community support for the pro-democracy struggle in China. Korean Americans responded to the massacre of civilians by the South Korean dictatorship in Kwangjuu with massive demonstrations and relief efforts, and established an important network of organizations in America, including Young Koreans United.[12]

While hitting high and low points, activism continued into the 1990s and the early 21st century through local organizations, such as the Korean Immigrant Worker Advocates in Los Angeles, that work to improve the economic and political options for Asian American workers.

In rethinking the contours of feminist history, it becomes apparent that the feminist project for women's empowerment was always infused with an expression of alliance to the project of Black racial equality. As a project for women's rights, feminism in its inception was a political endeavor fueled by the real life experiences of women who saw that the only way to attain their full identity as citizens was to make the personal political. Shifting the frame of reference for what a woman's place was in society in such a way that the status quo would always be contested and somehow less familiar, the political delineations and epistemological foundations of feminism caused waves in the otherwise still waters of the patriarchal status quo. Over a period of some 150 uphill years, feminism has evolved in three waves.

The sociopolitical climate that feminists in the first wave faced involved their alliances with the abolition movement. Realizing the marginalization they had experienced as they were fighting for the liberation of the enslaved Black populus, what resulted was the organization of various conventions during which the demand for full inclusion in the life of the nation, including the right to vote, was articulated and given public form. This was followed some time later, in the 1960s, by attention to the intersections of women's rights and the civil rights movement. Having learned from their first wave foremothers the importance of forming political alliances, second wave feminists came to the struggle equipped with the knowledge of coalition building. They realized that they needed the identity politics of others to provide a language to render intelligible the meaning of their struggle and to ensure, therefore, the support and outcome of their political standpoint and intent of liberation. Although second wave feminists benefited from their alliance with civil rights activists, the relationship was not reciprocal. This lack of mutuality was critiqued by Black women who had assumed allegiances with second wave feminism. The relationship between second wave and third wave feminism was solely generational, as it would privilege the dominant group's experience of being in any particular "generation."

The term "third wave" was used first by women of color in the late 1980s to position themselves outside of the second wave. The rise of third wave feminism can be attributed to reactions to public policy being made with regard to women's bodies, particularly concerning abortion rights, the threat of AIDS, and sexual harassment and rape. Not distancing itself from the goals and critiques of its second wave counterpart, third wave feminism sought diligently to rid American society of the structures of sexist oppression and the misogynist mentalities and ideologies that oppressed and exploited women in the United States. In addition, third wave feminists also enunciated an attack against all oppressions that confronted women, such as sexism, heterosexism, classism, and racism.[13]

Gay, lesbian, and transgender activists also tackle the heterosexism critiqued by the feminist movement. It was during the 1970s, according to historian Howard Zinn, that gay and lesbian rights came to the forefront, as notions of sexuality and personal liberties were challenged and altered. During this period, when the United States was being forced by racial minorities and women to radically alter the meaning of freedom and citizenship, the "gay movement then became a visible presence in the nation, with parades, demonstrations, and campaigns for the elimination of discriminating statutes" based on sexual orientation.[14] Some argue that the first organization concerned with gay rights was the Mattachine Society founded in 1951; the organization Daughters of Bilitis, with a concern for the agenda of lesbians, was formed in 1955. While these organizations are important, they did not have the political orientation and concerns that would mark gay and lesbian rights activism as of the 1970s. In part, this shift toward a more overtly political agenda stems from the successes of the civil rights movement in forcing legislation meant to safeguard civil rights.[15]

Although lesbians were overtly involved in the feminist movement as of its second wave, a widely recognized marker of this shift stems from an event at the Stonewall Inn located in New York City's Greenwich Village. In 1969, the police raided the bar, but rather than putting up with the abuse and harassment, as had been the norm up to that point, those in the bar fought back. The night after this event, hundreds gathered in Greenwich Village confronting the police and yelling "Gay Power!"[16] Fighting police brutality, exemplified by the Stonewall event, sparked the emergence of numerous organizations concerned with issues of sexual orientation and political power, including the Gay Liberation Front. By the 1980s, there were hundreds of such organizations, some local and others national in scope and reach. These organizations fought for the rights of gays and lesbians and also challenged normative notions of social relationships, family structures, and the nature of moral and ethical existence. Part of this challenge, of course, had to involve an interrogation of the assumed biblical basis for discrimination against gays and lesbians.

Theologizing Activism

It is clear that the social movements discussed here overlap and are linked in terms of strategy and other elements. However, they also differ and disagree. For example, the feminist movement was at times critiqued for racism in light of its poor response to the plight of Black women. And the gay and lesbian movement often failed to recognize the nature of its own racism. In addition, African American activism generally did not perceive the manner in which discrimination based on sexual orientation affected and influenced their agenda and response to ideas of solidarity. In spite of areas of disagreement, what has been shared is the manner in which these modalities of activism have all spurred theological responses in the form of liberation theology.

Theologians from these various contexts and communities recognized the merit of political struggle and also wanted to maintain an allegiance to the best of their religious commitments. Doing so required a synergy of religious thought and political ideology, most often presented in terms of a social Christianity: an understanding that religious faith demands struggle against sociopolitical injustice. In short, "true" religion demands liberation. As suggested in the chapters in this volume, this shared concern for liberation across the communities reflected in this book is expressed in a variety of ways. Liberation theology is contextual; it is enacted within a particular context and reflects the concerns and needs of a particular community. That situatedness explains the areas of agreement and disagreement among the various theologies linked to the social movements outlined in the preceding section.

For example, for Black theology, liberation has only slowly moved from a preoccupation with race and racism to a larger agenda that includes other forms of oppression. Feminist theologians have been slow to think of liberation outside the context of gender discrimination. Asian American theologians critique racism, but in a way that does not mirror the black/white dichotomy that all too often informs Black theology. Womanist theology (a bourgeoning discourse within religious studies that is accountable to the lived realities and practices of Black women by providing theories and methodologies that seek to unmask, debunk, and disentangle the interlocking forces of racism, sexism, and classism) is a liberation theology that critiques the sexism of Black theologians and calls for greater attention to issues of gender and class; but womanist theologians have been slow to address in a sustained way issues of sexual orientation. Latino/a theology is often pulled in the direction of class analysis as found in the Latin American context, but race—in light of the various contexts represented, such as Cuba and Puerto Rico—is not consistently addressed. Finally, many Native Americans debate the merits of theological analysis, arguing that it is a European conceptual framework that does not allow for proper attention to traditional spirituality.

The shared theological vocabulary of liberation theologies is not limited to the notion of liberation but also includes a joint concern with rethinking the nature and meaning of sin, which comes to mean not merely personal flaw but also social failure in the forms of racism, classism, sexism, homophobia, and so on. Salvation, by extension, does not mean simply the restoration of the individual in relationship with God as best reflected in the acquisition of heaven. Instead, salvation, in its realized eschatology, has a more "earthy" meaning as it reflects the securing of healthy life options on Earth. Such a reenvisioning of salvation and sin are possible because God is understood as siding with those who are suffering oppression; in this view, Jesus Christ is seen as the best representation of God's commitment to the oppressed because, through Jesus, God physically positions God's self with humanity in human history. These are only a few examples of the ways in which vocabulary and grammar reflect a desire to bring the theological in line with pressing social realities and political needs, making certain that theology speaks to the questions and concerns of those who suffer by reflecting in the very articulation of theology the existential context of the people.

Recognizing the public nature of political protest marked by these movements, liberation theologians have acknowledged the need to make public their theological agendas. This has meant presenting their ideas and theological arguments within their religious communities, but it has also meant demanding serious attention to liberation theologies within academia. Liberation theologians write their books and articles, but they also teach these materials in their classrooms as part of the standard curriculum. From a very early stage of their theological work, they refused to allow the academic study of religion and theological studies to present only the perspective of European theological formulations as offered by figures such as Karl Barth, Paul Tillich, Reinhold Niebuhr, and a host of others.

It is important to note the manner in which liberation theologies in the United States distinguish themselves from the tradition as represented by figures such as those just named. But it is just as important to note that liberation theologians are typically trained in the writings of European and white (male) American thinkers, and their work reflects this training. In a more general sense, liberation theologies in the United States are part of the larger liberal theological development and debate that marks the latter half of the 20th century. Liberal theology and the liberal religion movement to which it corresponds attempted to bring theological inquiry and religious faith into line with the pressing sociopolitical issues of the 20th century.

Within the North American context, early liberal theological thought is associated with Boston during the mid-1700s. Against the highly spiritual and supernatural assertions of the Great Awakening, certain ministers in Boston (including Charles Chuancy and Ebenezer Gay) argued for a connection between Christian faith and the best of Enlightenment thought. They argued that a modern Christianity—one that embraced reason—would better serve the needs of 18th-century Christians. From Boston, liberal religion and its theological platform was spread by Unitarians and other liberal Christians who embraced this orientation. Without supernatural authority to support religiosity and theological assertions, its proponents worked through elements of Christian faith in ways that kept Christians sensitive to the sociohistorical, political, and scientific realities of life. For example, evolution, a challenge to many, was seen by religious liberals as expressive of the unity of all life consistent with a Christian framework. That is, while rejecting a more general assumption that nature has "fangs," many liberal theologians and religionists argued that science, including evolutionary theory, did not destroy the Christian faith. Rather, it spoke to the workings of divine intelligence. Furthermore, in the teachings of liberal thinkers, Christianity was valued for its ethical and moral implications as opposed to its more fantastic claims, and human experience was seen as having fundamental importance as a source for religious understanding and theological inquiry.[17]

To be Christlike, then, involved a commitment to improving the historical arrangement of existence. Evangelical commitments of social gospelers entailed a requirement to spread the "good news" of Christ and salvation history, but in a way not disconnected from human history and pressing human need. Salvation in this regard had social-political and economic connotations, being both individually felt and communally enacted by its very nature. The kingdom of God was understood to entail a transformed society in which healthy life options reign. Such a theological perspective drew heavily from an understanding of the Christ-event as primarily concerned with ministry, as opposed to argumentation over the supernatural connotations of resurrection. In essence, Jesus is what he did, and Christians are to follow the example of his ethical ministry.[18] Liberal religion and liberal theology pushed for a democratic society premised on a sense of justice as Christian virtue.[19]

Even a quick read of the following chapters will suggest some overlap between this basic framework of liberal theology and liberation theologies. What the latter offer, however, is a corrective to liberal theology by bringing to the forefront a more complex and layered understanding of the nature and meaning of suffering. It maintains the commitment to human activity in the world, along with a preoccupation with an Earth-concerned approach to religious life and reflection on religious life. Liberation theologies have attempted to address the issues confronting their communities, but the work of theology must also be comprehensible by those who do not inhabit the social locations and do not share the experiences of the communities of concern represented in and by each liberation theology. It is this need to make the concerns, demands, and perspectives of liberation theologies available beyond their communities of interest that make this book necessary.

Why This Book?

Liberation theologies in the United States have matured over the past half-century, gaining both the attention of the publishing world and a solid place in the curriculum of seminaries and undergraduate and graduate institutions of higher learning. And while attention has been given to the genealogy of various forms of liberation theology, much of this work has revolved around introductory texts that treat each modality in isolation. This is certainly the case, for example, with the series of texts published by Orbis Books, including *Introducing Black Theology of Liberation*. Even surveys that seek to present a cross range of liberation theologies tend to understand these forms of theology within the context of a general framework of liberal religion.

In so doing, the unique theoretical and resource framework of liberation theologies such as womanist theology or Latina/o theology is lost amid a general ethos that theoretically privileges the dominant liberal and neoorthodox framework. This is problematic because liberation theologies such as feminist theology and those named above developed as a way to jettison the rather rigid and status quo concerns of the dominant theological paradigms in the United States.

In this volume, we provide a reader-friendly introduction to liberation theologies in the United States. Each chapter includes (1) the historical backdrop for the development of the particular theological approach in question; (2) a description of that particular theology; (3) sources for doing that form of theology; (4) an overview of the theoretical and methodological considerations at work; (5) a discussion of the ongoing issues of concern within that theological tradition; and (6) resources for further study.

The first element in this thematic structure, historical backdrop, situates the particular modality of liberation theology under discussion within sociopolitical and religious arrangements that inform its shape, purpose, and content. This is followed by information that will help readers understand the basic elements of that theological form: some of its defining characteristics, such as what it means when claiming to be a "liberation" theology. This is followed by a brief discussion of the resources used in constructing that particular theology, such as how scripture is used within that form of theology, how the Christian tradition is presented, and how the history and experiences of that particular community anchors that particular theology.

We recognize that these various liberation theologies all share at least implicit attention to questions related to what theology *is* and how one *does* theology. In short, these various theologies all wrestle with issues of theory and method. These questions are different from attention to the sources used in liberation theologies: theory relates to the ideas and overarching principles that shape how one thinks about the task of theology, and method relates to how the sources are "handled" or used in doing theology.

Because the contributors to this volume understand liberation theology as a continuously evolving and growing form of theological discourse, each chapter also contains a section addressing the ongoing challenges and concerns that inform that particular formation of liberation theology. Having generally described the historical experiences, sources, dispositions, and methodologies that inform these liberation theologies, each contributor invites readers to continue their exploration of liberation theology through further reading, and each chapter concludes with a list of sources of additional information readers might consider.

Concluding Considerations

The structure noted here points to a cohesive group of themes and topics through which to enter and evaluate liberation theologies in the United States in what we hope is a readily accessible fashion. However, we acknowledge that there are omissions and "thin" areas in this volume. Not all the possibilities are presented in these ten chapters, nor do the chapters cover all the possible theological angles represented in the various forms of liberation theology. Furthermore, the subheadings used by all the authors are meant to provide a similar organizational structure for the benefit of readers. However, readers will notice that the type and the detail of the information provided under each subheading vary from chapter to chapter. This inconsistency is unavoidable in that each liberation theology represented in the volume has its own growth pattern and prioritizes its own self-understanding and self-description. These theological traditions of liberation theology did not all develop at the same time and have not produced the same number of theologians. Such differences are reflected here in the way each chapter describes its subject. The ways in which and the reasons for which theology is done in each community determine how its history, sources, and theoretical and methodological concerns are expressed. Furthermore, there is also debate concerning the plausibility of a liberation theology within at least one of the communities. And this debate serves to add to the complexity and uneven development of liberation theologies in the United States.

But even these omissions within the volume and the variations among the information and presentation within the chapters provide an important lesson about liberation theologies: they are evolving and changing in light of existential conditions and concerns. Liberation theologies are uneven, flexible, and replete with shortcomings. Furthermore, they share numerous elements, but they are different because each represents a particular historical-cultural context.

This circumstance is not unique to this volume, nor is this reality unique to liberation theologies. All theological texts and all theological discourses are human discourses; they are the product of human inquiry, and they reflect the limits of human knowledge and imagination. Therefore, any attempt to address liberation theologies definitively would only further describe and reinforce such shortcomings.

There are important challenges in these chapters and opportunities to view the theological insights and concerns of numerous communities; in the process, readers are encouraged to bring their own theological perspectives into conversation with those in this book. Note the points at which you are in agreement with the theologians in this volume, and pay attention to the areas of disagreement. In short, enter into dialogue with the theological viewpoints presented. Ask questions as you read. Be influenced and affected by the insights offered in the following ten chapters. In short, engage.

1. James Cone, *Black Theology and Black Power* (Maryknoll, NY: Orbis, 1997 [originally published 1969]); Cone, *A Black Theology of Liberation,* 20th anny ed. (Maryknoll, NY: Orbis, 1990).

2. Ronald Takaki, *A Different Mirror: A History of Multicultural America* (New York: Little, Brown, 1993), 2.

3. Ian F. Haney Lopez, *Racism on Trial: The Chicano Fight for Justice* (Cambridge, MA: Harvard University Press, 2003), 178–204.

4. James S. Olson, *Equality Deferred: Race, Ethnicity, and Immigration in America Since 1945* (Belmont, CA: Thomson Wadsworth, 2003), 64–66.

5. Steve Talbot, *Roots of Oppression: The American Indian Question* (New York: International, 1981), 11.

6. Olson, *Equality Deferred,* 35–42.

7. S. Dale McLemore and Harriett D. Romo, *Racial and Ethnic Relations in America,* 5th ed. (Boston: Allyn and Bacon, 1998), 342.

8. Ibid., 72–73.

9. Takaki, *Different Mirror,* 191–204.

10. McLemore and Romo, *Racial and Ethnic Relations in America,* 158–159.

11. Glenn Omatsu, "The 'Four Prisons' and the Movements of Liberation: Asian American Activism from the 1960s to the 1990s," in *Asian American Politics: Law, Participation, and Policy,* ed. Don T. Nakanishi and James S. Lai (Boulder, CO: Rowman and Littlefield, 2003), 135–139.

12. Ibid., 145.

13. This section on the feminist movement is drawn from Ingrid Banks and Stacey Floyd-Thomas, "Feminist and Racial Formation in Three Waves," in *Black Renaissance/Renaissance Noire* 5, no. 2 (2004): 32–44; and Stacey Floyd-Thomas, "Feminism: An Overview," in *Encyclopedia of American Studies,* 4 vols. (New York: Grolier, 2001), 2:137–141.

14. Howard Zinn, *A People's History of the United States* (New York: Free Press, 1997), 454.

15. John D. Skrentny, *The Minority Rights Revolution* (Cambridge, MA: Belknap, 2002), 315–317.

16. Ibid., 316.

17. Gary Dorrien, *The Making of American Liberal Theology: Imagining Progressive Religion, 1805–1900* (Louisville, KY: Westminster John Knox, 2001).

18. Such thinking was not limited to liberal ministers within various denominations. Rather, with time, liberal theology would be represented in some of the most widely known schools of theology—such as the University of Chicago Divinity School, Boston University, and Union Theological Seminary (New York City). And, it would be debated in other locations.

19. Much of the information on liberal theology is drawn from Anthony B. Pinn, *Becoming "America's Problem Child": An Outline of Pauli Murray's Religious Thought and Theology* (Eugene, OR: Pickwick, 2008), chap. 3.

1

Black Theology

ANTHONY B. PINN

Historical Backdrop

The history of the United States involves the interplay of religion and political developments at numerous levels. From the religious rationale for the slave trade and the projection of the North American colonies as a "city on a hill," selected by God for political dominance and economic greatness, through 20th-century appeals to religion by politicians and the political participation of religious figures, the rhetoric of the United States has involved a certain religious ethos and has given some shape to the ethical and moral sensibilities in play during the development of this nation and its self-understanding.

In the case of African Americans, this synergy between religion and political forces has not always produced healthy life options and the ability to exercise "freedom" within the various venues of life. Rather, from the first arrival of Africans as indentured servants to their enslavement for better than three centuries, religion has often served as a mechanism by which to justify and sanction discriminatory patterns and practices. Colonists in the early years of European presence in North America often argued that Africans were properly used as chattel slaves in that biblical proclamations of their inferiority were merely played out through enslavement. To justify this stance, and maintain the illusion of proper Christian conduct, they often appealed to the story of Ham (Genesis), where Canaan, the son of Ham, is cursed because Ham saw his father (Noah) naked. The story goes, Ham sees his father drunk and naked and tells his brothers, who in turn cover their father. Upon awaking, Noah learns of his exposed state and Ham's viewing of him in that condition and punishes Ham's son, whose descendants are to become servants. Exegetes of the Hebrew Bible (or "Old Testament" as it is commonly called), who supported the institution of slavery, argued that modern Africans were the descendents of Ham and Canaan and therefore were slaves in keeping with the scriptural mandate. Others combined this Hebrew Bible account of servitude as divinely sanctioned with "New Testament" proclamations concerning the need for slaves to be obedient to earthly masters as unto God, as well as the recommendation by the Apostle Paul that a slave, in the epistle to Philemon, return to his master. In either case, historical context and the nature of social arrangements during the biblical period were overlooked, and religious commitment and biblical proclamations were used to justify sociopolitical discrimination based on race.

Even after the formal end of slavery during the 19th century, religious commitment usually tied to interpretations of sacred texts was used to justify continued patterns of discrimination such as formal and informal mechanisms of race-based restrictions on citizenship and civic opportunities in the form of what are commonly called "Jim Crow" and "Jane Crow" regulations that restricted certain services (e.g., the best sections of public transportation; public facilities such as diners and parks). White ministers and their churches often worked hand in hand with politicians to safeguard race-based discrimination, proclaiming on Sundays the moral and ethical "rightness" of separation of the races and the superiority of white Americans. Hate-based organizations such as the Ku Klux Klan, which monitored and worked to preserve the dominance of white Americans, considered themselves to be maintaining the Christian faith through their practices of intimidation and destruction. In fact, they did not see their activities as terroristic, nor did they understand themselves as doing harm. Rather, they thought of themselves as fighting off chaos and living out the best of the Christian tradition. Groups such as the Ku Klux Klan represent an extreme. Yet, it was consistently the case that religion was used as a way of sanctioning discriminatory practices in the United States.

Nonetheless, it would be false to conclude that an appeal to religion as justification for oppressive ideas and actions went without challenge. To the contrary, many African Americans (and white Americans) countered such arguments with a different reading of scripture and a different understanding of Christianity, one that made justice and equality the benchmark of Christian faith and conduct. During the early years of Black churches, for instance, ministers such as Richard Allen (the first bishop of the oldest African American denomination—the African Methodist Episcopal Church) argued in the 1700s for an end to slavery and the proper treatment of African Americans as children of God.

Bishop Allen's rhetoric was rather moderate in tone, but others were more forceful. In some instances, enslaved Africans used violence as a way to secure their freedom, in the process arguing that commitment to God required the securing of their liberation even if this meant killing white slaveholders. For example, Nat Turner (in 1831), Denmark Vessey (plotting before the July 14, 1822, rebellion started), and Gabriel Prosser (when the 1800 planned revolt was discovered and prevented) organized slave rebellions based on the assumption that God (vis-à-vis the Christian faith) required freedom and an end to discriminatory practices based on race. Although unsuccessful, these planned rebellions marked an alternate interpretation of the Christian faith, one by which destruction, not maintenance, of the status quo was the proper ethical and moral stance. During the period of slavery, African American women within churches also pushed for sociopolitical change. Maria Stewart, for instance, who was the first African American women to lecture publicly on political matters, in 1831 argued in Boston for increased participation of African Americans in the life of the United States, and she justified her critique of injustice through appeal to the teachings of Jesus.

After slavery's end, ongoing discrimination spurred African American Christians to continue to rethink the faith in ways that pushed for equality. Community leader and journalist Ida B. Wells-Barnett exposed lynching in the United States to an international audience and demanded through her lectures and writings greater rights for African Americans. Henry McNeal Turner, one of the most radical clergy persons of the late 19th and early 20th centuries, exemplifies this demand for sociopolitical transformation in the name of religion. He used the scriptural mandate for justice one finds in the Hebrew Bible and the teachings of Jesus the Christ in the New Testament to fight against modern injustice. Turner critiqued white and African American Christians alike who did not actively pursue a transformed society.

One should not believe, however, that African Americans consistently used Christianity as a weapon against injustice. To the contrary, historian Gayraud Wilmore argues for a substantial period of time during which many African American churches turned inward, demonstrating more concern with an abstract spiritualized gospel of individual salvation than with an interpretation of the gospel committed to social transformation as a marker of Christian commitment. Wilmore refers to this shift away from a "this-worldly" Christianity to an "other-worldly" orientation as the deradicalization of Black religion (and the de-Christianization of radicalism). Historically situated during the Great Migration (the mass movement of African Americans from the end of slavery through the middle of the 20th century to southern and northern cities), the deradicalization of Christianity within many African American churches meant somewhat isolated attention to issues of justice as a religious concern. Such, according to Wilmore, would be the case until the emergence of the civil rights movement beginning in the 1950s.

While figures such as Wells-Barnett and Turner hold important places in the legacy of religiously based social activism in the United States, perhaps the best-known example of Christianity used to fight injustice is found within the context of the late-20th-century civil rights movement, particularly in the ministry of Martin Luther King Jr. and the religiously based social activism of Malcolm X. Both King and Malcolm X understood their work for socio-political transformation as an outgrowth of their religious commitments. For King, the teachings and ministry of Jesus required of his followers continued effort to make life better for those who suffered most from injustice. And Malcolm X, particularly as he moved away from the Nation of Islam in 1963, saw Islam's ethical and moral commitments as directly transferable to activism. Yet no one who reads their writings would confuse the two. King and Malcolm X had radically different approaches to social transformation: King favored nonviolent direct action based on the transforming power of love for others consistent with God's love for all, whereas Malcolm X's approach was more rhetorically aggressive in that he saw nonviolent direct action and its commitment to countering violence with love and forgiveness as foolhardy. He did not rule out violence as an option, and he was more critical than King of one's ability to appeal to the moral conscience of a society grounded in inequality.

Both men, their rhetoric and practices, received a great deal of media attention and gained significant followings from those who attempted to model their teachings. It was an effort to create synergy between the Christian commitments of King and the social critique of Malcolm X that provided the framework for the emergence of Black theology in the late 1960s: How does one remain true to the best of the Christian faith while embracing the anger generated by injustice? How does one maintain the optimism embedded in Christianity and consistently critique white supremacy in all its forms? What is the proper balancing act, the best way to both critique and embrace King's philosophy and to critique and embrace Malcolm X's philosophy? In short, how does one maintain the relevance of one's faith within a context of absurdity and racial strife?

A group of ministers and academics began wrestling with these and related questions in the mid-1960s, and what eventually emerged was a new form of liberal theology—Black theology—that maintained the best of the Christian faith, as well as a critique of injustice and its religious supports. Black theology gave religious articulation to a synergy between Christian wings of the civil rights movement and the Black power movement.

Description

One of the first substantive attempts to appreciate and articulate the connections between Christianity and the demand for Black power against racial discrimination was the National Committee of Negro Churchmen's (NCNC) full-page statement in the *New York Times* on July 31, 1966.[1] This document addressed four groups: national leaders, white churchmen, Black citizens, and mass media. In each case, an appeal was made for rethinking the power dynamics that bred pain and suffering within African American communities. The riots and other events of the 1960s were presented as a minor threat to national security, the major threat being a failure of the nation to live in accordance with God's demand for justice and righteousness. A move into the full expression of God's will could not be achieved through rhetorical commitments to love (i.e., acceptance of the status quo) and appeals to U.S. individualism over community. In short, "powerlessness," as the statement goes, "breeds a race of beggars. We are faced now with a situation where conscienceless power meets powerless conscience, threatening the very foundations of our nation."[2] The oppressed, NCNC argued, must secure power in order to fully participate in the important processes of the nation, and securing such power was consistent with the demands of the Christian faith.

This pronouncement in the *New York Times* was followed by other declarations, including the "Black Manifesto" authored by the national Black Economic Development Conference (Detroit, April 26, 1969) and presented at Riverside Church in New York City by James Forman. This document called for white churches and others who have benefited from the oppression of African Americans to make funds available that would be used to support the economic growth of African American communities. Fueled by events—most notably the assassination of King in 1968—and rhetorically powerful statements such as the Black Manifesto, Black clergy wrestling with the relevance of the Christian gospel were confronted in a manner that could not be ignored. So, in response, the National Committee of Black Churchmen (formerly NCNC) began articulating a theological response, one that summed up the frustration and anger over injustice, the importance of Black consciousness, and the demands of the Christian faith.

The name given this theology was "Black theology." This new theological development, with its unapologetic focus on race and racism, did not go unnoticed in churches and organizations of professional scholars of religion. It challenged the very notion that theology (and the interpretation of the gospel) was universal: applicable to all. The name and pronouncement of this new form of liberal theology—a theology committed to addressing lived experience and human need—promoted an appreciation for the particular socioeconomic, political, and racial context in which theology is done:

> Black theology is a theology of black liberation. It seeks to plumb the black condition in the light of God's revelation in Jesus Christ, so that the black community can see that the gospel is commensurate with the achievement of black humanity. Black Theology is a theology of "blackness." It is the affirmation of black humanity that emancipates black people from white racism, thus providing authentic freedom for both white and black people. It affirms the humanity of white people in that it says No to the encroachment of white oppression. The message of liberation is the revelation of God as revealed in the incarnation of Jesus Christ. Freedom IS the gospel.[3]

Furthermore,

> The word "Black" in the phrase was defined by the life and teachings of Malcolm X—culturally and politically embodied in the Black Power Movement. The term "theology" was influenced by the life and teachings of Martin Luther King, Jr.,—religiously and politically embodied in the Black Church and the Civil Rights Movement. The word "liberation" was derived from the past and contemporary struggles for political freedom and the biblical story of the Exodus, as defined by the Black religious experience in the United States.[4]

The same year that this statement on Black theology was issued, James H. Cone published the first full-length discussion—*Black Theology and Black Power* (1969). This book was quickly followed by *A Black Theology of Liberation* (1970), the first systematic liberation theology ever published in English. In these two books, Cone, the first of the professional Black theologians of liberation, theologically links the plight of African Americans and God's commitments as expressed in scripture. Perhaps the most challenging component of Cone's theology is the assertion of God's ontological blackness. In other words, God is so strongly identified with the oppressed—in this case, African Americans—that God's very being is defined by this relationship: "The blackness of God means that God has made the oppressed condition God's own condition."[5] God becomes defined by this Blackness—becomes one with the Black oppressed—and this is the centerpiece of Black theology. "There is no place in black theology," Cone argues, "for a color-less God in a society where human beings suffer precisely because of their color."[6] By extension, commitment to God's will as expressed in the Christian faith requires Christians to maintain this same strong connection to the oppressed. Hence, true Christians in the context of the United States are also ontologically Black.

This doctrine of God tied to African Americans oppressed because of race requires as strong a statement concerning the nature and meaning of the Christ-event—of Jesus—as the primary mode of God's interaction with humans within history. For Cone, and consistent with scripture as he understands it, Jesus is the Black Messiah: a revolutionary concerned with the destruction of injustice. Hence, as one should assume, only a Black Jesus can be associated with an ontologically Black God. From Cones's perspective, depiction of the white Jesus is so intimately connected historically with white supremacy and the oppression of people of color that it is of no use to those seeking freedom. In a word, a rather strong word, "If Jesus the Christ is white and not black, he is an oppressor, and we must kill him."[7] Put differently, conceptions of Jesus as white and all the sociopolitical baggage associated with that depiction of the divine manifest in humanity mean they are of no value to those who suffer because of their race. And, what is more, if such a white Jesus is the only option, the oppressed are better off without him. Fortunately, this is not the case: the "Black Christ" is alive and well, working with the oppressed and in him reflecting God's commitment to liberation as a historical happening. As in the New Testament, for Black theology, Jesus is found where people suffer, and his presence speaks to a divine demand for their liberation.

Doctrine of God and Christology (the nature and meaning of Jesus the Christ) in Black theology begs the question of humanity. In the form of a question—What is the nature, purpose, and meaning of humanity?—Black theology gives primary attention to an understanding of humanity as containing the image of God (*imago dei*). That is, humans were created by God and are meant for freedom, not oppression. Furthermore, this is not simply a matter of individual success. Instead, humanity is meant to enjoy community—relationship with others—and it is in the context of community that freedom and liberation are most forcefully and fruitfully acknowledged and expressed. Indeed, humans must enjoy development as individuals within the context of healthy community. One must also acknowledge, Black theology is wont to inform, that humans are capable of, and in fact prone to, misdeeds, to oppression and injustice. Here the concern is not with individual misdoing such as lying but with the manner in which humans participate in corporate or collective wrongdoing (e.g., racism and white supremacy) that hampers life options. Furthermore, African Americans who do not struggle for freedom, who surrender to racism, are also guilty of sin. On the one hand, white Americans sin by overemphasizing their importance (their humanity against the importance and value of others), and this is expressed by white supremacy and participation in racism. On the other hand, African Americans can sin by underestimating their importance, their humanity, and this is manifest through participation in one's oppression.

Those who read Black theology looking for discussion of salvation and heaven in deeply spiritual and nonhistorical terms will be greatly disappointed. There is nothing resembling an "other-worldly" orientation in Black theology. To the contrary, salvation is not seen as the individual's ability to connect with God through a surrender of sin and a proper Christian life without social consequences. Rather, salvation is understood as liberation: as the production of new sociopolitical and economic developments not marked by injustice and oppression. And heaven (or the kingdom of God) is associated with the historically situated society in which justice reigns. This perspective does not rule out hopefulness. It simply situates this hope within the context of historical developments and arrangements: "The future is still the future." According to Cone, "This means that black theology rejects elaborate speculations about the end. It is just this kind of speculation that led blacks to stake their whole existence on heaven—the scene of the whole company of the faithful with their long robes. Too much of this talk is not good for the revolution."[8]

Cone was not alone in this work; J. Deotis Roberts, Cecil Cone, Gayraud Wilmore, and William R. Jones, among others, also articulated a vision of Black theology. Roberts, for example, provided philosophical underpinning for Black theology and offered, in addition, a corrective to Cone's emphasis on liberation over reconciliation. For Roberts, the will of God at work in the world required a simultaneous commitment to liberating African Americans and reconciling them with white Americans. According to Roberts, one could not move in a linear fashion from liberation to reconciliation because the two are mutually dependent. The emphasis remained on race, but in a way that emphasized mutuality and dialogical developments. The latter concern was emphasized in texts dealing with a comparative analysis of Black theology and other forms of liberation theology such as South American liberation theology.

Roberts's emphasis on synergy between liberation and reconciliation was not the only challenge to the trajectory of Black theology marked by Cone's work. Cone's brother, Cecil Cone, and Gayraud Wilmore raised questions concerning the very nature of Black theology: What is *Black* about *black* theology? Both suggested that Black theology was too heavily indebted to the thought and conceptual frameworks of European theologians such as Karl Barth—whom Cone referenced often in his early writings. From their perspective, Black theology seemed nothing more than traditional, Europe-centered theology with the rhetoric of Blackness awkwardly layered on top. Hence, it did not seem organic to African Americans, drawn from their thought, practice, and intellectual traditions. Both men, in their own way, pushed for a change in orientation. They noted a need to turn attention to sources for theological thinking found within traditions of African Ameri-can thought and practice. For example, Wilmore offered traditional Afri-can practices, ethical and religious, as a potential source for doing theology. Cecil Cone suggested attention to the protest thought of African Americans articulated and preserved over the centuries as the basis for Black theology. In short, both suggested that Black theology's future success depended on its ability to more intimately connect to the thought and practices of Afri-can Americans: to move away from materials gathered from formal training within the dominant (and, from their perspective, dangerous) tradition and develop a theology that was organic and consistent with the language and concerns of African Americans.

While the correctives offered by Roberts, Cecil Cone, and Wilmore do not challenge the basic principles of Black theology and the Christian tradition to which it is wed, instead of simply attempting to further express its potential more fully, William Jones posed a challenge to the underlying assumptions guiding Black theology. Up to 1973, when Jones published *Is God a White Racist? A Preamble to Black Theology,* it was assumed by Black theologians of liberation that God sided with the oppressed in the struggle for freedom and would assist them in making this freedom felt within the realm of human history. That is, they argued for a good, loving, kind, just, and compassionate God who guaranteed success for those who followed God's will and fought for the welfare of those who suffer. However, Jones raised questions: What is the historical evidence for such a God? How does one explain the contin-ued suffering of the oppressed in spite of assistance from a powerful God? In essence, doesn't the continued oppression of African Americans just as easily suggest that God is concerned with their destruction and the success of white Americans?

Jones challenged the response to moral evil offered by Black theology in the form of theodicy (which addresses the question of how one speaks to the justice of God in light of human suffering). Black theologians were loyal to the idea of a God working for good, one whose biblical record suggested an end to unjust suffering as consistent with God's will. Jones cut this perspective to the quick and in its place offered a theological system that emphasized human accountability and responsibility for moral evil and downplayed the work of God in this area. He named this approach "humanocentric theism." Black theologians objected to Jones's rejection of Christianity as they understood and embraced it, but they had to respond and more sharply address the implication of their commitment to a certain understanding of God in light of continuing modalities of oppression.

In spite of this challenge and the correctives offered by figures such as Roberts, James Cone's take on Black theology has dominated, in part because he was one of few Black theologians working with graduate students and thereby producing the next generation of Black theologians committed to his theological agenda. This "second generation" of Black theologians maintained the focus put in place during the 1970s, with little movement outside the Christian orientation and commitment to economic and political justice for the oppressed expressed earlier. In fact, in reading the work of second-generation theologians like Dwight Hopkins and James Evans, one hears echoed the theological platform that informed Cone's two major texts early in Black theology's development. According to most, Black theology is currently in its third generational incarnation, but what was said of the second generation is for the most part true for the third.[9] This is not to say that there have been no innovations, that second-generation theologians have not made their mark on this enterprise. Rather, it is to say that innovations, their particular take on the issues, fit firmly within the paradigms and conceptual frameworks inherited. God remains ontologically Black, with few exceptions; Jesus the Christ remains defined by ministry to the oppressed of society; humans are still defined by the image of God in them; and there is still little attention in most circles to "other-worldly" depictions of salvation and heaven. Rather than large shifts in Black theology's dominant discourse, there has been more attention given to the non-Protestant ways in which Black theology might develop.

Whereas Black theology during its first decade was defined by the assumption of Protestantism as the Christian orientation for African Americans, more recent work suggests the importance of both Protestantism and Roman Catholicism. Even so, this increased attention to a liberation theology agenda from the Roman Catholic perspective (representing some three million African Americans) involves only a slight shift in emphasis.[10] For example, liberation from socioeconomic and political oppression remains the focus of theological concern, and Jesus' ministry remains the litmus test for proper Christian conduct. However, Roman Catholic theologians do give more attention to the importance of Mary, consistent with Mariology as a Catholic focus, for an understanding of God's work within history.

Put in more general terms, there is some attention given to the religious pluralism marking African American communities, along with the need for Black theology to take seriously and respond to this diversity of religious commitment expressed by African Americans. Outside more work by Catholic theologians of Black liberation, some within Black theology have also turned attention to African-based religious traditions, Islam, and nontheistic orientations such as humanism as a religious basis for liberative theology. In spite of historian of religion Charles Long's three-decade push for a more general understanding of African American religion as a matter of ultimate concern not tied to a particular tradition, this emphasis on "non-Christian" orientation is a point of slow growth within Black theology because of a long-standing debate over the nature of theology, with most assuming it is by its very nature a theistic (and most properly Christian) enterprise. This premise is matched by a sociological assumption on the part of many within Black religious studies in general and Black theology in particular that the most significant and noteworthy religious orientation for African Americans over the centuries has been Christianity. Again, this orientation has been slow to change, but due to the work of theologians such as Josiah Young (an emphasis on Afrocentric resources) and Anthony Pinn ("non-Christian" orientations), to name only a couple, the necessity of a Christian framework for doing Black theology has been called into question, and alternate approaches to those proposed during the early years of Black theology have been put forth.[11]

In addition to rethinking the religious commitments marking Black theology, recent developments have raised questions concerning the nature of Blackness as an ontological category assumed in early formations of this theology. To be sure, the notion of ontological Blackness as articulated by Cone and embraced by a host of others limits the ways in which one can be authentic and authentically committed to the struggle for liberation. Blackness as defined by Black theology has tended to emphasize a certain relationship to lack of economic resources and a certain connection to African American culture. However, what of the middle-class person: Can this person be ontologically Black? Or, what about the gay or lesbian who is not typically mentioned within the context of Black theology: Is that person ontologically Black? Black theology has tended to assume the recognition of the truly Black person according to the essential nature of particular characteristics in ways that do not allow for much diversity of interests or concerns. Thus, from the perspective of some Black theologians like Victor Anderson, ontological Blackness denies African Americans the ability to exercise notions of liberation in a diverse manner: all African Americans are rendered the same, with the same interests, concerns, and relationships to the structures of society.

As noted here, certain changes have taken place within Black theology, but what has remained consistent over the better than three decades of its existence as a field of academic inquiry in universities and seminaries around the country is its male orientation. Indeed, Black theology has developed from the perspective of Black men and gives priority to the modes of oppression that affect them. Like the civil rights movement and the Black power movement that informed it, Black theology has concentrated on racism as the dominant mode of oppression. Only recently, in large part spurred by philosopher Cornel West, who introduced the social theory of Marxism to theological inquiry, has Black theology embraced class as an important and related mode of oppression. As Stacey Floyd-Thomas makes clear in her chapter in this book, Black theology has been even slower to give attention to sexism as a pressing issue of concern. Assuming that the correction of racism served as the linchpin for social transformation, Black theology has not tended to recognize the manner in which it privileged a male orientation and, in the process, has tended to ignore the modalities of oppression affecting more than one-half the African American population. Its language (e.g., God as "He") and orientation (e.g., framed by a male-dominated Black church tradition) betrayed a narrow agenda that was actually counterproductive.

While Rev. Dr. Pauli Murray[12] and others began pointing out this dilemma within the civil rights movement and the first several years of Black theology's existence, it was not until 1979, with the publication of an article by Jacquelyn Grant, one of James Cone's students, that the sexism of Black theology was acknowledged and noted for the contradiction it posed. Cone and others would begin to use inclusive language and address (at least in rhetoric) sexism as a problem internal to Black theology and as a major source of injustice on the societal level. In the mid-1980s, as Stacey Floyd-Thomas notes in her essay, through publications by Katie Geneva Cannon and Delores Williams, the critique of Black theology and the constructive work of Black women scholars of religion took on a name that spoke to its orientation: womanist ethics and womanist theology. Borrowing from Alice Walker's definition of "womanish," womanist thought marks perhaps one of the most innovative African American brands of theological work. While predominantly Christian in orientation, through attention to Alice Walker, womanist theologians have also given attention to issues of the environment and sexuality in important and groundbreaking ways. From that point forward, Black male theologians have worked mindful of the weblike nature of oppression and in dialogue with womanist scholars. Such collaborative posture is most obvious in the work of second- and third-generation Black theologians.

Sources

Black theology from its start argued for an approach that recognized theology as done within a particular cultural context. James Cone, J. Deotis Roberts, and others asserted that theological opinions were not universal but, rather, grew out of the thought and practice of particular communities and must reflect the existential context and needs of that community. Black theology argued that a theology appropriate for oppressed African Americans must draw from resources or source materials intimately connected to that community. Although there is no firm consensus on the matter, over time, a basic collection of sources for doing Black theology, with only slight variation, came to define much of what was published and includes the following: (1) African American experience and history, (2) the Christian tradition, (3) sacred texts, and (4) African American cultural production. All of these sources are read through an understanding of liberation as normative, as the standard expression of God's will for humanity. Mindful of this norm, sources are ranked and used, depending on how the particular theologian sees them as contributing to the push for liberation.

African American Experience and History

Beginning with the first formulations of a working Black theology, there has been a concern with using the "stories" and life circumstances of African Americans as raw material for doing theology. Theology was formulated in light of what African Americans have encountered in the world: it speaks to and from the vantage point of African American struggle for existence and advancement. In this way, it seeks to answer the questions African Americans ask concerning the divine in light of their existential condition. This is not a simple appeal to the activities and stories of individual African Americans. While individual "testimonies" (such as slave narratives) are important, Black theologians as part of their theological work have drawn lessons from the collective experiences of African Americans in chattel slavery, along with the various moments of struggle and happiness that mark their history. Black theology is formulated in such a way as to render African Americans subjects of history: to read their presence in North America from their perspective, as opposed to assuming the authority of the dominant account of life in the United States provided by the dominant culture. Black theology attempts to be historical in its outlook, paying attention to the various intellectual, historical, social, political, economic, and religious institutions and movements that have shaped African American life. It is not a theology based on abstractions but draws from and is guided by the concrete realities of African American existence in North America.

Christian Tradition

Most of those doing Black theology are Christian, and they shape their work in accordance with the teachings and practices of the best of the Christian faith. In general, they draw from the teachings, insights, and practices of Christianity as found within the writings of early church leaders such as St. Augustine, as well as the general ethos that marks the ministry of Jesus Christ as interpreted by the Christian church over the course of centuries. In particular, however, Black theology draws from the rich tradition of African American Christianity as expressed in the various denominations (e.g., African Methodist Episcopal Church; National Baptist Convention, USA; Church of God in Christ). One sees this influence in the frequent attention given to liberation themes in the writings and speeches of leaders from these various denominations, such as Bishop Henry McNeal Turner of the African Methodist Episcopal Church and Martin Luther King Jr. of the Progressive Baptist Convention.[13] Furthermore, the African American church tradition as a resource for doing Black theology is also played out by many through a long-standing effort to be personally involved in the life and inner workings of various African American denominations. Many proponents argue that Black theology is a church theology written by those who are intimately associated with the African American churches both as ordained ministers and as lay leaders. For example, James Cone is an ordained minister in the African Methodist Episcopal Church, Dwight Hopkins is an ordained Baptist minister, and James Evans is an ordained Baptist minister.

Sacred Texts

According to Black theologians working from the Christian tradition, the Bible serves as a significant resource for their work in that it outlines God's involvement with humanity and does so in a way that provides proper moral and ethical guidelines for life. Biblical stories in the Hebrew Bible and the New Testament have spoken in strong ways to an assurance that liberation is normative and that God works on behalf of suffering humanity. In scripture, Black theology finds revelation of God's self, or the historical markings of God's presence with humanity. African American Christians in general and Black Christian theologians in particular have not given equal attention to all biblical stories; in fact, they have found some of them problematic in that they do not clearly suggest the types of liberation themes and concerns they hold dear. Certain stories such as the Exodus account and the ministry of Jesus have been highlighted in African American Christian circles and in Black theology because of their clear statements concerning the evil nature of oppression and God's compassion and commitment to those suffering injustice.

By and large, Black theology does not take scripture literally; nor does it understand the Bible to be without errors—infallible. God, according to Black theologians, did not write the Bible. Rather, God used humans to record the materials that make up the Hebrew Bible and the New Testament. Hence, the Bible bears the marks of its historical and cultural context and reflects that context. And our interpretation and use of scripture must be mindful of this fact. The Bible provides life lessons—moral and ethical insights—that are gleaned from the various stories, but they are best secured and understood when scripture is engaged critically rather than being accepted as the literal word of God. From God's activities in the biblical world, we are able to gather some sense of God's intentions within the historical moment: "The meaning of scripture is not to be found in the words of scripture as such but only in its power to point beyond itself to the reality of God's revelation. . . . The Bible is inspired: by reading it a community can encounter the resurrected Jesus and thus be moved to risk everything for earthly freedom."[14]

African American Cultural Production

While African American scholars gave attention to the artistic production of African Americans as an important source for deep intellectual work long before the mid-20th century, scholars of Black religion have been a little slower to appreciate and unpack these materials. Yet, as of the 1970s, Black theologians have worked based on the premise that African Americans have expressed themselves religiously inside and outside the context of formal religious organizations and activities. The fourth and final resource for doing Black theology is the cultural production of African Americans: the literature, visual arts, expressive culture, music, and so on. Beginning with attention to the spirituals and the blues, mining them for their statements concerning the religious commitments of African Americans, Black theologians have also given attention to the slave narratives and other modalities of literary expression found within African American communities. Using these sources, Black theologians gauge and trace the religious sensibilities of African Americans outside the context of formal church leadership. For example, rather than simply privileging the sermons of famous religious leaders like Martin Luther King Jr., use of cultural production (commonly called popular culture) affords an opportunity to determine what the "masses" of African Americans understand and say about their religious lives.

Theoretical and Methodological Considerations

Sources for doing Black theology must be selected and used according to some set of guidelines, and this brings up the question of theory and method. What one says about the nature of Black religion and its resources is an issue of theory, and how one goes about using or applying resources is an issue of method.

For much of Black theology's history, issues of theory and method received little explicit attention. Instead, Black theologians concentrated on the urgency of struggle for liberation and often assumed that any formal and sustained attention to such issues was a luxury they did not possess. Most simply assumed a common understanding, a shared theory of African American religion, based on a shared Christian orientation. In short, they knew African American religion when they saw and experienced it. One notable exception during the early years of Black theologies development came from the challenges posed by Charles Long, who raised questions concerning the very nature and meaning of Black religion. Long argued for more explicit attention to a working theory of religion. Drawing from philosopher of religion and theologian Paul Tillich, Long suggested that Black religion could be described as the ultimate orientation for African Americans: the signs, symbols, language, rituals, and so on that African Americans use to make meaning and answer the large questions of existence.

While Long's position is noteworthy, few in Black theology have done more than quote his perspective. Anthony Pinn, however, has attempted to develop an interdisciplinary theory of African American religion, drawing from Long and others. He argues that Black theology should move away from its problematic assumptions that tie African American religion and Black churches too closely together. Instead, Black churches should be seen as merely one dimension, one expression of African American religion. Pinn suggests this theory: African American religion, of which Black churches are a part, is the quest for complex subjectivity, reflecting the deep impulse in everyone human for a sense of his or her own meaning and the relationship of their existence to the larger realities of life.[15]

Once the nature and meaning of African American religion is understood and the resources for doing theology are identified, methodologies help the Black theologian "handle" or use these resources. Again, while Black theology texts give little sustained attention to issues of methodology—in part, because of assumptions concerning the lack of utility represented by such abstract conversations—texts do imply and at times explicitly state a methodological element that is clearly linked to Black theology's self-identified and fundamental task of tracing and proclaiming God's agenda for liberation of the oppressed: a hermeneutic of suspicion.

Hermeneutics involves interpretation, and a hermeneutic of suspicion involves interpreting documents and events with an assumption that there is an underlying power dynamic at work. It assumes that things are not as they appear and as they are recorded in that history is "written by the winners" and is meant to proclaim and support their assumptions and attitudes. Within the context of Black theology, a hermeneutic of suspicion involves reading the Christian tradition with an eye toward the ways in which Christianity has been used to support the status quo and justify oppression. From Christian endorsements of slavery to more recent church involvement in anti–civil rights activities, Black theology argues that one cannot assume the righteousness of Christian teachings and practices; one must recognize both the harm and good that mark Christianity's presence in African American communities. Black theology uses this mode of interpretation as a way of discerning oppressive power dynamics that must be fought and countered.

In addition to the hermeneutic of suspicion present in various forms of Black theology, this work has also been informed in an inconsistent manner by other methodological approaches borrowed from other disciplines. For example, some in Black theology refer to postcolonial studies, postmodernism, or cultural studies, among other recent methodological developments that seek to raise questions concerning how knowledge is produced and disseminated, as well as the ways in which life is constructed and arranged. Attention to such methodological tools is still recent, however, and the strength of appeal to them and the continuity of their use remains an open question. Nonetheless, their use does point to growth with respect to the methodological and theoretical underpinning of Black theology. It suggests that Black theology is not an isolated endeavor but is developing conversation partners and drawing from the growing body of knowledge that represents the academy.

Ongoing Issues

Black theology continues to grow and change in ways that reflect the changing nature of African American communities, as well as its place within academia. This growth highlights important issues for continued attention, of which we will highlight only a few here. They are audience, use of popular culture, and the problem of moral evil and the nature of liberation.

Audience and Conversation Partners

For much of its history, Black theology has assumed the African American churches were its primary conversation partners, and it assumed that Black theologians were connected in an intimate fashion to these churches. What has become clear over the years, however, is the gap between these churches and Black theology. In fact, few within African American church membership—across denominations—are aware of Black theology and have read it. Like most professional theologies, it is really the terrain of a select (and self-selecting) group of highly informed laity and ministers, students in higher education, and professionals in the study of religion.

Black theology is coming to grips with this and is beginning to assess how it defines its audience. The key has been recognition of multiple (and at times overlapping) audiences, including attention to a religiously diverse audience. Reflecting this, one is seeing an increase in attention to Black theologies as opposed to Black theology. For example, some like Dale Andrews and Lee Butler are writing Black practical theologies geared toward the demands of church ministry; others like James Evans and Anthony Pinn are writing theology in ways that speak to the academic nature of the enterprise, with a primary focus on shaping conversation in light of and in response to an academia-based audience. Evans and Pinn assume that Black theology must be written with a particular audience in mind and that, in different texts, the theologian can address different audiences. Others, like Dwight Hopkins, are attempting to maintain a theological platform and practice that speaks simultaneously to a church-based and an academia-based audience. Yet, this approach, based on sociological studies, is proving a difficult task at best.

On a somewhat related note, Black theologians have been slow to form substantial conversations with others in North America working on issues of theologically articulated justice. For example, African Americans and Latino/as share a great deal with respect to history within the United States as minority groups. (By Latino/a I do not mean those living in Latin America but, for instance, Puerto Ricans and Cubans living in the United States.) Also, their theologies of liberation have taken hold in the same geography and make use of similar resources on occasion; yet, there is little evidence of "cross-fertilization," or dialogue. Both forms of liberation theology would grow through such an exchange. The synergy and solidarity that could emerge from sustained conversation between theologians in these two communities is impressive.

Furthermore, tied to the great potential present in cross-community dialogue is recognition of the need to reconsider the geography for Black theology. An ongoing issue involves the need for Black theology to begin thinking about its resources, norms, and overall agenda in light of not just the United States but also the Americas as a hemisphere. Put differently, cultural developments in the Caribbean have reached African Americans in the United States (e.g., rap music and its Jamaican roots). Along these lines, there is increased work being done that links Black theology in the United States to portions of the African diaspora in Europe. For example, numerous Black theologians in the United States are involved with *Black Theology,* a journal published in the United Kingdom. In addition, Black theologians in the United Kingdom regularly participate in conference programs in the United States organized by U.S. Black theologians. Black theologians are also beginning to explore notions of liberation and oppression in light of the larger political and economic developments across the Americas—moving north and south, as well as east toward Europe and Africa. For centuries, the various nations within the Americas have had certain cultural and economic links, and Black theology would benefit from an exploration of its work from the vantage point of these links as they extend beyond the boundaries of particular countries.

Use of Popular Culture

While Black theology has given some attention to popular culture for over thirty years, that attention has remained on a limited range of forms of popular culture. For example, little sophisticated attention has been given to the religious content and implications of hip-hop culture. Instead, hip-hop remains a relatively misunderstood form of cultural expression, and too many Black theologians assume it has little to recommend it. This seems a rather odd position, however, when one considers the similarities between the blues (which receive ample attention) and rap music. Both are often nihilistic in tone and can lack any strong appeal to the reality of God that many Black theologians embrace. Rap music offers a similar challenge to Black theology as that promoted by the blues, but the latter has been embraced and the former ignored at a great loss. What is lost is simple: the most complex and layered understanding of how African Americans express themselves and express themselves religiously.

The Problem of Evil and the Question of Liberation

From the work of William Jones to the present, Black theology has been vulnerable to questions concerning its take on the problem of evil, particularly theodicy: What can one say about divine justice in light of human suffering in the world? Much of what Black theology has offered in response to this question has involved "redemptive suffering": the notion that human suffering has secondary benefit, that God uses it for some great purpose. While this might seem harmless enough, such a theological position raises questions concerning the need for struggle—if, in fact, God makes use of suffering to bring about justice. It also raises questions concerning the sustainability of struggle for liberation, if the oppressed are told that their pain and suffering has some benefit in the cosmic plan for them. There is also the possibility that redemptive suffering arguments might lessen a sense of accountability and responsibility on the part of oppressors in that they see the pain they cause through harsh economic policies and the like as part of the "stuff" out of which God will bring good. They, then, are acting in accord with the will of God. At the very least, the redemptive suffering argument that has emerged in Black religious thought and Black theology from the 1700s to the present opens up less than ideal possibilities. For Black theology, the persistence of moral evil despite the presence of a good and just God raises a question that demands more sustained attention.

African American communities are diverse in all respects: economically, politically, spiritually, culturally, and so on. Thus, Black theology must continue to revise its sense of liberation in ways that allow it to appeal to the largest cross-section of African Americans possible. This is important because it allows Black theology to address the diversity of the Black community and its range of socioeconomic and religious needs. Tied to this is the question of oppression: Are all African Americans oppressed? Are they all oppressed in the same manner? If not, what is the nature of Black theology's struggle for social transformation, for liberation? In short, from what exactly do African Americans seek freedom? Is it economic for all African Americans? Or is Black theology really focused on a certain group of African Americans who suffer from certain forms of poverty? As the rhetoric of some Black theologians might suggest, is Black theology's primary (if not exclusive) concern economic poverty? Black theology as it moves forward will need to continuously sharpen its take on the nature and signs of oppression and the shape of liberation.

NOTES

Some of this essay and its general structuring of the presentation are drawn from Anthony B. Pinn, "Black Theology: A Survey of Its Past, Present, and Future," in *Religious Compass*, available at http://www.religion-compass.com.

1. A small portion of this "description of Black theology" section is drawn from Anthony B. Pinn, "Black Theology in Historical Perspective: Articulating the Quest for Subjectivity," in Anthony B. Pinn and Benjamín Valentín, eds., *The Ties That Bind: African American and Hispanic American/Latino/a Theology in Dialogue* (New York: Continuum, 2001), chap. 1.

2. "Statement by the National Committee of Negro Churchmen, July 31, 1966," *New York Times*, July 31, 1966; reprinted in James H. Cone and Gayraud Wilmore, *Black Theology: A Documentary History*, Vol. 1: *1966–1979*, 2nd ed., rev. (Maryknoll, NY: Orbis, 1993), 19.

3. "Statement by the National Committee of Black Churchmen, June 13, 1969"; reprinted in James H. Cone and Gayraud Wilmore, *Black Theology: A Documentary History*, Vol. 1: *1966–1979*, 2nd ed., rev. (Maryknoll, NY: Orbis, 1993), 38.

4. Ibid., quoted in Pinn, "Black Theology in Historical Perspective," 25.

5. James H. Cone, *A Black Theology of Liberation*, 2nd ed. (Maryknoll, NY: Orbis, 1986), 63.

6. Ibid.

7. Ibid., 111.

8. Ibid., 142.

9. Generations of Black theologians are determined and categorized based on a variety of factors. While there is no one approach, most will distinguish generations in light of questions such as the following: By whom was the theologian trained, and whose theological agenda informs the theologian's work? What are the theoretical and methodological commitments of the theologian?

10. Cyprian Davis and Jamie T. Phelps, eds., *Stamped with the Image of God* (Maryknoll, NY: Orbis, 2004); Diana L. Hayes and Cyprian Davis, *Taking Down Our Harps: Black Catholics in the United States* (Maryknoll, NY: Orbis, 1998).

11. Anthony B. Pinn, *Varieties of African American Religious Experience* (Minneapolis: Fortress, 1998); Josiah Young, *Pan-African Theology: Providence and the Legacies of the Ancestors* (Trenton, N.J.: Africa World Press, 1992).

12. Anthony B. Pinn, ed., *Pauli Murray: Selected Sermons and Writings* (Maryknoll, NY: Orbis, 2006).

13. Henry McNeal Turner, *Respect Black: The Writings and Speeches of Henry M. Turner*, ed. Edwin Redkey (New York: Arno, 1971); Martin L. King Jr., *Where Do We Go from Here: Chaos or Community* (Boston: Beacon, 1968).

14. Cone, *Black Theology of Liberation*, 32–33.

15. Anthony B. Pinn, *Terror and Triumph: The Nature of Black Religion* (Minneapolis: Fortress, 2003).

FURTHER STUDY

Anderson, Victor. *Beyond Ontological Blackness: An Essay on African American Religious and Cultural Criticism*. New York: Continuum, 1999.

Andrews, Dale P. *Practical Theology for Black Churches: Bridging Black Theology and African American Folk Religion*. Nashville, TN: Westminster John Knox, 2002.

Cone, James H. *God of the Oppressed*, rev. ed. Maryknoll, NY: Orbis, 1997.

Cone, James H., and Gayraud Wilmore. *Black Theology: A Documentary History*, 2 vols. Maryknoll, NY: Orbis, 1993.

Cummings, George C. L. *A Common Journey: Black Theology and Latin American Liberation Theology*. Maryknoll, NY: Orbis , 1993.

Evans, James H. *We Have Been Believers: An African American Systematic Theology*. Minneapolis: Fortress, 1992.

Hopkins, Dwight N. *Head and Heart: Black Theology, Past, Present, and Future*. New York: Palgrave Macmillan, 2002.

Jones, Major. *The C.O.L.O.R. of God: The Concept of God in African American Thought*. Athens, GA: Mercer University Press, 1987.

Jones, William R. *Is God a White Racist? Preamble to Black Theology*. Boston: Beacon, 1996.

Paris, Peter. *The Social Teachings of the Black Churches*. Minneapolis: Fortress, 1985.

Pinn, Anthony B. *Terror and Triumph: The Nature of Black Religion*. Minneapolis: Fortress, 2003.

Roberts, J. Deotis. *A Black Political Theology*, new ed. Nashville, TN: Westminster John Knox, 2005.

West, Cornel. *Prophesy Deliverance! An Afro-American Revolutionary Christianity*, anny ed. Nashville, TN: Westminster John Knox, 2002.

Wilmore, Gayraud S. *Black Religion and Black Radicalism: An Interpretation of the Religious History of African Americans*, rev. 3rd ed. Maryknoll, NY: Orbis, 1998.

Young, Henry. *Hope in Process: A Theology of Social Pluralism*. Minneapolis: Fortress, 1991.

Young, Josiah U. *A Pan-African Theology Providence and the Legacies of the Ancestors*. Baltimore: African World, 1992.

2

Womanist Theology

STACEY M. FLOYD-THOMAS

Historical Backdrop

In her sermon titled "Has the Lord Spoken to Moses Only?" Pauli Murray raises critical questions pertinent to the womanist theological project: "Does the future of humanity depend upon how quickly . . . feminine principles can be incorporated into our religious life and thought? Is God calling women to reassert prophetic leadership and ministry before it is too late?"[1] Murray uses the story of Miriam, sister of Moses and Aaron, the first woman identified as blessed by God with the gift of prophecy. Foreshadowing much of the womanist vision, Murray's invoking of Miriam's prophetic stance as an example of how the questions of gendering power dynamics and perspectives with Black religious life may have always existed yet awaited women of great faith, courage, and wisdom to call attention to and ultimately end such injustice. The conditions and circumstances of our contemporary era are just as needful of a prophetic critique of the racialized and gendered oppression that still plagues Christianity, both Black and white.

Furthermore, womanist theology reveals itself to be an organic discourse inasmuch as it is faithful to the church while also seeking to remake this most central and cherished institution. This is not viewed as an innovation by womanist theologians but is deemed a continuation of Black women's traditional culture of struggle, survival, and celebration that represents the likes of womanist muses such as Maria Stewart, Jarena Lee, Sojourner Truth, Harriet Jacobs, Ida B. Wells-Barnett, Anna Julia Cooper, Nannie Helen Burroughs, Zora Neale Hurston, Pauli Murray, Rosa Parks, Fannie Lou Hamer, Septima Clark, and countless others in affirmation of themselves of the Black community and their relationship to the divine. Also embedded in the work of these theologians is an emphasis on bringing together elements of Black literature, visual art, music, and sacred testimonies to make an urgent and impassioned plea to Black churches to address not only racism and classism in mainline Christianity but also sexism and anti-intellectualism in the historic Black church tradition.

Womanist theology was formed not only in a context in which white men controlled the public spheres of academia and the church but also within a generally embraced standpoint where, to use Gloria Hull's words, "all the women are white, all the Blacks are men."[2] The same efforts within Black theology and feminist theology that were forging a discourse to deconstruct the normative gaze of white male dominance resulted in obscuring and obliterating the exigent realities and liberative aspirations of Black women within the church, academy, and society as well.

During most of the 20th century and the development of Black denominations, Black studies discourse in general, and Black liberation theology in particular, alongside the establishment of the women's movement, women studies in general, and feminist theology in particular, a dualism increasingly emerged between Black men and women on the one hand and white women and Black women on the other. After each of these movements and ideologies established itself in America off the sweat equity and grassroots activism of Black women, the hope was that the institutions and ideologies that emerged would be inclusive of all Blacks on the one hand and all women on the other. As these movements and discourses evolved, however, the roles and agency of Black women were exploited while their needs and experiences were ignored.[3]

From abolitionism to reconstruction to the civil rights movement to the Black power movement, a dualism between Black men and women increasingly emerged. While Black men found themselves at the helm of movements and institutions that were for, by, and about Black people, Black women continued to endure the stereotypes and oppressions of an earlier period. As if by divine appointment or by the inheritance of a male-dominated society, Black men deemed it proper for them to speak for the entire community, male and female. Consequently, the interests and concerns of Black women were divided and subverted. While Black male theologians identified tensions between white Christianity and a liberating gospel, that same gospel did not bespeak any concern for the liberation of women from patriarchal Christianity.

The women's movement and feminist theology proved to be little different in effect. From the popularized liberation of women from domesticity embodied by Betty Friedan and Gloria Steinem to the political activism and theological discourse endorsed by Mary Daly to its present academic incarnation, there was a failure to acknowledge the realities of Black women throughout the three evolutionary waves of modern feminism. The interests of the movement were more geared toward the needs and concerns of predominantly educated white middleclass and upperclass women and less with the needs and concerns of women of color in general and Black women in particular. Confronted with this growing reality, there were decisions to be made. For African American women, the increased oppression they suffered because of their race, as well as their gender, demanded a response not found in feminist thought and theology.

Although feminist movements and ideologies launched a strident critique against patriarchy, in all its forms, marked differences in the experiences of Black and white women in America remained. For example, Black women did not have to fight for the right to work in the public sphere because this burden was forced on them. Nor was "motherhood" contested in the same way for Black women as it was for white women. The predominance of female-dominant households in the Black community, despite the views of the "The Negro Family in America: The Case for National Action" by Daniel Patrick Moynihan and of other writers, served to preserve the Black family, not destroy it. Also, while Black women's economic lot may have stabilized or improved based on greater gender equity, their options for education, housing, employment, and health care were and are still considerably limited in a racist society. Black women's sexuality and reproductive control was also historically and still today is mythicized, manipulated, and mangled to varying degrees. Black women are generally not afforded the immediate hope to access political power because such political institutions tend not to be in place within the Black community. Feminists largely deal with the political and ideological, while Black women are in need of a discourse and movement that also embraces the spiritual and personal because these are the means to meet their common objective—the elevation and empowerment of women. While Black men and white feminists are seeking more public privilege, Black women must still struggle to ensure essential rights for themselves and their communities.

In this context, Black feminist scholarship deemed it imperative to examine Black women in modern America. In *Ar'n't I a Woman? Female Slaves in the Plantation South*, Deborah Gray White discusses how Black women's fertility and motherhood were fostered by slaveowners as a means of capital growth, as well as social control. Motherhood superseded marriage in the slave community, not because of some propensity of Blacks toward oversexed, immoral lifestyles but because this priority was imposed by "superior" white men. From the point of slavery on, Black women's sexuality became a commodity and, by controlling it, white patriarchy was able to gain and exert power over white women and Black men. Antagonism, according to White, developed between Black and white women during this period due to these sexual politics: the intersection between sexuality and power. Under the plantation system, Black women became more embodied and sexualized, while their white counterparts became aestheticized and revered. Black women were angered because they had to bear the brunt of the responsibilities and realities that were not part of the white woman's "cult of true womanhood."[4]

White women, in contrast, were resentful of the distinctions that placed them on a pedestal and made Black women "real." A number of controlling and damaging images of Black womanhood were socially constructed by white women in order to neutralize or denigrate the Black woman's sexuality, while bolstering "true womanhood." These included the desexed, nurturing mammy; the domineering, emasculating matriarch; the hardworking, stubborn, and unattractive mule; and the promiscuous, sexually aggressive Jezebel. In time, more portraits of Black womanhood, equally harmful and unfounded, would be created. Such stereotypes were injurious because they were rooted in the monstrously manipulated, unasked-for realities of Black women. Moreover, these images were so insidious, enduring, and pervasive that they helped perpetuate the means for the economic exploitation and political oppression of Black women in America. This dichotomy of the "real" woman and the "true" woman has established an adverse dynamic in the relationship of Black and white women.

In *Women, Race, and Class* (1981)—an illustration analysis of women's activism against the evils of white patriarchy in America, from abolition and women's suffrage to civil rights and women's liberation—Angela Davis poignantly demonstrates how the relations between Black and white women in these given movements have been repeatedly damaged at crucial junctures by racism. She discusses how white women, when pressed to align themselves either by race or gender, usually opted for unity along racial lines. Feminist scholar Sara Evans states in *Personal Politics* (1979) that the civil rights movement was key to the revitalization of the women's liberation movement. She discusses how white Southern women became more involved and political by being part of the civil rights movement, and she describes the great indebtedness white women owed to the Black power movement. She does not mention the monumental debt owed to Black women, such as Ella Baker or Septima Clark, however, who were the foundation of the civil rights movement, except to say that "these black women became 'mamas' in the sense of being substitute mother figures, new models of womanhood" for these young white women.[5] This reference to such noteworthy Black women is reminiscent of the stereotypical "mammy" imagery that these women were trying to combat and the notion of surrogacy that womanist discourse would later take on as being at the root of demonarchy found in Black male theology and feminist discourse.

Tensions between Black and white women during the civil rights movement took on a more pronounced aspect. Black women were central yet unseen forces behind most civil rights organizations such as the Student Non-violent Coordinating Committee (SNCC) and the Southern Christian Leadership Conference (SCLC), but it was not until the entrance of white women to the movement that it truly gained recognition. Black women were further slighted by having their leadership of these organizations usurped by Black men, who then proceeded to become sexually involved with white women. This additional stress on the already strained relationship between Black and white women desperately needed to be resolved before any collective effort toward gender equality could take place.

The need for African American women to form their own ideology and find their own vehicle for empowerment stems from the reality that the history, issues, and contexts confronting them are markedly different from those facing white women and Black men. Feminism, in its politics and scholarship, was firmly enmeshed in an all-white, bourgeois context that had little or no relevance to Black women. Even when Black feminists tried to bridge the growing gap between Black and white women, white ideology was still used to impart some mythical aspect to Black womanhood which could be useful to feminism on a whole.[6] Meanwhile, racial progress all too often had been equated with the reconstitution of a much maligned and abused Black manhood. This has led to a masculinization of Black thought and a growing neglect for the concerns and needs of Black women.

By the 1970s, Black women were not afforded many options to further their legitimate causes because the movements they had been so instrumental in forming were now suppressing their input. In *Black Macho and the Myth of the Superwoman*, Michele Wallace stated that if there is to be a Black women's movement, it must both distinguish itself from white feminism and debunk the hurtful images and myths of the Black woman that are present in modern America. Such an endeavor has to put forth a positive, self-defined concept of Black women that deals with their real-lived experiences without the imposition of white women's realities and concerns. By the 1980s, there was a growing demand for just such a movement and ideology among Black women.

Black feminism was an immediate response to mainstream feminism. In *Sister Outsider* (1984), Black feminist scholar Audre Lorde criticizes white feminism's failure to incorporate the marginalized "outsider," especially Black women, lesbians, the old, and the poor. There seemed to be great contradictions present: "If white American feminist theory need not deal with the differences between us, and the resulting difference in our oppressions, then how do you deal with the fact that the women who clean your houses and tend your children while you attend conferences on feminist theory are . . . poor women and women of Color?"[7] By becoming more politicized and ideological, Black feminist thought strives to place the Black woman at its center and gain greater equality in much the same fashion as mainstream feminism.

The definition of Black feminism is somewhat slippery and ambiguous because it was important to designate who could be a Black feminist and what such a distinction meant. In *Feminist Theory: From Margin to Center* (1984), bell hooks boldly articulated a number of vital aspects that feminism must deal with in order to be effective. First, she states that there is no way to deal solely with sexism; activism must consciously vie to eliminate all hetero-patriarchal forms of oppression. Second, in order to provide the oppressed with a realized definition and destiny, personal power must be usurped. Third, echoing the view of Audre Lorde, hooks states that the voices of men as well as "Others" are needed in women's politics if its end is to be truly universal and humanistic. Fourth, and most important, there is a need to reconcile the notion of the good society as based on each group's reality with observed imbalances rectified by revolutionary process. Her demands challenged a new generation of Black women in academia to assert their right not only to be free and equal but also to make themselves a formidable force to be reckoned with.

However, hooks's desire to contest the firmly ensconced institutions of white patriarchy through political activism only seems practical when following the framework designated by white feminism. Patricia Hill Collins states in *Black Feminist Thought: Knowledge, Consciousness, and the Politics of Empowerment* (1990) that "Black feminist thought is *of* African-American women in that it taps the multiple relationships among Black women needed to produce a self-defined Black women's standpoint. Black feminist thought is *for* Black women in that it empowers Black women for political activism."[8] Collins agrees with hooks that "by advocating, refining, and disseminating Black feminist thought, other groups—such as Black men, white women, white men, and other people of color—further its development."[9] Black feminism requires a level of commitment and shared experience, as well as perspectives, that may not be possible for those who are not Black women.

There is a compensatory and conciliatory nature to this inclusive vision that is not expressly the Black women's concern since they have historically been "the most vulnerable and exploited members of American society."[10]

Historical analyses of Black women's lives and experiences take previously unexplored or negative depictions of these women and present more positive and empowered images of them; in this regard, Black feminist scholarship is comparable to such formative contributions of their white counterparts. Black feminist scholarship, such as Christie Farnham's "Sapphire? The Issue of Dominance in the Slave Family, 1830–1865," Elizabeth Clark-Lewis's "'This Work Had an End': African-American Domestic Workers in Washington, DC, 1910–1940," and Evelyn Brooks Higginbotham's *Righteous Discontent* came from an increasing need to have the Black women's historical presence recast in a manner other than simply having been helpless slaves and victims of an unjust society.

However, a problem with Black and white feminisms is the fact that women are taken out of their historic and cultural context and appropriated as model "feminists" in posthumous support and promotion of the movement. The use of these womens' identities, vocations, and experiences in this manner has an inherently manipulative aspect to it. The refusal of feminism to leave the contributions of these historic women politically unencumbered is worsened by the fact that these women must adhere to criteria of intellectualism that may not have been their reality. By not recognizing the lives of these women within their given contexts, feminist movements both deny them the full agency of their actions and diminish those accomplishments that do not fit into the overall feminist vision. This feminist standard that all women, past and present, must meet is neither universal nor mutualistic. The Black woman never had the opportunity to impart an Afrocentric ideology on America in the same way in which her white counterpart was able to reinforce Eurocentrism.

Consciously or not, Black feminism was in search of something more, as evident in the work of its premier theorists, Patricia Hill Collins and bell hooks. Despite hooks's assertion that Black women should remain an active part of the mainstream feminist movement, it seems that "as long as the white-male experience continues to be established as the ethical norm, Black women, Black men and others will suffer unequivocal oppression. The range of freedom has been restricted by those who cannot hear and will not hear voices expressing pleasure and pain, joy and rage as others experience."[11] White feminists have been bound to the heteropatriarchal systems of institutions in ways that still bias and hinder the dismantling of privileges and advantages they share with their male counterparts in American society. The reality that "all African-American women share the common experience of being Black women in a society which denigrates women of African descent"[12] will bring forth unity between Black feminism and womanism.

In the hopes of initiating Black women's return to Afrocentric thought and practices, Alice Walker, in *In Search of Our Mothers' Gardens* (1983), provided the definitive criteria and basis for womanism. Walker defines "womanist" both with regard to the individual and the movement, as

1. From womanish. (Opp. of "girlish," i.e., frivolous, irresponsible, not serious.) A Black feminist or feminist of color. From the Black folk expression of mothers to female children, "You acting womanish," i.e. like a woman. Usually referring to outrageous, audacious, courageous, or willful behavior. Wanting to know more and in greater depth than is considered "good" for one. Acting grown up. Being grown up. Interchangeable with another Black folk expression: "You trying to be grown." Responsible. In charge. Serious.

2. Also: A woman who loves other women, sexually and/or nonsexually. Appreciates and prefers women's culture, women's emotional flexibility (values tears as natural and counterbalance of laughter), and women's strength. Sometimes loves individual men, sexually and/or nonsexually. Committed to survival and wholeness of the entire people, male and female. Not a separatist, except periodically, for health. Traditionally universalist, as in: "Mama why are we brown, pink, and yellow, and our cousins are white, beige, and black?" Ans.: "Well, you know the colored race is just like a flower garden, with every color flower represented." Traditionally capable, as in: "Mama, I'm walking to Canada and I'm taking you and a bunch of slaves with me." Reply: "It wouldn't be the first time."

3. Loves music. Loves dance. Loves the moon. Loves the Spirit. Loves love and food and roundness. Loves the struggle. Loves the Folk. Loves herself. Regardless.

4. Womanist is to feminist as purple is to lavender.[13]

In Walker's definition, a number of characteristics emerge, unique to African American women's virtues, such as a sense of community, a longing for justice, and a deep and personal love of oneself, of others, and of the Spirit. In combination, these elements not only create a complete and fully realized depiction of Black womanhood but also call for an epistemology and vocation for Black women to self-define and self-determine both themselves and the discourses to which their destinies are delineated and affixed. Thus the womanist also has an interest in knowledge production in the hope of not merely being informed *by* her context or given reality but *of* this context as well. With this newfound knowledge of herself and her reality, the womanist makes an informed choice in how she is going to improve both her life and the lives of loved ones and how they are studied.

Unlike feminism, womanism is not an overarching paradigm that all women must ascribe to but a guide to self-definition and self-determination to which a Black woman chooses to adhere. Womanism is not a form of revolutionary asceticism, nor does it impose intellectual or moral superiority, but it is a means of putting Black women in contact with a more subjective, communal, redemptive, and critical means of dealing with her reality, within both the African American community and America at large. The personal and spiritual qualities of womanism can be attributed to the fact that "the confessional element of 'womanist' means that it is a term which cannot be imposed, but must be claimed by the Black woman who is engaged in the eradication of oppression from her own faith perspective and academic discipline."[14] The definition of the "womanist" that Alice Walker presents is a prototypical and evolving one, as womanist scholars seek to revise and redefine its real-life applications.

Where Black male theology and feminist theology invited the church and the academy to an ethical analysis that expanded the theological moral purview to include a systemic social analysis of the working of Eurocentrism on the one hand and patriarchy on the other, so, too, a later generation of Black female theologians shone a light brightly on the death-dealing intersection of race, sex, and class as a central site for theological and ethical reflection. In much the same way that Reinhold Niebuhr's *Moral Man and Immoral Society* (1960) and Dietrich Bonhoeffer's *The Cost of Discipleship* (1959) presciently called forth new modes of analysis for the then-dominant liberal theologies and that James Cone's *Black Theology and Black Power* (1969) and Mary Daly's *Beyond God the Father* (1973) challenged liberal and progressive forms of white male theology, what we have with the dawn of womanism is the necessary voice of critique that constructs new understandings of a more thoroughgoing and inclusive liberation theology in the 21st century.

By claiming this radical space, womanist theology is doing a bit more than recognizing the "mainstreaming" of an insurgent movement within academia. What is highlighted, instead, is the character of womanist theological discourse as that which is best able to interrogate and subvert contemporary systems and discourses of domination in the context of late-modern North America. As a liberationist discourse (one that was nurtured by and grew in critical dialogue first and foremost with the works of James Cone and Bev Harrison among a host of others), the role of womanist theology has helped to identify and challenge the pervasive white and male biases that are deeply embedded within the field of study; in turn, it has reshaped the traditional inquiry and raised candid questions between the two locales of whiteness and maleness. Womanist theology insists that new questions guide the research so that Black women's moral wisdom and experience of the divine and evil can provide answers to the existential questions that face marginalized persons and communities. Womanist theology is so keenly aware of those people withstanding the destructive onslaughts of the demonic systems of oppression, within both the church and society, and those who stand in solidarity with their struggle, because we have confronted the very same withering realities.

Therefore, Black women's moral wisdom becomes a resource for all of humanity and not merely a repository exclusively available to Black women themselves. Moreover, womanist theology distinguishes between "possibilities in principle" and "possibilities in fact." This is essential for theological discourse in that notions of faith, eschatology, and redemptive suffering have been used by dominant discourse as a legitimizing trope for forestalling justice, freedom, and liberation. At the same time, womanist theologians are cognizant of the need to find incarnation, redemption, and resurrection in "the struggle." Womanist theological reflection as struggle resonates with the experiences of preceding generations of Black women like Jarena Lee, Julia Foote, Mary Jane Smalls, and Prathia Hall, to name a few, who fought on the front lines of racial and gender justice in the church and in society. Often these women did not and were not going to improve materially, yet they had an abiding faith and steadfast hope that, by their righteous living, a "change was going to come," even if it was one inherited by future generations.

These Black Christian women brought their social concerns and plights to the forefront of religious discourse. They used progressive language and biblical precedents for theological justification of women's rights and suffrage. They deemed that it was impossible to claim divine justice without social justice, which included upholding dignity and respect for Black women as fearfully and wonderfully made in the image of God. Black women's real-lived experience was an affirmation of God's mothering ability to be a God of the oppressed who is intentional in mandating that social transformation is a requirement of the gospel. These predecessors gave meaning to a theology of relationship that was concerned with human participation as a vital part of the struggle for the liberation God desires, and social transformation was a consequence of redemptive suffering. These preaching Black women activists asserted that God rejects oppression and surrogacy of Black women.

Description

The term and concept "womanist" began to take on a life of its own when Katie Cannon, in the article "The Emergence of Black Feminist Consciousness" (1985), employed it as an accurate and necessary interpretive principle through which Black women's theology could be assessed experientially and critically as more than discourse but as a theology native to Black women that provides "the incentive to chip away at oppressive structures, bit by bit" while "hold[ing] on to life in the face of formidable oppression."[15] Cannon described the early stage of womanist theology while she was a doctoral student as survival-work: "drawing on the rugged endurance of black folks in America who outwit, outmaneuver, and outscheme social systems and structures that maim and stifle mental, emotional, and spiritual growth."[16]

Long before Katie Cannon's *Black Womanist Ethics* (1988), Jaquelyn Grant's *White Women's Christ and Black Women's Jesus* (1989), Delores Williams's *Sisters in the Wilderness* (1993), and other estimable works within the womanist corpus, womanist theology was *lived* out. The groundbreaking efforts that helped carve out this intellectual legacy emerged along the fault lines of a Eurocentric academy and the heteropatriarchal ranks of male clergy which were charted by Black female students at Union Theological Seminary in New York City (a major location for Black liberation theology and feminist liberationist ethics) who were committed to unraveling and naming the systems of oppression that made mental and physical casualties of eleven of their Black female colleagues. According to womanist pioneer Delores Williams, who was a student at that time, Black parents kept coming to get the spiritually and physically scarred bodies of their Black daughters while the remaining Black women were continually challenged to justify by many of their classmates "how in the hell God could call [them] to preach let alone be worthy of a Ph.D."[17]

Black women were confronted with the fact that, although they may be in the higher echelons of academia, their plight still touched the realities of the rank and file. They were prepared to experience the grave uncertainty and isolation that comes with being pioneers in their own right. As an intergenerational cadre of Black women in the form of Katie Cannon, Delores Williams, and Jacquelyn Grant, not only were they dismantling the "master's house" but also they were using the "master's tools," to use Audre Lorde's words,[18] to build new houses on old foundations. They were ready to develop their own modes of control and mined the motherlode of their own experiences that was God-conscious, community-minded, racially proud, and womanishly intuited in order to break the strongholds of the centuries-old patterns of racism, sexism, and overall exploitation to ensure the survival of an entire people, male and female.

Steeped in Black family virtues and schooled in the moral tradition of the Black church that taught that trouble doesn't last always, that the weak can gain victory over the strong (given the right planning), that God is at the helm of human history, and that the best standard of excellence is a spiritual relation to life obtained in one's prayerful relation to God, womanism challenged later "more pragmatic" claims that justice had to be meted out and instead held out for the standards and excellence that only tenacity can bring. It is this womanist tradition born in the face of chaos and nurtured in fervent hope that facilitates the thinking-being-doing continuum that gives oppressed people the self-esteem and courage to strive and to achieve great heights amid seemingly insurmountable odds. These ethical insights and social teachings are what help to further the unfinished work of the liberal, progressive, and liberationist vision of normative theology in an effort to keep academia and the church alert to what standards should be and what constitutes excellence for our discipline, church, and society.[19]

Womanist theology strips away false, objectified conceptualities and images of the divine and evil that undergird the apparatuses of systemic oppression and replaces them with images and cultural discourses that provide life-giving hope in the face of these webs of domination. To this end, womanist theology serves as a clarion call for a new heuristic and academic enterprise that focuses the power of Blackness (Black theology) and the personal as political (white feminism) as it shifts the margins to the center (Black feminism); more important, it seeks to debunk, unmask, and disentangle in order to place the most marginalized experiences of Black women at the heart of a burgeoning narrative of religious awareness and spiritual empowerment that makes it easier to see the radicality of the gospel from the aspect of the outsider/within and the least of these. Womanist theology is a movement and an ideology that places the African American woman at its center and strives to improve the lot of the African American community at large.

By defining herself as a womanist, the womanist theologian takes on the responsibility of improving the life chances for Black women by enumerating principles and insights gained from the moral wisdom of Black women who were able to foster love for all and the building of relationships that heal and set individuals and the community free. She calls for the church to transform embodied relationships by taking society from domination to partnership, alienation to connection, despair to hope. Womanist spirituality encourages following the example of a Jesus who befriended the marginalized and oppressed and who stood for developing relationships that respect bodies and souls.

Following Cannon's groundbreaking text *Black Womanist Ethics*, early womanist scholarship emerged that provided a concrete basis for the rationality of a womanist movement within the American Academy of Religion (AAR) and the Society for the Study of Black Religion (SSBR), as well as the methodologies and resources that could be readily utilized. Cannon's text and subsequent writings highlight a conceptual framework that is vital for understanding the nature and meaning of Black women's experience. To womanist theology, Delores Williams offers the framework of surrogacy as a way of understanding the historically situated abuse of Black women's bodies and the manner in which this abuse was justified by a turn to religiously defined intervention.

Beginning this analysis with an interrogation of the Hagar story, Williams turns to the central figure of the New Testament: as Jesus offered himself for the sins of the world, Black women were expected to offer themselves for the benefit of the status quo. This alternate perspective on the theologically arranged abuse of Black women brought an important critique against religious discourse as developed by white men, white women, and Black men, and it problematized their often uncritical appropriation of scripture. In so doing, Williams, and womanist theology by extension, forced a reevaluation of the nature and meaning of suffering and liberation and pushed for an appreciation of the Christ-event as opposed to a concern with the person of Jesus (trapped in maleness). According to Williams:

> If black liberation theology wants to include black women and speak on behalf of the most oppressed black people today . . . theologians must ask themselves some questions. Have they, in the use of the Bible, identified so thoroughly with the theme of Israel's election that they have not seen the oppressed of the oppressed in scripture? Have they identified so completely with Israel's liberation that they have been blind to the awful reality of victims making victims in the Bible? Does this kind of blindness with regard to non-Hebrew victims in the scripture also make it easy for black male theologians and biblical scholars to ignore the figures in the Bible whose experience is analogous to that of black women?[20]

Williams's challenge of uncritical use of scripture and other resources forced self-evaluation on the part of other liberation theologies, but it also provided a way of developing a unique theological cartography. For example, the move beyond the gender-bound Jesus, critiqued by Jacquelyn Grant and then Williams, to the Christ of Community allowed for a more-sustained modeling of behavior by privileging what the Christ-event means for the transformation of life options within the context of existential circumstances. Sin, then, had to do with the mistreatment of Black women through racism, sexism, classism, and other modalities of discrimination and oppression. Suffering, as Williams notes, should not be understood as the proper reality for Black women; surrogacy is to be rejected. And salvation involved the restoration of proper life options consistent with Alice Walker's definition offered above. Scholars such as Grant, Cannon, and Williams offered an initial framing of womanist theology, one that would be refined and extended as womanist theology developed over the decades.

Subsequent womanist publications—such as Renita J. Weems's *Just a Sister Away: A Womanist Vision of Women's Relationships in the Bible* (1988), Jacquelyn Grant's *White Women's Christ, Black Women's Jesus* (1989), Delores S. Williams's *Sisters in the Wilderness: The Challenge of Womanist God-Talk* (1993), Emilie M. Townes's *Womanist Justice, Womanist Hope* (1993), and Kelly Brown Douglas's *The Black Christ* (1994)—emerged from the theological disciplines to add to the range of issues to address within the context of the Black church and the greater realities of African Americans in American society. *A Troubling in My Soul: Womanist Perspectives on Evil and Suffering* (1993), the first anthology of womanist theological discourse, edited by Emilie M. Townes, addresses the question of theodicy by employing a critical, deconstructive methodology that integrates race, class, and gender analysis of the issue of evil and suffering in a manner that traditional, feminist, and Black scholars have often missed. It is in such a manner that womanist theology continues to challenge existing ontological (ways of being) and epistemological (ways of knowing) theologies that confront and eradicate the injustice and oppression facing Black women in America.

Sources

Black Women's Real-Lived Experience

More than scripture or (Black male or feminist) theories, African American women's experience is the primary lens through which womanist theology is assessed ontologically and epistemologically. In large part, womanist theology stems from the experiential process of Black female scholars of religion who have tried to carve out meaning in theological discourse. To wit, in addition to being religious scholars, womanist theologians are also predominantly ordained ministers, which means not only have they themselves experienced the disconcerting reality of living at the interstices of racism, sexism, and classism in the church and academia, but also they have direct access to the primary institution that could capture the range of Black women's experience and agency. That is, Black churches are the one institution totally controlled by Blacks wherein Black women make up the majority of its congregants and provide most of its human and fiscal resources but lack a space in which they can express themselves freely and take independent action. Thus, central to womanist theology was the need to unmask sacred spaces and debunk the living laboratory where patriarchal surveillance, sexist treatment, and economic exploitation of Black women was simultaneously proclaimed and practiced.

Black Women's Literature

To assess the experience and give voice to Black women outside of one's specific context, womanist theologians turned to the literary tradition of African American women writers as a constant resource and means of discourse in womanist theology. The wealth of writings found in "the Black woman's literary tradition documents the 'living space' carved out of the intricate web of racism, sexism and poverty. The literary tradition parallels Black history. It conveys the assumed values in the Black oral tradition. And it encapsulates the insularity of the Black community."[21] The works of African American women writers, such as Zora Neale Hurston, Alice Walker, Gloria Naylor, and Toni Morrison, to name a few, serve as both a rich, unexplored repository of experience and knowledge to be studied and an untapped inspiration and shared testamonies for womanist theologians. Black women's literature aids in an alternative reading and deconstructive analysis of how the Bible takes one of the most important tools of Eurocentric patriarchal oppression, Christianity, and extracts its positive and liberating elements. Both Black and white textual sources can be used to deal with the reality of sexual politics as they relate to Black women. Womanists' use of these texts is an innovative and effective means of addressing issues such as domestic violence, prostitution, sexual abuse, and rape, all of which are increasingly pressing concerns in the lives of Black women. Black women's writings were regarded as sacred texts that examine racism, sexism (or male supremacy or patriarchy), and economic exploitation not simply as acts of violence but as social sin.

Once brought to light, Black women's experiences and the problems that ensue can be dealt with realistically and constructively. Womanist theology honors and centers Black women's experiences as sacred worlds that make possible the analysis of ways in which race, gender, and class give meaning to religious experience. Therefore, these hidden traditions retain power in the hands of Black people, function socially to influence domestic relationships for women and girls, and offer supernatural assets for strength and survival for all of humanity.

Theoretical and Methodological Considerations

While Walker's four-part definition of "womanist" has been adopted as a standpoint that adequately names the self-avowed identity of womanist theologians, the reflection used for cultivating methodologies and coming to theological conclusions is found in the discourse of "womanism." Thus, while Walker has defined what it means *to be* womanist, Black womanist theologians have defined what it means *to do* womanism.

As a leading voice in the womanist movement, Delores Williams states:

> Womanist theology is already beginning to define the categories and methods needed to develop along lines consistent with the sources of that theology. Christian womanist theological methodology needs to be informed by at least four elements: (1) a multidialogical intent, (2) a liturgical intent, (3) a didactic intent, and (4) a commitment both to reason *and* to the validity of female imagery and metaphorical language in the construction of theological statements.[22]

Multidialogical intent allows womanist theologians to advocate in praxis and discourse with a wide array of sociopolitical, cultural, and religious communities focused on the survival and empowerment of the oppressed. *Liturgical intent* within womanist theology ensures that the fruit of womanist labor will be a relevant reflection of the action, thought, and worship of the Black church tradition. The *didactic intent* in the womanist theological perspective contends that theology should have a pedagogical dimension. *Theological language*, generated by womanist theology, illustrates the amalgam of Black women's history, culture, moral wisdom, and religious experience that is instrumental for transforming academia, church, and society. Following Williams's schema, the womanist theological project is indicative of its intentionality: Black women asserting themselves in the fullness of their historical reality, social conditions, and religious experience as the core of their theological interpretation.

Why does this matter? As womanist theology takes full account of racism, sexism, and classism inherent to mainline Christian theology, it refuses to surrender to an interpretive method that insists on compartmentalizing race, class, gender, and sexuality as separate and even singular concerns in the analysis of Black women's faith. This makes womanist theology clearly distinguishable from other theologies of the oppressed that preceded it—namely, Black liberation theology and feminist theology. Therefore, although rooted in their quest for social transformation and the end of human oppression, womanist theological interpretation does not take for granted that all of these theologies can be lumped into a single box yet contributes critical insights and interventions that have challenged other theologies to their God-talk.

With the publication of the edited volume *Deeper Shades of Purple: Womanism in Religion and Society* (2006), womanist theological ethicist Stacey Floyd-Thomas illuminates how womanism has been used as a vantage point for the theoretical orientations and methodological approaches of the Black women scholar-activists who brought this discourse from the church to academia and from experience to scholarship. While keeping the foundational elements of Walker's four-part definition intact, womanist scholars have essentially explored the four tenets of "womanism":

1. RADICAL SUBJECTIVITY

   a. A process that emerges as Black females in the nascent phase of their identity development come to understand agency as the ability to defy a forced naiveté in an effort to influence the choices made in their life—how Black women's conscientization incites resistance against marginality.

   b. An assertion of the real-lived experiences of one's rites of passage into *becoming* a Black woman, *being* "womanish"; the audacious act of naming and claiming voice, space, and knowledge.

   c. A form of identity politics that is not a tangible, static identity that measures and gauges the extent to which one is or is not what others had planned or hoped for one to be.

2. TRADITIONAL COMMUNALISM

   a. The affirmation of the loving connections and relational bonds formed by Black women—including familial, maternal, platonic, religious, sexual, and spiritual ties. Black women's ability to create, remember, nurture, protect, sustain, and liberate communities which are marked and measured not by those outside of one's own community but by the acts of inclusivity, mutuality, reciprocity, and self-care practiced within it (opposite of the biological deterministic assumption that a woman's role is to serve as nurturer and protector).

b. The moral principles and practices of Black women living in solidarity with and in support of those with whom they share a common heritage and contextual language; having a preferential option for Black women's culture, esp. their constructive criticism, "tragicomic hope," "in/visible dignity," and "un/shouted courage" which furthers the survival and liberation of *all* Black women and their communities.

c. The synthesis of double consciousness which occurs via the mastery of striking a balance between diametric opposites and the ability to address and readdress, deconstruct and reconstruct while simultaneously subverting the forces that destroy Black communities and devastate the lives within them.

d. The ability of Black women to wrest younger Black women from the strongholds of internalized oppression (i.e., colorism) and self-delusion (i.e., exceptionalism) and restore them with self-awareness, collective memory, and communal pride.

e. The inherited and shared legacy of Black women who have "made a way out of no way" from generation to generation.

3. REDEMPTIVE SELF-LOVE

a. An assertion of the humanity, customs, and aesthetic value of Black women in contradistinction to the commonly held stereotypes characteristic of white solipsism. The admiration and celebration of the distinctive and identifiable beauty of Black women.

b. A reaffirmation of Black womanhood in all of its full creation. The essence and freedom of Black women's cultural, physical, and spiritual expression.

c. Black women's unconditional and relentless resolve to enjoy the range of their common sense and the pleasures of their individual senses.

4. CRITICAL ENGAGEMENT

a. The epistemological privilege of Black women borne of their totalistic experience with the forces of interlocking systems of oppression and strategic options they devised to undermine them.

b. An unequivocal belief that Black women hold the standard and normative measure for true liberation; the capacity of Black women to view things in their true relations or relative importance; and while expected to be among the chief arbiters of accountability, advocacy, and authenticity, they, too, must be faithful to the task of expanding their discourse, knowledge, and skills.

c. A hermeneutical suspicion, cognitive counterbalance, intellectual indictment, and perspectival corrective to those people, ideologies, movements, and institutions that hold a one-dimensional analysis of oppression; an unshakable belief that Black women's survival strategies must entail more than what others have provided as an alternative.

This notion of womanism marks the essential features of the numerous interdisciplinary methods (literary analysis—biomythography, virtue ethics, and diasporic analysis; sociological methods—case study method, sociohistorical methodology, emancipatory metaethnography; and historiography— slave narratives, moral biography and autobiographical method, and emancipatory historiography) employed by womanist theologians to unearth the untapped resources found in the Black women's real-lived experiences and literature.[23] Consequently, womanism shifted from a solo enterprise to a broad field of inquiry. This transition is representative of how Black women's moral wisdom can be a vantage point for apprehending scholarly context, criteria, and claims.

While it remains a discourse produced by Black women, womanism is open to intentional allies who seek to work in solidarity with and on behalf of Black women who have made available, shared, and translated their wisdom, strategies, and methods for the universal task of liberating the oppressed and speaking truth to power in both the church and society.

Ongoing Issues
Appropriating Walker's Definition

The question of whether Alice Walker's definition of womanist can be faithfully applied within a Christian theological framework, a concern that Cheryl J. Sanders posed at the dawn of the womanist movement, remains a point of concern for womanist theology.[24] While specific to Sanders's critique was Walker's emphasis on self-assertion, the secular nature of womanist, and the incorporation of lesbian experience, the overarching appropriation of a nonscholar and a non-Christian is striking. Many inside and outside of womanist camps continue to resolve the dissonance caused by Black Christian women's theological development and scholarship appropriating the self-avowed expression of a confessed pagan. Taking this observation even further, non-Christian womanist scholars have critiqued much of womanist theology as a de facto Christian discourse that has silenced Walker's focus on "love for the Spirit" regardless of what form it takes, thus claiming that womanist scholars have stymied the working for the healthy perpetuation of all faith groups.

With the publication of her anthology, *Deeper Shades of Purple,* Floyd-Thomas, along with over twenty other scholars, made the claim that Walker's articulation of the definition and identity of "womanism" does not exclusively guide womanist discourse. Floyd-Thomas contends that much of the bourgeoning discourse within womanist scholarship is of women who celebrate religious pluralism and other expressions of the divine, to include African traditional religion, humanism, and Islam, as illustrated exceptionally in the work of womanist theologians and historians such as Debra Mubashir Majeed, Dianne Stewart, and Tracey Hucks.

Embodiment and Sexuality

Another perennial concern within womanist theology is that, while Walker's vision celebrates lesbianism and many of the scholars, themselves, are lesbians, issues of embodiment and sexuality, particularly as they address this group, have failed to punctuate the discourse. Based on the sense of compassion and accountability that emerges from womanist theology and progressive scholarship, many scholars—like Kelly Brown Douglas and Renee Hill—have decided to do the radical work of bringing the issue of sexuality, homophobia, and heterosexism from the margins of womanist analysis to the center, while the mainstream of womanist discourse has remained silent on this issue.

Accessibility and Practical Implications

A weakness of womanist theology, alongside other marginalized theological discourses, has been moving from dialogue into the practical problems of its nonacademic community. Although social and ecclesiastical change originated as the primary aim of womanist theology, many have noted that most of its impact has been merely theoretical. Many have cited the need for a political program to stop sexism and an alliance between womanist scholars and women's organizations in Black churches in order for change to be implemented. Because womanist theology has developed in predominantly white seminaries, suspicion and the independent status of Black churches has prevented much impact on the local level.

In an effort to bridge this gap, inroads have been made for womanist theology to not only have the Black church in mind but also be accessible to it.

The works of womanist biblicist Renita Weems (*Just a Sister Away: A Womanist Vision of Women's Relationships in the Bible*) and womanist theological ethicist Marcia Riggs (*Plenty Good Room: Women versus Male Power in the Black Church*) are of note in this regard as they have focused attention on fostering dialogue between Black church laywomen and womanist scholars. Consequently, the leadership taken by these well-regarded womanist scholars has inspired other scholars to either make their scholarship more accessible or intentionally write texts that can and should be used for Bible studies among the laity.

NOTES

1. Pauli Murray, "Has the Lord Spoken to Moses Only?" in *Pauli Murray: Selected Sermons and Writings*, ed. Anthony B. Pinn (Maryknoll, NY: Orbis, 2006), 75.

2. Gloria T. Hull, Patricia Bell Scott, and Barbara Smith, eds., *All the Women Are White, All the Blacks Are Men, But Some of Us Are Brave: Black Women's Studies* (New York: Feminist Press, 1982).

3. For further exemplification, see Nancy Cott, "What's in a Name? The Limits of 'Social Feminism'; or Expanding the Vocabulary of Women's History," *Journal of American History* 76, no. 3 (1989): 809–829.

4. Deborah Gray White, *Ar'n't I a Woman? Female Slaves in the Plantation South* (New York: W. W. Norton, 1999).

5. Sara Evans, *Personal Politics: The Roots of Women's Liberation in the Civil Rights Movement and the New Left* (New York: Random House, 1979), 53.

6. These efforts are aptly chronicled in works such as Gerda Lerner, ed., *Black Women in White America: A Documentary History* (New York: Random House, 1972).

7. Audre Lorde, *Sister Outsider* (Freedom, CA: Crossing, 1984), 112.

8. Patricia Hill Collins, *Black Feminist Thought: Knowledge, Consciousness, and the Politics of Empowerment* (New York: Routledge, 1990), 32.

9. Ibid., 78.

10. Katie G. Cannon, *Black Womanist Ethics* (Atlanta: Scholars, 1988), 4.

11. Ibid., 3.

12. Collins, *Black Feminist Thought*, 22.

13. Alice Walker, *In Search of My Mothers' Gardens* (San Diego, CA: Harcourt, 1983), xi–xii.

14. Emilie M. Townes, "Voices of the Spirit: Womanist Methodologies in the Theological Disciplines," *Womanist* 1, no. 1 (1994): 1.

15. Katie G. Cannon, "The Emergence of Black Feminist Consciousness," in *Feminist Interpretation of the Bible*, ed. Letty N. Russell (Oxford: Blackwell, 1985), 40.

16. Quoted in M. Shawn Copeland, "A Thinking Margin," in *Deeper Shades of Purple: Womanism in Religion and Society*, ed. Stacey M. Floyd-Thomas (New York: New York University Press, 2006), 228.

17. Delores S. Williams, interview with author, New York, April 30, 2004.

18. Audre Lorde, *Sister Outsider: Essays and Speeches* (New York: Crossing Press, 1984), 110.

19. Delores Williams, "Excellence beyond Standards (Is. 25:6–9; Phi1. 4:4–13; Mt. 22:1–10)," *Christian Century,* October 17, 1990, p. 931

20. Delores S. Williams, *Sisters in the Wilderness: The Challenge of Womanist God-Talk* (Maryknoll, NY: Orbis, 1993), 149.

21. Cannon, *Black Womanist Ethics,* 7.

22. Delores S. Williams, "Womanist Theology: Black Women's Voices (1986)," in *The Womanist Reader,* ed. Layli Phillips (London: Routledge, 2006), 121.

23. For a detailed examination of these methodologies, see Stacey M. Floyd-Thomas, *Mining the Motherlode: Methods in Womanist Ethics* (Cleveland: Pilgrim, 2006).

24. More recently, like Cheryl Sanders in 1989, Monica Coleman has raised the question in her essay "Must I Be a Womanist?" which has sparked a lively debate within and beyond womanist theological circles concerning Black female religious scholars and the authenticity of womanist identity. See Cheryl J. Sanders, "Christian Ethics and Theology in Womanist Perspective," *Journal of Feminist Studies in Religion* 5, no. 2 (1989): 83–112; and Monica A. Coleman, "Must I Be a Womanist?" *Journal of Feminist Studies in Religion* 22, no.1 (2006): 85–96.

FURTHER STUDY

Baker-Fletcher, Karen. *Dancing with God: The Trinity from a Womanist Perspective.* St. Louis, MO: Chalice, 2007.
———. *A Singing Something: Womanist Reflection on Anna Julia Cooper.* New York: Crossroad, 1994.
———. *Sisters of Dust, Sisters of Spirit: Womanist Wordings on God and Creation.* Minneapolis: Fortress, 1998.
Baker-Fletcher, Karen, and Garth Baker-Fletcher. *My Sister, My Brother: Womanist and Xodus God-Talk.* Maryknoll, NY: Orbis, 1997.
Brown, Teresa L. Fry. *God Don't Like Ugly.* Nashville, TN: Abingdon, 2000.
Cannon, Katie G. *Black Womanist Ethics.* Atlanta: Scholars, 1988.
———. *Katie's Canon: Womanism and the Soul of the Black Community.* New York: Continuum, 1995.
———, et al. (The Mudflower Collective). *God's Fierce Whimsy: Christian Feminism and Theological Education.* New York: Pilgrim, 1985.
Copeland, M. Shawn. *Enfleshing Feedom: Body, Race, and Being.* Minneapolis: Fortress, 2009.
Douglas, Kelly Brown. *The Black Christ.* Maryknoll, NY: Orbis, 1994.
———. *Sexuality and the Black Church: A Womanist Perspective.* Maryknoll, NY: Orbis, 1999.
———. *What's Faith Got to Do with It: Black Bodies/Christian Souls.* Maryknoll, NY: Orbis, 2005.
Floyd-Thomas, Stacey M. *Black Church Studies: An Introduction.* Nashville, TN: Abingdon, 2007.
———. *Deeper Shades of Purple: Womanism in Religion and Society.* New York: New York University Press, 2006.
———. *Mining the Motherlode: Methods in Womanist Ethics.* Cleveland: Pilgrim, 2006.

Gilkes, Cheryl Townsend. *If It Wasn't for the Women . . . : Black Women's Experience and Womanist Culture in Church and Community.* Maryknoll, NY: Orbis, 2000.

Grant, Jacquelyn. *White Women's Christ, Black Women's Jesus.* Atlanta: Scholars, 1989.

Hayes, Diana L. *And Still We Rise: An Introduction to Black Liberation Theology.* New York: Paulist, 1996.

———. *Hagar's Daughters: Womanist Ways of Being in the World.* New York: Paulist, 1995.

———. *Trouble Don't Last Always: Soul Prayers.* Collegeville, MN: Liturgical, 1995.

Holmes, Barbara A. *Joy Unspeakable: Contemplative Practices of the Black Church.* Minneapolis: Fortress, 2004.

Kirk-Duggan, Cheryl. *Exorcising Evil: A Womanist Perspective on the Spirituals.* Maryknoll, NY: Orbis, 1997.

———. *Misbegotten Anguish: A Theology and Ethics of Violence.* St. Louis, MO: Chalice, 2001.

———. *Soul Pearls: Worship Resources for the Black Church.* Nashville, TN: Abingdon, 2003.

Martin, Joan M. *More Than Chains and Toil: A Christian Work Ethic of Enslaved Women.* Louisville, KY: Westminster John Knox, 2000.

Mitchem, Stephanie Y. *Introducing Womanist Theology.* Maryknoll, NY: Orbis, 2002.

Phelps, Jamie T. *Black and Catholic: The Challenge and Gift of Black Folk—Contributions of African American Experience and Thought to Catholic Theology.* Milwaukee: Marquette University Press, 1998.

Riggs, Marcia T. *Awake, Arise, and Act: A Womanist Call for Black Liberation.* Cleveland: Pilgrim, 1994.

———, ed. *Can I Get a Witness? Prophetic Religious Voices of African American Women: An Anthology.* Maryknoll, NY: Orbis, 1997.

———. *Plenty Good Room: Women versus Male Power in the Black Church.* Cleveland: Pilgrim, 2003.

Ross, Rosetta E. *Witnessing and Testifying: Black Women, Religion, and Civil Rights.* Minneapolis: Fortress, 2003.

Terrell, JoAnne Marie. *Power in the Blood? The Cross and the African American Experience.* Maryknoll, NY: Orbis, 1992.

Thomas, Linda E., ed. *Living Stones in the Household of God: The Legacy and Future of Black Theology.* Minneapolis: Fortress, 2003.

———. *Under the Canopy: Ritual Process and Spiritual Resilience in South Africa.* Columbia: University of South Carolina Press, 1999.

Townes, Emilie M. *Embracing the Spirit: Womanist Perspectives on Hope, Salvation, and Transformation.* Maryknoll, NY: Orbis, 1997.

———. *In a Blaze of Glory: Womanist Spirituality as a Social Witness.* Nashville, TN: Abingdon, 1995.

———, ed. *A Troubling in My Soul: Womanist Perspective on Evil and Suffering.* Maryknoll, NY: Orbis, 1993.

———. *Womanist Ethics and the Cultural Production of Evil.* New York: Palgrave, 2007.

———. *Womanist Justice, Womanist Hope.* Oxford: Oxford University Press, 1993.

Weems, Renita J. *Battered Love: Marriage, Sex and Violence in the Hebrew Prophets.* Minneapolis: Fortress, 1995.

———. *I Asked for Intimacy: Stories of Blessings, Betrayals and Birthings.* San Diego: Luramedia, 1993.

————. *Just a Sister Away: A Womanist Vision of Women's Relationships in the Bible.* West Bloomfield, MI: Walk Worthy, 2005.

————. *Showing Mary: How Women Can Share Prayers, Wisdom and the Blessings of God.* West Bloomfield, MI: Walk Worthy, 2002.

Williams, Delores. *Sisters in the Wilderness: The Challenge of Womanist God-Talk.* Maryknoll, NY: Orbis, 1993.

3

Latina Theology

NANCY PINEDA-MADRID

Historical Backdrop

The significance and contribution of Latina theology becomes clear when read in light of the contentious histories of Latina/os in the Americas. No single historical narrative line exists for Latina/os, as the term serves as an umbrella representing many distinct groups of people, each with their own history (Mexican Americans, Puerto Ricans, Cuban Americans, etc.).[1] Frequently, dominant political and economic powers have used religious ideas to bolster their own legitimacy and to provide a veneer of moral righteousness for their ideas. Throughout Latina/o history, this fusion of political power and religious ideas became more poignant during periods of significant transition (e.g., the conquest of "New Spain," the Treaty of Guadalupe-Hidalgo in 1848, the civil rights movement). While these had a direct impact in the lives of all Latina/os, Latinas experienced the brunt of these political transitions acutely.

In the years after Christopher Columbus's "discovery of America" in 1492, he and many others interpreted his arrival in the "new world" to be part of God's plan, a plan to create a new, pure Catholic Christian church in the Americas, one that would stand in marked contrast to the corrupt Catholic church of Europe and as a Catholic bulwark in the face of the reformations sweeping many European countries. Spain's Catholic rulers, Ferdinand and Isabella, promoted these ideas. Early in the 16th century, Spanish Protestant communities began to take root in Seville and Valladolid, but the inquisition completely suppressed them by 1562. In 1524, shortly after the conquest of the Aztecs and much of Mesoamerica, the Catholic church in Spain sent twelve Franciscan priests, widely known as "Los Doce," to the "new world" to represent the biblical twelve apostles and begin the work of evangelizing the indigenous population. This became a pointedly ambiguous endeavor in that it prevented the complete annihilation of the indigenous in many regions, but not all, yet it also legitimized the conquest and the resulting enforced labor of the indigenous population. In some regions of the Americas, like Cuba, the conquest led to the extermination of the indigenous population within decades. As indigenous populations plummeted, the Spaniards increasingly brought more and more Africans to the Americas, enslaving them in order to maintain a steady labor force.

Throughout the middle of the 16th century, debates raged in Spain's most celebrated universities concerning the conquest. Did the pope have authority over the lands occupied by nonbelievers? How could the "Americas" be "discovered" if they were not abandoned lands? If the indigenous rejected the Christian faith, then didn't the Spanish have the right to punish the indigenous and force acceptance of Christianity? Do Christians have the right to impose morality on "barbarians"? Are the indigenous fully human beings and therefore capable of receiving the sacrament of baptism? All of these debates were attempts to come to grips with whether or not the conquest of the Americas was morally justified. Needless to say, the political and economic power interests of the Spanish Crown ultimately trumped all other concerns. The point is that this coalescence of politics and religion repeatedly functioned to the detriment of the indigenous and the enslaved Africans, who, in addition to the Spanish, are foremothers and forefathers of Latina/os.

While the history of Latina/os in what is today the United States has had many contentious moments, the early 19th century would certainly be among the more poignant. By and large, the United States of the late 18th century (and perhaps still today) understood itself as an "elect nation," which for the vast majority meant a white Anglo-Saxon Protestant nation. In the early 1800s, this self-understanding developed into an aggressive nationalism and became codified in the doctrine of "manifest destiny." This idea of America's providential calling and mission fueled westward expansion and cloaked it in a mantel of extending the "kingdom of God." When white settlers confronted Mexicans in the West, these white Americans formulated an idea of themselves as racially Anglo-Saxon, as a people superior to others and therefore entitled to economic and political domination from the Atlantic all the way to the Pacific. In the process, lands historically populated by indigenous and Latina/os were taken. In 1821, Spain was forced to cede Florida. In 1836, recently arrived Anglo-Saxon settlers finally won Texas's independence from Mexico. In 1848, Mexico lost half of its territory, being forced to cede all of what is today California, New Mexico, and Nevada, as well as major portions of Colorado, Arizona, and Utah.

All the Latina/os living in these lands automatically became U.S. citizens; in fact, however, their status and standing was diminished. Only white males had rights before the law (e.g., land rights, language rights). This provoked a stinging awareness, not only of the social restrictions faced by women in general but also those faced by Latina/os. Former Mexican nationals, regardless of their skin color, were not considered white. In the 1860s, Anglo-Saxon recent arrivals organized the lynching of long-settled former Mexican nationals (who were now U.S. citizens) living in the southwest. This became a strategy for Anglo-Saxons to gain control of the land and its resources. The lynching continued until the 1920s.

But the United States was not finished. In 1898, the United States forced Spain to cede the island of Puerto Rico. The United States sought the willing assistance of Protestant churches in the colonization of Puerto Rico. Long before the war with Spain was over, these churches had a plan set to carve up the island among themselves for missionary purposes. The United States christened this missionary work a "sacred calling" and then claimed that it justified its colonization of Puerto Rico. That is, the United States claimed that it was not so much acting on its colonial and economic interests but was serving the higher purpose of evangelization. Many years later, Bernardo Vega, a Puerto Rican social activist in New York City, summarized the prevailing sentiment of U.S. citizenry in the early decades of the 20th century as follows: "Cuba and Puerto Rico were just two islands inhabited by savages whom the Americans had beneficially saved from the clutches of the Iberian Lion."[2] U.S. colonial interest did not end with Puerto Rico. Between 1898 and 1909 the United States twice occupied Cuba, which went on to become an independent nation. Even so, after 1909 the United States continued, rather freely, to exert capital and influence in Cuba until the communist revolution of 1959.

Indeed, the doctrine of manifest destiny fostered a climate of collaboration between the colonial and economic interests and the religious interests of Christian denominations within the United States, Protestant and Catholic alike. As the United States took control of these lands, mainline Protestant denominations introduced the Protestant faith to Latina/os living in the Caribbean and other parts of Latin America, as well as those living in the new southwest territories of the United States. The first generations of Latina/o Protestants emerged in the 19th and 20th centuries. While Catholicism had been rooted in these lands for centuries, significant conflicts within the church developed as white clergy from the eastern United States displaced the sitting Latino bishops and clergy. Perhaps the most well known conflict was the one that erupted between Bishop Jean-Baptiste Lamy and the Catholic clergy and people of the New Mexican territories. This protracted conflict began in 1851 shortly after Lamy was appointed bishop of Santa Fe, and he publically suppressed the devotional practices and religious culture that had grounded New Mexican Catholicism for more than two centuries.

The situation of Latina women shifted dramatically when these lands came under the control of the United States. Under Spanish and Mexican governance, the settlers occupying these lands included people of Spanish, African, and indigenous heritage who lived under a rigid hierarchy based on class, color, and labor that privileged the Spaniards. Even though indigenous and Blacks were relegated to the bottom rungs of the social scale, there is evidence that free Blacks, non-elites, and Latina women could and did own property. Along these lines, married Latinas were at an advantage in that they kept control of their property: even after they married, they held a one-half interest in the community property they shared with their husbands; then, when they became widows, they inherited the land and wealth of their deceased husbands. Such was not the case for their Euro-American counterparts. Under English common law, when women in the United States married, all their property was automatically held in common with their husbands, and they could not own property separate from their husbands. So when the Mexican and Spanish lands came under U.S. control, Latina women lost considerable property and wealth.

In the early 1960s, the Roman Catholic Church in the United States launched its most significant effort ever on behalf of an immigrant population. In this case, it was to assist Cuban refugees and immigrants in the aftermath of the overthrow of Fulgencio Batista in 1959. By the end of 1962, the Catholic Church in Florida offered several Masses with sermons in Spanish and had spent over $1 million to assist refugees with their resettlement. Many additional Catholic institutions were soon established for the purpose of serving the needs of the Cuban Catholic community.

In contrast, within the same decade of the 1960s, a critical consciousness intensified among many Mexican Americans living in the southwest. Anti-foreign hostility led to a wave of intense and open repression against Mexican Americans throughout the 1950s. Eventually, this fueled an explosion of civil rights organizing. In 1968 a high school student strike in Los Angeles triggered the Chicana/o movement, or El Movimiento, one of several social protest movements that led to an accelerated critical awareness relative to race, gender, and class. Within El Movimiento, however, a division among the Chicana leaders emerged between those utterly committed to the liberation of Chicanas as women and those for whom liberation meant liberation of *la raza* as defined by the male leadership of El Movimiento, meaning that liberation for women would have to wait.

Many practicing Catholic Chicanas and Latinas supportive of El Movimiento confronted yet another layer of conflicts. During the late-1960s, the institutional Catholic Church positioned itself as opposed to all that El Movimiento represented. Latina/o sisters, priests, and other church leaders were typically and explicitly instructed by Anglo church leadership *not* to celebrate Mass or offer any ministry in Spanish. Yet, El Movimiento stirred pride and ethnic consciousness around being Mexican American by directly challenging overt racism, not only of society at large but also within the institutional church. Latinas, particularly women religious, found themselves caught in the middle. Would they remain within the church, challenging its blatant racist practices, or would they leave? In 1971, led by Sr. Gregoria Ortega and Sr. Gloria Graciela Gallardo, some fifty women religious gathered in Houston, Texas, and formed Las Hermanas, whose mission was to promote effective ministry among Latina/os. From its inception, the projects of Las Hermanas focused on the injustices experienced by Latinas, particularly at the hands of the church.

With this as a backdrop, Latinas began writing theology in the late 1970s (Ada María Isasi-Díaz, María Pilar Aquino, and Marina Herrera), roughly a decade after Virgilio Elizondo (the originator of U.S. Latina/o theology) and Orlando E. Costas (the originator of Latina/o evangelical theology) each began their own publications. Two phases in the development of Latina theology can be distinguished: the first, from about 1980 to 2001; and the second, from roughly 2001 to the present.

Description

The first attempts to theologically articulate Latinas' desire for liberation grew out of the visionary soil that generated Las Hermanas (1971), the Womenchurch movement and the Women's Ordination Conference (1970s), the founding of the Mexican American Cultural Center (1971) and the three National Encuentros of Catholic Latina/o leadership (1972, 1977, and 1985). The National Encuentro process, along with other Catholic Church movements among Latina/os, furthered the leadership skills of thousands, if not tens of thousands, of Latina/o Catholics.

The early 1980s likewise marked a significant time for the development of Protestant theology with the inauguration of the journal *Apuntes*, which became one of the first journals where Protestant Latinas published their work. The *Journal of Hispanic/Latino Theology*, which has published most of the Latinas discussed in this article, did not begin publication until 1993.

The 1980s was a heady time; it ushered in the formative and first phase of Latina theology. While working as a lay parish minister, Ada María Isasi-Díaz (born in Cuba, Catholic), attended the 1975 Women's Ordination Conference, where her eyes were opened to the reality of sexism in the Catholic Church. In reflecting on this experience, she observed:

> The Womanchurch movement . . . became my home . . . however, [this] brought me into conflict with the sisterhood. As long as I toiled in the garden of Euro-American feminism, I was welcomed. But as I started to claim a space in the garden to plant my own flowers, the ethnic/racist prejudice prevalent in society reared its head within the Womanchurch movement. . . . What took me totally by surprise was the inability or unwillingness of the Euro-American feminists to acknowledge their prejudice.[3]

Isasi-Díaz turned to her pen in an effort to resist the compounding forces—political, racial, cultural, religious, and economic—that silence Latinas, making them invisible. It was no fluke that Isasi-Díaz began one of her first articles, "Toward an Understanding of Feminismo Hispano in the U.S.A." (1985) with the words, "How more invisible than invisible can you be? And yet there is a quality of invisible invisibility. . . . Invisible invisibility has to do with people not even knowing that they do not know you. . . . We are so irrelevant that the mind constructs needed to think about us do not exist. Society at large thinks of us as Hispanic and the majority of Hispanics think of us as women."[4] During the same time period, a gender analysis played no part in U.S. Latina/o theological discourse. Consequently, she began the process of inserting Latinas into feminist theology and privileging Latina experience in U.S. Latina/o theology.

Claiming the power that comes from naming oneself and acknowledging the influence of womanist theologians, Isasi-Díaz in collaboration with Yolanda Tarango coined the term and originated the concept "mujerista theology." While others have contributed, Isasi-Díaz remains mujerista theology's persistent driving force. She contends that using the term "feministas hispanas" lacks a sense of Latina particularity and ignores at least two problems. First, this term conceals the consistent marginalization of Latinas within feminist circles; second, this term alienates some within the Latina/o community for whom sexism remains a central Latina/o concern but for whom the term "feminism" cannot signify more than a Euro-American response. In selecting the name "mujerista," Isasi-Díaz endeavors to move beyond both these limitations. In brief, she defines mujeristas as Hispanic women who "struggle to liberate (themselves) not as individuals but as members of a Hispanic community."[5]

Mujerista theology assumes a preferential option for Latina women and thereby offers a response to the question, "What would theology look like if it was genuinely life-giving or liberating for Latinas?" To conceive a response, this discourse roots itself in liberative praxis, meaning "reflective action that has as its goal liberation."[6] Accordingly, mujerista theology encourages Latinas in their development of moral agency, in their desire to give public voice to their theological insights, and in their struggles not simply to survive but to flourish. This vision constitutes liberation. It furthers this vision by enabling Latinas in (1) the development of conscientization regarding deeply internalized oppressions, (2) the transformation of oppressive societal structures, and (3) the continuous conversion from sin. Her book *Mujerista Theology: A Theology for the Twenty-First Century* (1996) offers the most systematic treatment of this theology.

In the very early 1980s, while doing pastoral work and teaching in Mexico City, María Pilar Aquino (born in Mexico, Catholic) began publishing. The title of one of her first articles, "El culto a María y María en el culto" ("The Veneration of Mary and 'Mary' of the Veneration"),[7] published in the widely touted Mexican feminist publication *FEM* in 1981, is suggestive of Aquino's incisive, critical approach to theology. While both Aquino and Isasi-Díaz privilege a feminist hermeneutic, they frame their projects distinctly. A reader of their works quickly discovers a sharp distinction between mujerista theology and Latina feminist theology, the name used by Aquino and others. Neither of these two terms used alone accurately represents the writings of all Latina theologians committed to feminism.

Isasi-Díaz views the term "feminist" as alienating. Aquino, in contrast, points to critical feminist theories developed in Latin America and to the long history of feminist movements in various Latin American countries to argue that the term "feminist" must not be constructed as a concept transplanted from a white, feminist, first-world context. Aquino's use of the term "Latina feminist theology" affirms the importance of the historical roots of Latina feminism. The difference here is more than semantic. For Aquino, the theological project necessitates a critical analysis of systems that impoverish and marginalize women (and men), which then informs the development of a liberative theological vision: in other words, an interpretation. For Isasi-Díaz, the theological project concerns giving increasing numbers of individual women public voice for the benefit of the whole community, an endeavor facilitated by the use of the sociological method of ethnography. She shies away from interpretation for fear that it will objectify and essentialize women's voices and experience.

Aquino's theological writings offer a critical analysis of sociopolitical and economic injustices with the intention of transforming relations of domination and the structures that sustain domination, be they social or religious. Gender oppression, consequently, is analyzed in an extended and in-depth fashion that theorizes racial, class, cultural, ecological, and religious hegemonies. Her work foregrounds a serious critique of the imperialistic, globalized economy that destroys the lives of poor women (and men) and of marginalized people in the geopolitical South. Yet her analytical commitment extends beyond socioeconomic and historical forces to include ideological worldviews. In her 1992 book, *Nuestro clamor por la vida* (*Our Cry for Life*), Aquino mapped the contours of her feminist liberation theology. Here she followed a liberation theology method and considered Latin American women's experience of oppression as the point of departure for the question of liberation, conceived as both historical and theological. She posits:

> Theological work by women is interested in gathering the historical and spiritual experiences of oppressed women, looking at them, and interpreting them in the light of faith in order to contribute to their own liberation and the liberation of all humanity. Therefore everything that has to do with the creation, re-creation, and defense of life for the poor and for women's work of solidarity has theological significance for their particular way of understanding the faith.[8]

Actual human experience as the point of departure has enormous implications for Latinas, both in the United States and throughout Latin America. The daily lives of Latinas are often marked by immense suffering and, until recently, have been largely invisible. The near absence of women's experience in Latin American liberation theology and U.S. Latino theologies is a glaring omission. If, as has happened in these theologies, women's voices are collapsed into the voice or the experience of the community as a whole, then women's liberation becomes overlooked and subsumed, hence negated. But Aquino interprets this historical moment as the moment of the "eruption of the poor," particularly women, onto the stage of history. The poor are no longer objects of concern but are subjects and agents who shape their own history.

Throughout her work, Aquino not only identifies and examines Latinas' particular ways of knowing but also makes clear their resulting contribution to Latina feminist theology. When women's "vision and speech" stretch the otherwise narrower outlook of liberation theology, Latinas inevitably criticize this theology's androcentric predisposition as they offer a corrective by transfiguring the meaning and force of liberation. Thus, the inclusion of Latinas's vision and speech must not be interpreted as exclusively a matter of language. Fundamentally, the inclusion of Latinas' vision and speech concerns the expansion of "liberation theology's *epistemological horizon.*"[9] How we come to know, and what can be known, changes.

Aquino and Isasi-Díaz are not the only theologians employing a feminist hermeneutic. During this early phase of Latina theological writings, Jeanette Rodríguez-Holguin (Ecuadorian American, Catholic) extended this discourse with an original approach. She turned to psychological theory to frame human experience. A great part of Rodríguez-Holguin's early research was devoted to examining the influence and significance of the symbol of Our Lady of Guadalupe in the lives of Mexican American women that resulted in her book, *Our Lady of Guadalupe: Faith and Empowerment among Mexican-American Women* (1994). This research led Rodríguez-Holguin to develop the category of "cultural memory." Cultural memory includes elements of tradition, worldview, historical memory, and myth, each in their own way responding to the human need for "identity, salvation, hope and resistance to annihilation."[10]

In this initial and formative phase of Latina theology, while some Latina theologians employed a feminist hermeneutic, others published in the field of pastoral theology. This second group of Latina theologians focused their attention on making theological sense of the various ministerial needs of the Latina/o community. So they discussed, among other ministerial foci, questions of religious education, spiritual growth, liturgical practice, and youth ministry. While these Latina theologians expressed interest in both how the faith has been understood throughout history (historical theology) and how the coherency and significance of revelation are interrelated (systematic theology), their overriding concern remains how to respond to the pastoral needs of individual Latina/os and their communities.

Latina pastoral theologians have a long and rich history of publications dating from Marina Herrera's (Dominican-born, Catholic) first article, "La teología en el mundo de hoy" (Theology in Today's World), published in 1974. Since then, Herrera has authored numerous articles primarily in the field of multicultural catechesis and ministry and has reflected on the role of women in the church.

Ana María Pineda (born in El Salvador, Catholic) has published several articles and essays since the late 1980s. For her, the distinctiveness of and, accordingly, the contemporary ministerial concerns of the U.S. Latina/o faith community can only be understood in light of their historical experience. Her research, therefore, sheds much needed light on the Mesoamerican oral tradition, clarifying how this tradition can be revelatory of the sacred for U. S. Latina/os today.

Latinas *evangélicas* and Latinas *protestantes* make up a third group of Latina theologians. They began publishing in the mid-1990s, roughly more than a decade after their Catholic colleagues. These Latina theologians operate at the margins of three realities. They are Protestants in the midst of a Latina/o culture that is predominantly Catholic; they are Latinas in the midst of Protestant denominations that are basically Anglo; they are Latina theologians working in universities, seminaries, and churches deeply imbued with a patriarchal worldview. Most of them are ordained and have many years of experience as ministers and pastors. Their theological work vividly reflects these realities.

In this initial phase, as well as the next, these theologians have made contributions in diverse theological areas. Daisy Machado (born in Cuba, ordained minister of the Disciples of Christ) has written on church history in the southwestern borderlands, Latina/o Protestantism, ecumenism, justice, and historical imagination. In her writings, Elizabeth Conde-Frazier (Puerto Rican, ordained minister of the American Baptists) has addressed questions of spiritual formation, practical theology, and religious education. Teresa Chavez Sauceda (Chicana Mexican American, ordained pastor of the Presbyterians) has written on racial and gender justice, the doctrine of God, and social ethics. Arlene Sánchez Walsh (Mexican American, Latina Pentecostal) writes on Pentecostal history, Pentecostal identity, Latina/o evangelical youth culture, Protestant ministry, and evangelicalism. Loida Martell-Otero (Puerto Rican, ordained minister of the American Baptists) has published on Latinas *evangélicas*, ministry, and soteriology.

While not theologians, another group of Latina scholars deserves mention because they have made such a significant contribution to the development of Latina theology. Since the early 1990s, sociologists of religion Ana María Díaz-Stevens and Milagros Peña have both studied and analyzed the role of Latinas in religious institutions, in social movements, and as practitioners of popular religious practices. Much of Díaz-Stevens's work has focused on detailed historical and social portraits of the Latina Puerto Rican Catholic experience. Peña, alternatively, has attended to a wide range of concerns related to Latinas, activism, religious practices, and the challenges of living along the U.S.-Mexico border.

By 2001 a subtle shift began to occur, and it accelerated over the course of the following years. Before 2001, fewer than ten monographs (in addition to a number of essays and articles) delineated the Latina theological conversation. All the monographs before 2001 were written by a few Catholic theologians. Since 2001, Latina theologians have contributed to published conversations with African American and womanist theologians, and with Latin American and Caribbean feminist theologians. With increasing frequency, Latina Protestant and Latina Catholic theologians have published their work together. A number of Latina Protestant theologians have published monographs. A couple of Latina Catholic theologians have published their first monographs. An even larger new group of Latina theologians, Catholic and Protestant, have begun publishing their work, bringing a wide array of critical tools of analysis to Latina theology. Many of these theoretical and methodological tools were not in use in Latina theological discourse before 2001. All of this is to say that the parameters of the Latina theological conversation have been substantially redefined, inaugurating the second phase of Latina theology. This growth and deepening phase began in 2001 and takes us up to the present.

The nature of edited collections played a role in the transition to the second phase. *The Ties That Bind: African American and Hispanic American/Latino/a Theologies in Dialogue* (2001)[11] signaled the coming change when Latina/o theologians and African American theologians, women and men, each contributed articles on a given theme and entered into dialogue. Latino/a theological writing had now bridged a racial divide. Furthermore, *Religion, Feminism and Justice: A Reader in Latina Feminist Theology* (2002)[12] represented several "firsts": not only is it the first collection focused exclusively on Latinas and theology, but also only Latina theologians made contributions. This volume contains the writings of many emerging Protestant and Catholic Latina theologians, so it furthered the ecumenical conversation and introduced readers to the coming generation of Latina theologians. Only Latina theologians served as editors: two Catholics (María Pilar Aquino and Jeanette Rodríguez-Holguin) and one Protestant (Daisy Machado). In 2004, a team of four scholars convened the first symposium of Latina feminist theologians from the United States, Latin America, and the Caribbean, which eventually led to *Feminist Intercultural Theology: Latina Explorations for a Just World* (2007).[13] It is the first edited collection that includes Latina theologians from throughout the Americas: north, central, and south. María Pilar Aquino was the driving force behind both of these collections.

During these same years, the nature of monographs shifted dramatically. Beginning in 2003 and over the next several years, a number of Latina Protestant theologians published monographs for the first time (Daisy Machado, Arlene Sánchez Walsh, Elizabeth Conde-Frazier, and Mayra Rivera Rivera). During this same time period, two Latina Catholics likewise published their first monographs (Michelle González and Anita de Luna). González then proceeded to publish two additional books over the following four years. As a result of all of these developments, the Latina theological conversation has stepped into an even brighter spotlight: it has moved beyond its initial boundaries along several distinct fronts, and it has deepened significantly through a rich infusion of substantive monographs. In the process, the conversation has been transformed.

In a brief period of time, Michelle A. González Maldonado (Cuban American, Catholic) has emerged as one of the most productive scholars among Latina theologians. In a span of fewer than four years, she published three books and has many articles to her credit, which, taken together, reveal her wide-ranging theological interests. Indignant with Octavio Paz's observation that Latin America has "no Kant, no Robespierre, no Hume, no Jefferson,"[14] González wrote *Sor Juana: Beauty and Justice in the Americas* (2003) in which she excavated Sor Juana's theological, scholarly contribution in the areas of aesthetics, ethics, and epistemology. She concludes with an examination of the connections between ethics and aesthetics in contemporary theology and the ways this connection could prove fecund for liberation theologies. Long concerned with the absence of a theological examination of the Afro-Cuban or Cuban American experience, González wrote a second book in which she examines questions of identity construction and religiosity that emerge at the intersection of Blacks and Latina/os. She concludes by raising some questions for a future Cuban American anthropology.[15] For her third book, González wrote an introductory text for feminist theological anthropology, mapping the questions that orient feminist theology today and into the future.[16]

In many respects, it is appropriate to begin a discussion of the second phase of Latina theology with the work of Daisy Machado. She is the first Latina *protestante* to earn a Ph.D. in a theological field, and she is among the first to publish a monograph, *Of Borders and Margins: Hispanic Disciples in Texas: 1888–1945* (2003).[17] In this work, Machado examines the limited success of the Christian church (Disciples of Christ) in attracting Mexican coreligionists when compared with the success of other Protestant denominations during the same time period in Texas. Further, she considers the dissonance created by the theological vision of the Disciples, on the one hand, and their uncritical, perhaps even tacit, acceptance of the ideology of manifest destiny, on the other. Machado calls on her fellow Disciples, and all of us, to think long and hard about the relationship between Christianity and nationalism and about the ways in which racist convictions often play a role.

At roughly the same time, Elizabeth Conde-Frazier and Arlene Sánchez Walsh each articulated a vision of theology that responded to the queries of Pentecostals and Evangelicals. Conde-Frazier, in her two monographs, addressed the educational and theological challenges of particular local churches from the perspective of Hispanic Protestant missiology. She offered a serious examination of how to focus local churches ever more clearly on the "kingdom of God" in the midst of American biases and ideologies shaping perceptions of race, ethnicity, gender, class, nationalism, and sexuality. Sánchez Walsh focused on the ambivalent relationship that Mexican American Pentecostals have with their ethnic identity as it relates to their religious identity. Her study was localized in southern California and traced a history of the troubled race relations in the wake of the Azusa Street Pentecostalism of the early 20th century. These authors directed our attention to the church's understanding of its mission and the ways in which ethnic and racial identity functions in churches.[18]

In addition to these Latina Protestants, there are two other theologians whose work belongs in this second phase. Mayra Rivera Rivera (Puerto Rican, Methodist), well versed in postcolonial theory, "radical orthodoxy," and liberation theologies, developed the first sustained constructive work on the doctrine of God by any Latina theologian. In her first monograph, she offers a reformulation of divine transcendence in which relationality and intimacy play a preeminent role. She wants us to understand how human creatures encounter divine transcendence and the necessity of this encounter for the purpose of imagining and creating ethical human relationships.[19] Nancy Elizabeth Bedford (Argentinean, Mennonite), a recent transplant to the United States (2003) from a university in Buenos Aires, has, since 1996, published numerous articles and three books, primarily in the field of systematic theology. In her recent work she examines the intersections between economy, theology, and feminist theory.[20]

Since 2001, some of the Latina theologians mentioned in the first phase have published additional books. Besides the two edited collections already mentioned, María Pilar Aquino coedited two additional volumes addressing questions of large-scale conflicts, reconciliation processes, and the just war doctrine.[21] Jeanette Rodríguez-Holguin coauthored a book on the religious, cultural, and social aspects of cultural memory.[22] Ada María Isasi-Díaz published a book that explores further some of the fundamental themes of mujerista theology (i.e., *mestizaje-mulatez, lo cotidiano,* justice, and reconciliation, among others),[23] and she coedited a volume on Jesus and ministry. For Nancy Pineda-Madrid (Mexican American, Catholic) theological construction necessarily strives for a critical interpretation of historical experience in light of gospel faith for the historical and spiritual liberation of all. Currently she is working on a book that argues for a social doctrine of salvation in light of the suffering of Latinas. Her research focuses on feminist soteriologies.[24]

The field of pastoral theology, too, continued to unfold during the second phase, largely due to the innovative contributions of Carmen Nanko-Fernández (Spanish-Czech, Catholic) and Anita de Luna (Mexican American, Catholic). Even though Nanko-Fernández published a short volume on ministry with Catholic college students in 1997,[25] she rightly belongs in this second phase. Since 2001 Nanko-Fernández has published articles on the church, theological reflection, immigration, justice, youth ministry, Catholic social teaching, and popular culture. In 2002, de Luna (now deceased) published her first monograph in which she offered an in-depth analysis of several catechisms, with particular attention to the Hispano catechisms used at different points in Texas history. She then shows how these catechisms can serve as an entry point into the spiritual life of Tejanos.[26]

Sources

The move beyond preliminary theological boundaries serves as the hallmark of this second phase of Latina theology. Indeed, at the dawn of the 21st century, Latina theologians have begun to address an expanding horizon of questions and interests.

Latina theologies obviously draw on sources common to all Christian theologies (i.e., human experience, scriptures, and tradition). Even so, every expression of Latina theology emerges out of a distinctive cultural milieu⊠ that is, an interrelated network of symbols, semantic fields, attitudes toward life, shared core myths, and tacit political and social relationships. A cultural milieu consists of all the ways a given group understands and expresses its identity. Latina theological discourse, likewise, contends with larger forces: the operative political, economic, gendered, class, and sexual realities that define the world of its social location. Indeed, Latina theologians invariably approach the sources they select (whether those common to all Christian theologies or those that provide access to some dimension of Latina experience) from within some concrete given: namely, some tangible sociocultural and political world.

While Latina theology grows out of a concrete given world, this does not mean that the term "Latina" stands for an essentialized experience supposedly common to every female human being of Latin American background. Rather, "Latina" represents a group of women who for politically strategic purposes use this term to stand for a culturally, racially, economically, and socially diverse set of experiences and histories. While a Mexican American, a Salvadorian, and a Cuban American will all use the term "Latina" to identify their work, the concrete given worlds *from which* and *for which* they write typically differ significantly. Consequently, the sources, as well as the theological questions considered, reveal the enormous differences among "Latinas." Latina theologians also draw on a wide range of sources for the purpose of developing theology. These sources are grouped under (1) experience, history, and cultural material; (2) Hebrew and Christian scriptures; and (3) tradition.

Experience, History, and Cultural Material

Latina theologians often take the "lived experience of Latinas" as a point of departure for developing theology. Yet, this notion is in quotation marks because it stands for the diverse nature of Latina experience. Moreover, the "lived experience of Latinas" does not come in some transparent given form, but, like all human experience, it is invariably mediated through culture and language. All human experience is interpreted experience.

Latina theologians have interpreted this experience through categories like *mestizaje* and *mulatez*. *Mestizaje* references the racial and cultural mixing of Spanish and Amerindian peoples and *mulatez* the mixing of Spanish and Black African peoples. *Mestizaje* and *mulatez* are primal and pervasive inasmuch as Latinas (and Latinos) have survived precisely through this mixing. From the perspective of the Protestant faith experience and ecclesiastical practice, Latina theologians consider their experience as *evangélicas* and provide a new interpretation of the experience of *mestizaje* (mixing of two realities): namely, the experience of being both "Hispanic" and "Protestant."

The lived experience of Latinas has also been interpreted through the category of *lo cotidiano* (the daily experience of living). The stories and narratives that Latinas tell of their lives are part of *lo cotidiano*. This category has been used by Latina theologians to call attention to the transitory and incomplete nature of the struggle of daily life; to make explicit the social location of all knowledge; to highlight the experiences of Latinas that resonate among them— injustices in terms of race and class, as well as gender; and to signal that in the daily experience of living we come to know grace and sin. *Lo cotidiano* emerges in the dynamic web of *la familia*, of *la comunidad;* it belongs neither to the strictly private nor the strictly public spheres of life but pertains to both. Latina theologians use other sources as well to read the lived experience of Latinas. Some have noted the way in which the Spanish language both reflects and shapes Latinas' experience. Others privilege sociological and anthropological portraits of Latinas' experience.

For Latina theologians, the histories of Latina/o communities both in the United States and in their Latin American countries of origin have served as a significant theological resource on many levels. Some theologians have focused on the historically decisive events (e.g., the occupation of Puerto Rico [1898], the Treaty of Guadalupe-Hidalgo [1848], the communist revolution in Cuba [1959]) that shaped their community's identity and stirred Latina/os to look to their faith for a way to make sense of their experience. Others have re-read historical accounts, attempting to uncover and piece together the myriad ways that Latina/os have acted on behalf of their communities. Still others have followed a similar line of thought, one focused more specifically on the ways Latinas have asserted themselves. The importance of history as a source for Latina theology has been affirmed through the development of ideas like *the irruption of history* (historical consciousness in the lives of women)[27] and the category of *proyecto histórico* (the hoped-for future in the lives of women).[28]

Yet another important and emerging source is cultural material. Many Latina theologians have mined the rich vein of literary works written by Latinas, both contemporary and historical. Latina literature has been used to explore themes of voice, authority, grace, spirit, salvation, loss, and suffering, to name a few. The visual arts have also played a large role. Latina theologians have deliberated on the symbolism found in public murals in many cities in the United States and that found in the paintings of contemporary Latina artists. Similarly, religious iconography and art have also served as a source (e.g., *retablos, milagritos,* Caridad del Cobre, Guadalupe).

Hebrew and Christian Scriptures

The scriptures play a preeminent role in Latina theological discourse, as the primary resource for mediating an understanding of the mystery and workings of God. Latina theologians look to scripture to break open the lives of Latinas: that is, their struggle for liberation in the face of oppression, their desire to survive when survival is in question, and their hope for the coming kingdom of God in the midst of crushing poverty. As such, Latina theologians turn to particular passages that resonate with the existential reality of Latinas' lives. The first chapters of Genesis, the Exodus event, the concubine in Judges 19, the prophetic books, the stories of Jesus' healings, the accounts of Pentecost and the early church in Acts, among other passages, have all been used by Latina theologians to reflect on the meaning of grace, liberation, suffering, social sin, conversion, and other theological concerns.

By and large, Latina theologians understand the scriptures to be the "word of God," not in a literal sense but in the sense that, for believers, the scriptures can mediate an experience of the living God so powerful that it transforms lives. For Latina theologians, the "word of God" is that which brings life; that which nourishes the lives of Latinas, of all humanity and of creation; and that which continually summons believers, through the work of the Spirit, to ever-greater intimacy with God and to ever-greater love for one another.

Tradition

Latina theologies also draw from the wisdom expressed in the writings of a long line of outstanding Christian believers and from the practices of individuals who, and communities which, have sought to live lives as Christian disciples ever more deeply committed to gospel faith. This tradition of two thousand years carries rich insights as the experience of being Christian has been clarified and reclarified many times in widely diverse circumstances and during radically distinct historical periods. Latina theologies have turned to prominent Christian thinkers such as Augustine, Irenaeus, Anselm, Aquinas, and Sor Juana to inform their writings. Official church teachings and documents have likewise been used frame theological concerns. Given the liberationist orientation of much of Latina theology, many contemporary works in Latin American liberation theology, feminist theologies, womanist theology, Black theology, and moral theology, among others, have been used to stretch and deepen Latina theological discourse.

Popular religious practices—meaning religious practices created by the people for the purpose of their spiritual growth and their appropriation of the Christian faith—have been a rich tradition since the dawn of Christianity in the Americas. These practices have taken scriptural stories and insights and brought them to life through theological dramas, through the use of images and iconography, and through short ritual celebrations. Reflection on this rich dimension of the Christian tradition has enlivened Latina theologies.

In addition, many Protestant Latina theologians bring the added dimension of their experience as ordained leaders of faith communities to bear on their theological writings. By way of contrast, Latina Catholic theologians do not have experience as ordained leaders.

Theoretical and Methodological Considerations

Latina theologians make decisions not only about the sources they will employ but also about what they understand the theological task to be. Simply put, what are they doing when they write theology? A theologian's understanding of the theological task will inform her selection of sources. In other words, a theologian assumes a theory in the writing of theology, selects particular sources to use, and then makes decisions about how she will engage the sources she selected. What will be considered important from a given source? How will the sources be used in relation to each other? What is the best way to use the selected sources to accomplish the task of theology?

Latina theologians assume that the theological task is to reflect critically on the experience of Christian faith for the sake of liberation. Latina theology assumes that this reflection is *from within* and *for* the liberation of the Latina/o community so that the community may realize a world more free of all that is dehumanizing and unjust, which necessarily means a world more in harmony with God's love. Furthermore, such a theological assumption presumes a preferential option for poor and oppressed people, meaning that the injustices of the world are to be understood first from the vantage point of the most vulnerable among us. The theological task is an intellectual endeavor in service of bringing about a more just, transformed, God-filled world—not simply for Latina/os but for all humanity and creation. While Latina theologians generally agree on this basic orientation, there remain significant methodological differences. The differences stem from more subtle understandings of the theological task and from a difference in strategy for realizing that task (method).

By and large, Latina theologians using a feminist hermeneutic agree that the diversity of Latinas lived experience must be taken seriously and that it is necessary to examine and critique the ways in which social and discursive systems foster an interlocking web of oppression. This web of oppression consists of inequities of gender, race, class, sexual orientation, and colonialism. Yet this same group of Latina theologians disagree on how "feminism" is to be regarded and, therefore, on which methodological tools to use. For some theologians, the term "feminist" is useful and historical. Feminist theories from Latin America, the United States, and elsewhere offer the best range of approaches for engaging sources and theorizing the diversity of Latinas' lived experience. When theologians theorize this lived experience well, then the possibility of liberation is advanced. For other Latina theologians, ethnography and metaethnography, which are socioanthropological resources, offer the most useful method for realizing the liberative desires of Latinas. Liberation is realized by encouraging Latinas to act in the world with greater moral agency and to give public voice to their theological insights. For these theologians the term "feminist" carries problematic baggage. Mujerista theology employs this latter method.

Any methodological approach that does not make clear from the onset that "scripture is authoritative for faith and practice" would be regarded as suspicious by many of the Latina theologians who identify as *evangélicas* or *protestantes*. For this second group of Latina theologians, scripture "needs to be reread with the guidance of the Holy Spirit in order to rediscover God's Word of affirmation and liberation for all people, especially the marginalized and oppressed. Together with liberation theologies, [these Latina theologians] critique the excessive privatism, individualism, and false spiritualization of the gospel that has traditionally been sustained by Protestant thought and belief."[29] They claim that the gospel understands salvation to be both God's promise of a future life in the fullness of time and what we experience in our lives here on Earth. Among these theologians, methods of exegesis and methods for the discernment of the Holy Spirit play a paramount role.

A third group of Latina theologians, while in agreement with the liberative task of Latina theology, consider the immediate pastoral needs of the Latina/o, believing community to be central. They concern themselves with how to witness to, and communicate the faith to, Latina/os in this historical moment. These theologians gravitate toward a methodological approach that enhances religious education, spiritual growth, liturgical practice, youth ministry, and the practice of the church.

Yet, even though several distinctions in methodological approaches can be made, the writings of many Latina theologians straddle more than one of these approaches. The distinctions in approaches serve simply as a guide to the range of methodological commitments in Latina theology. As Latina theological discourse has matured over the past two decades plus of its existence, the discourse has clearly expanded and deepened. One reflection of that growth can be found in the increasing and sophisticated use of a wide range of methodological resources. Latina theologians today use postcolonial theory, postmodern theory, critical theory, critical race theory, feminist theory, economic theory, intercultural philosophy, U.S. pragmatism, and Latin American philosophy, to name only some of an expanding list of resources employed.

Ongoing Issues

Of late, Latina theology has expanded and deepened in ways not imagined even a short decade ago. Historical circumstances have created new opportunities and challenges that have propelled this discourse to a new level. The following areas represent merely a few of the many theological issues that Latina theology will continue to face in the coming decades: (1) diversity of Latina/os communities, (2) the expanding conversation, and (3) operative gender ideologies.

Diversity of Latina/os Communities

We have already mentioned that the term "Latina" functions as an umbrella term to refer to women who reside in the United States yet trace their roots to the countries of Central America, the Caribbean, Latin America, or Mexico and that the term "Latina" continues to be adopted for politically strategic purposes. The name "Latina theology" garners more political weight in academia and in our churches than would designations such as Dominican American theology, Cuban American theology, and so forth. The term "Latina theology" suggests that those who write this are part of a larger discourse. Yet the term "Latina theology" presents problems because of the enormous differences in histories, cultures, religious beliefs and practices, racial and ethnic mixing, intellectual histories, economic circumstances, and so on. Some Latinas identify with the experience of exile, others with the experience of being a colonized people, and still others with being in the United States *sin papeles* (without papers).

A brief current statistical portrait of U.S. Latina/os will provide a further context. In 2005, the Pew Hispanic Center reported that of the 296 million people who make up the population of the United States, Hispanics or Latina/os comprise 14%, or 41 million. By 2050, the Pew projects that Hispanics or Latina/os will make up 29% of the U.S. population. Also for 2005, of all Hispanics or Latina/os living in the United States, 63.9% are of Mexican origin, 9.1% are Puerto Rican, 3.5% are of Cuban origin, 3.0% are of Salvadorian origin, 2.7% are of Dominican origin, and all other Hispanic/Latina/o groups make up less than 2.0% of the U.S. Hispanic or Latina/o population. In 2006 Pew conducted a survey and determined that of all Hispanics or Latina/os living in the United States, 68% are Roman Catholic, 15% are Evangelical Protestant, and 8% (the third largest group) includes those who identify with either "no affiliation" or as agnostic or atheist.[30]

Given this diversity, Latina theologians need to sort out how Latina theology may be constructed such that it respects the multiplicity of Latinas' experience yet does not empty the umbrella term "Latina" of meaning, thereby compromising the vital political, strategic purpose that a term like "Latina" affords this theological discourse. Short of addressing this challenge directly, Latina theologies run the risk of falling into new internal hegemonies based perhaps on racial privilege, religious dominance, class influence and privilege, demographic dominance, or some other distinction of power. Internal hegemonies would, in time, undermine the liberation that Latina theologies profess to seek. Recently Latina theologians have begun addressing this challenge, the importance of which will only grow with time.

The Expanding Conversation

Latina theologians have now begun to engage in conversations with other theologians committed to liberationist discourse. As might be anticipated, initial exchanges with African American and womanist theologians revealed several overlapping areas of interest and similar historical concerns. These exchanges have prodded Latina theologians to rethink the boundaries of their writings. For example, where do the theological concerns of Latina feminist theologies and womanist theologies converge? diverge? How would Asian American feminist theologies contribute to, challenge, or affirm these concerns? How might Latina theologians understand differently what it means to write theology if this work is intentionally linked to the projects of African American and Asian American theologians? In 2004 and again in 2008, some Latina feminist theologians from the United States engaged in a dialogue with feminist theologians from Latin America and the Caribbean. This dialogue pushed participants to reimagine what it means to write Latina feminist theology. Questions of globalization, economic power, and imperialism moved to the fore, recontextualizing how Latina theologians perceive the social location of their work. No doubt, the frame of reference for Latina theology is shifting; the overarching goal of liberation is taking on new meaning.

Operative Gender Ideologies

Latina theologians writing feminist theology have already analyzed the dynamic way that the patriarchal world in which Latina/os live and its attendant sexist practices subordinate Latina females, rendering them of a lesser humanity. These same feminist theologians named this reality "social sin" and called for a world that genuinely supports the full humanity of Latinas, as well as that of all human beings. Yet, by and large, the theological discourse of Latina/os reflects a lack of critical consciousness of the extant gender ideologies which this same discourse discloses. It is true that many Latino theologians will occasionally cite the work of Latina theologians in their theological writings and will note the importance of women and women's contributions. In fact, in the edited collection *Protestantes/Protestants*, four different Latino theologians call specific attention to Latinas' experience; some even voice concern that Latinas have been systematically excluded from public roles and denied recognition for the leadership they offer.[31]

Notwithstanding all of this evidence and more that could be brought to bear, there is still a problem. Orlando Espín got it right when he observed that "much Latina/o theology pays lip service to feminism, while ignoring it methodologically."[32] Latinas who employ a feminist hermeneutic would be well served to take the next step and use the feminist theoretical tools with which they are well acquainted to make clear the ways that gender ideologies function throughout Latina/o theological discourse and the ways in which these operative ideologies ultimately impoverish the humanity of women and men alike.

On a related note, Latina theologians need to dig deeper into the roots, nature, and character of Latina/o patriarchy and sexism. This particular form of patriarchy bears its own unique marks. Even though Latina theologians have put forward an in-depth analysis of the ways in which patriarchy and sexism have been detrimental to Latinas, much more work needs to be done on clarifying the Latina/o form(s) of patriarchy. We do not yet have a clear picture of the Latina/o version of this social sin.

NOTES

Brief portions of the sections titled "Historical Backdrop" and "Description" are taken from Nancy Pineda-Madrid, "Latina Roman Catholic Theologies," in *Encyclopedia of Women and Religion in North America*, ed. Rosemary Skinner Keller and Rosemary Radford Ruether (Bloomington: University of Indiana Press, 2006), 1193–1200.

1. Before proceeding, it is necessary to clarify the meaning of certain terms. For example, a number of different terms are used to designate Latin American or Hispanic ancestry. The majority of theologians represented in this article prefer the term *Latina* because it highlights the communities' Latin American roots. It recognizes the Spanish, Amerindian, African, and Portuguese origins of contemporary Latina/o communities, and it is a self-selected term. Other terms frequently used are *Hispanic, chicana, mestiza,*

and *mulatta*. A number of Latina/o theologians do not use the term "Hispanic" because the U.S. government designated this term for Spanish-speaking and Spanish-surnamed people and intended, by its use, to elevate the Spanish ancestral roots and dismiss the Amerindian and African roots. For many, "Hispanic" is not a self-selected identifier. "Chicana" designates not just a woman born in the United States of Mexican or Mexican American heritage but also a woman who critically assumes a political consciousness of class, race, and gender as framing the way she views the world. "Mestiza" means a woman whose identity emerges from the biological, cultural, and religious mixing of the Spanish and the Amerindian; and "mulatta" arises from the mixing of the Spanish and the African. Neither term is inclusive of all women of Latin American heritage.

2. Bernardo Vega and César Andreu Iglesias, *Memoirs of Bernardo Vega: A Contribution to the History of the Puerto Rican Community in New York* (New York: Monthly Review, 1984), xiv.

3. Ada María Isasi-Díaz, *Mujerista Theology: A Theology for the Twenty-First Century* (Maryknoll, NY: Orbis, 1996), 18.

4. Ada María Isasi-Díaz, "Toward an Understanding of Feminismo Hispano in the U.S.A," in *Women's Consciousness, Women's Conscience: A Reader in Feminist Ethics,* ed. Barbara Hilkert Andolsen, Christine E. Gudorf, and Mary D. Pellauer (Minneapolis: Winston, 1985), 51.

5. Isasi-Díaz, *Mujerista Theology,* 61.

6. Ibid., 62.

7. María Pilar Aquino, "El Culto a María y María en el Culto," *FEM Publicación Feminista* 5, no. 20 [Mexico City] (1981–1982): 41–46. Aquino's title does not translate easily into English. The second half of her title suggests that she will address the social construction of "Mary" through the practice of her veneration.

8. María Pilar Aquino, *Our Cry for Life: Feminist Theology from Latin America* (Maryknoll, NY: Orbis, 1993), 117.

9. Ibid., 109.

10. Jeanette Rodríguez[-Holguin], *Stories We Live: Cuentos Que Vivimos* (Mahwah, NJ: Paulist, 1996), 13.

11. Anthony Pinn and Benjamín Valentín, eds., *The Ties That Bind: African-American and Hispanic American/Latino/a Theologies in Dialogue* (New York: Continuum, 2001).

12. María Pilar Aquino, Daisy L. Machado, and Jeanette Rodríguez, eds., *Religion, Feminism and Justice: A Reader in Latina Feminist Theology* (Austin: University of Texas Press, 2002).

13. María Pilar Aquino and María José Rosado-Nunes, eds., *Feminist Intercultural Theology: Latina Explorations for a Just World* (Maryknoll, NY: Orbis, 2007).

14. Michelle A. González, *Sor Juana: Beauty and Justice in the Americas* (Maryknoll, NY: Orbis, 2003), xi.

15. Michelle A. González, *Afro-Cuban Theology: Religion, Race, Culture, and Identity* (Gainesville: University Press of Florida, 2006).

16. Michelle A. González, *Created in God's Image: An Introduction to Feminist Theological Anthropology* (Maryknoll, NY: Orbis, 2007).

17. Daisy L. Machado, *Of Borders and Margins: Hispanic Disciples in Texas, 1888–1945* (New York: Oxford University Press, 2003).

18. Elizabeth Conde-Frazier, *Hispanic Bible Institutes: A Community of Theological Construction* (Scranton, PA: University of Scranton Press, 2004); Elizabeth Conde-Frazier, S. Steve Kang, and Gary A. Parret, *A Many Colored Kingdom: Multicultural Dynamics for Spiritual Formation* (Grand Rapids, MI: Baker Academic, 2004); and Arlene M. Sánchez Walsh, *Latino Pentecostal Identity: Evangelical Faith, Self, and Society* (New York: Columbia University Press, 2003).

19. Mayra Rivera Rivera, *The Touch of Transcendence: A Postcolonial Theology of God* (Louisville, KY: Westminister John Knox, 2007).

20. Nancy Elizabeth Bedford's books include *Puntos de Encuentro* (Buenos Aires: ISEDET, 2005).

21. María Pilar Aquino's publications include María Pilar Aquino, Daisy L. Machado, and Jeanette Rodriguez[-Holguin], eds., *A Reader in Latina Feminist Theology* (Austin: University of Texas, 2002).

22. Jeanette Rodriguez[-Holguin] and Ted Fortier, *Cultural Memory: Resistance, Faith, and Identity* (Austin: University of Texas Press, 2007).

23. Ada María Isasi-Díaz, *La Lucha Continues: Mujerista Theology* (Maryknoll, NY: Orbis, 2004).

24. Nancy Pineda-Madrid's publications include numerous articles such as "Traditioning: The Formation of Community, the Transmission of Faith," in *In Futuring Our Past: Explorations in the Theology of Tradition,* ed. Orlando Espín and Gary Macy (Maryknoll, NY: Orbis, 2006), 204–226.

25. Carmen Nanko, *Campus Ministry: Identity, Mission and Praxis* (Washington, DC: National Catholic Education Association, 1997).

26. Anita de Luna, *Faith Formation and Popular Religion: Lessons from the Tejano Experience* (Lanham, MD: Rowman and Littlefield, 2002).

27. Aquino, *Our Cry for Life,* 9–25.

28. Isasi-Díaz, *Mujerista Theology,* 153–158.

29. Elizabeth Conde-Frazier and Loida I. Martell Otero, "U.S. Latina Evangélicas," in *Encyclopedia of Women and Religion in North America,* ed. Rosemary Skinner Keller and Rosemary Radford Ruether (Bloomington: University of Indiana Press, 2006), 1:479.

30. This section is based on Pew Hispanic Center, *U.S. Population Projections: 2005–2050,* report dated February 11, 2008, available at http://pewhispanic.org/reports/report.php?ReportID=85; Pew Hispanic Center, "A Statistical Portrait of Hispanics at Mid-Decade, Table 3: Detailed Hispanic Origin: 2005," report dated August 29, 2006, available at http://pewhispanic.org/files/other/middecade/Table-3.pdf; and Pew Hispanic Center, *Changing Faiths: Latinos and the Transformation of American Religion,* chap. 1: "Religion and Demography," page 7, report dated April 25, 2007, available at http://pewhispanic.org/files/reports/75.1.pdf.

31. David Maldonado Jr., ed., *Protestantes/Protestants: Hispanic Christianity within Mainline Traditions* (Nashville, TN: Abingdon, 1999), 116, 156, 258–259, 287.

32. Orlando O. Espín, "The State of U.S. Latina/o Theology: An Understanding," in *Hispanic Christian Thought at the Dawn of the 21st Century: Apuntes in Honor of Justo L. González,* ed. Alvin Padilla, Roberto Goizueta, and Eldin Villafañe (Nashville, TN: Abingdon, 2005), 104.

Aquino, María Pilar. *Our Cry for Life: Feminist Theology from Latin America*. Maryknoll, NY: Orbis, 1993.

Aquino, María Pilar, and María José Rosado-Nunes, eds. *Feminist Intercultural Theology: Latina Explorations for a Just World*. Maryknoll, NY: Orbis, 2007.

Aquino, María Pilar, Daisy L. Machado, and Jeanette Rodríguez, eds. *Religion, Feminism and Justice: A Reader in Latina Feminist Theology*. Austin: University of Texas Press, 2002.

Conde-Frazier, Elizabeth. *Hispanic Bible Institutes: A Community of Theological Construction*. Scranton, PA: University of Scranton Press, 2004.

de Luna, Anita. *Faith Formation and Popular Religion: Lessons from the Tejano Experience*. Lanham, MD: Rowman and Littlefield, 2002.

González, Michelle A. *Afro-Cuban Theology: Religion, Race, Culture, and Identity*. Gainesville: University Press of Florida, 2006.

———. *Sor Juana: Beauty and Justice in the Americas*. Maryknoll, NY: Orbis, 2003.

Isasi-Díaz, Ada María. *En la Lucha/In the Struggle: A Hispanic Women's Liberation Theology*. Minneapolis: Fortress, 1993.

———. *La Lucha Continues: Mujerista Theology*. Maryknoll, NY: Orbis, 2004.

———. *Mujerista Theology: A Theology for the Twenty-First Century*. Maryknoll, NY: Orbis, 1996.

Machado, Daisy L. *Of Borders and Margins: Hispanic Disciples in Texas, 1888–1945*. New York: Oxford University Press, 2003.

Pineda-Madrid, Nancy. "Traditioning: The Formation of Community, the Transmission of Faith." In *Futuring the Past: Explorations in the Theology of Tradition*, ed. Orlando Espín and Gary Macy, 204–226. Maryknoll, NY: Orbis, 2006.

Rivera, Mayra Rivera. *The Touch of Transcendence: A Postcolonial Theology of God*. Louisville, KY: Westminister John Knox, 2007.

Rodríguez, Jeanette. *Our Lady of Guadalupe: Faith and Empowerment among Mexican-American Women*. Austin: University of Texas Press, 1994.

Rodríguez, José David, and Loida I. Martell-Otero, eds. *Teologia en Conjunto: A Collaborative Hispanic Protestant Theology*. Louisville, KY: Westminster John Knox, 1997.

Sánchez Walsh, Arlene M. *Latino Pentecostal Identity: Evangelical Faith, Self, and Society*. New York: Columbia University Press, 2003.

4

Hispanic/Latino(a) Theology

BENJAMÍN VALENTÍN

Historical Backdrop

Even though it has existed alongside other theologies of liberation and alongside other forms of contextual religious discourse since at least 1975, Hispanic or Latino theology still remains unknown or undiscovered by many in the wider arena of theological and religious scholarship.[1] I suppose that this neglect is related to and continues a long history of disrespect toward Latino/as and of their being rendered invisible or insignificant in the United States. However, I suspect that the neglect of Latino/a theology could also be tied to the failure to make a distinction between it and Latin American liberation theology. In other words, it is possible that people who study, follow, or do theology may mistakenly identify, equate, or lump together Latino/a theology with the liberationist theologies that have emerged in Mexico and in the Spanish-speaking countries of the Caribbean Basin and of Central and South America. But this is a faulty assumption, not only because each of the theological expressions that has emerged from these countries on the southern side of the U.S.-Mexican border deserves mentioning and study in its own right but also because Hispanic/Latino(a) theology should be seen as a distinctive form of theological colloquy in itself.

Although influenced in certain respects by the mode of liberation theology or justice-seeking theological address that emerged in different parts of Latin America, Latino/a academic theology exemplifies the religious and theological inflections of Hispanic people living in the United States of America. In other words, Latino/a theology is a North American theological tradition—a theological tradition that is bred and based in the United States. This theological voice flows from the thought, writings, and activities of a heterogeneous group of theologians, comprised of people who can trace their ancestry in some way or another to different parts of Spanish-speaking Latin America but yet call the United States their home. The written and oral presentations of this group of theologians deserve attention and appreciation in mainstream theological study, both because they provide a window into a distinctive form of contextual and justice-seeking theological address that emerges from and relates to the social milieu of the United States and because they provide insight into the confounding realities of life in the United States and the varieties of Christian and other religious expressions found within it.[2]

To begin, it is important to note that Hispanic/Latino(a) theology grows out of and responds to the complex experience of Latino/as in the United States. That being the case, I believe that it would be worthwhile to look at the intricate cultural history and set of experiences that generally informs and gives rise to this theology.

If one allowed oneself to be informed only by the insinuations that often underlie recent debates over culture, language, and immigration, one could come to think that Latino/as are all foreign newcomers to the United States. But the truth is that Latino/a history in North America actually predates the history of the United States. The history of Latino/as in North America, and the commencement of the Hispanic/Latino(a) people as a whole, begins with the Spanish exploration and colonization of the Caribbean islands and then of the North and South American continents that began with Christopher Columbus's arrival in the Americas in 1492. His journey to the "east" transpired at a time when Spain was seeking to expand its colonial borders and strengthen a faltering economy with resources from unexplored lands. Consequently, following Columbus's discovery of a route from Europe to these areas, a series of Spanish explorers sailed to the Americas with the intention of surveying and settling its territories. As a result of their takeover of these lands and of their subjugation of the native peoples that inhabited them, a good part of the territory that comprises the Americas—including much of Central and South America, Mexico, large segments of the Caribbean, and most of what is now the southern and western United States—gradually came to be claimed for Spain.

Spain's boon, however, would be the bane of the different American indigenous populations as they were forcibly conquered, had their lands taken away, were exposed to new diseases brought over from Europe that proved to be devastating, were systematically mistreated, and had a different language, culture, and worldview imposed on them. One aspect of this wide-ranging oppression involved the exploitation of the indigenous populations. Historians of the Spanish colonial period have established that much of the early Spanish interest in the New World centered on mining.[3] But the development of these mines required a larger supply of labor than the Spanish colonizers were willing or able to provide on their own. Hence, the conquered indigenous populations were forced into mining labor. The oppressive labor conditions, scant nourishment, broken family life, and disease that were part of this harsh life of indenture under Spanish rule combined to bring about a swift and significant decline in the native populations. This not only affected the native population but also had tragic consequences for the people of Africa, because, in order to replace or supplement the decreasing indigenous labor force, the Spaniards took to forcibly introducing large numbers of African slaves from the western coast of Africa to the Americas.

This overall historical happenstance should certainly be deemed as grievous and tragic because it led, among other things, to the subjugation and decimation of peoples, to disruption and forced transmigration, to enslavement, and to the destruction of preexisting cultures or ways of life. But, ironically, the upheaval brought about by the Spanish conquest of the Americas gave birth to something new and becoming—the formation of new cultures and new populations out of the intermingling and fusion of three distinct groups of peoples and cultures in the Americas (i.e., the Spanish, Amerindian or Native American, and African peoples and cultures). In brief, sexual encounters, both forced and consensual, between men and women of these three different groups of people occasioned the emergence of a new biological and cultural context as the Spanish, Native American, and African populations increasingly intermingled, creating through the centuries new cultures and large populations of mestizo/a and mulatto/a peoples (i.e., peoples of mixed ancestry). Present-day Latin American and U.S. Latino populations have been especially marked by this racial and cultural mixture and are in some way or another the result of the adventitious encounter and amalgamation of these peoples and cultures during the Spanish colonial period.

As this last statement implies, the Hispanic or Latino/a world has not only been marked by but could in fact be said to have been produced by the encounters of these three disparate groups of peoples and cultures during the approximately three hundred years of Spanish colonialism. In this sense, one has to make a distinction between the Spanish and the Hispanic/Latino(a) peoples. The reason for this is simple: Hispanics/Latinos(as) are more than just descendants of the Spanish conquistadors that colonized the Americas; they are also descendants of the Native American or Amerindian peoples who had already been living in the Americas and of the peoples whom the Spanish brought from Africa to the Americas as slaves. Thus, the Hispanic/Latino(a) peoples and their cultures can be said to be a new reality, a new creation, an offshoot of the violent and unequal encounter of these varied peoples and cultures during the Spanish colonial period. In short, it is this peculiar or distinctive merging of peoples and cultures of the Americas that gave rise to the Americans known as Latino/as or Hispanics. This implies two things: first, that U.S. Hispanic/Latinos(as) and Latin Americans more generally can be said to be new "children of the Americas"; second, that U.S. Hispanic/Latino(a) and Latin American identity cannot be understood apart from *mestizaje* or *mulatez*—that is, apart from the reality of racial or ethnic and cultural mixture.

The *mestizaje/mulatez,* or complex racial and cultural mixture, that marks the Hispanic/Latino(a) heritage has affected practically every dimension of the lives of present-day U.S. Latinos and Latin Americans from race and religion to food, language, music, and most everything else in between. It certainly reveals itself in different ways within this community of persons, but it does not fail to reveal itself in some way or another. Among certain groups of Latin Americans and U.S. Hispanics or Latino/as such as the Cubans, Dominicans, and Puerto Ricans, as well as Venezuelans and Pan-amanians, for instance, the African component of this racial and cultural mélange may sometimes prevail. Among other groups of Latin Americans or U.S. Hispanic/Latinos(as) such as the Mexicans and others from the larger area of Central American influence, the indigenous element may perhaps prevail. And in some cases it may be the Spanish or Iberian component that is notable. But, one way or the other, Hispanic/Latino(a) identity has been, is, and will continue to be a function of the cataclysmic process of the forced encounter between Iberian, Amerindian, and African peoples and cultures during the Spanish colonial period.

In any case, returning to our historical narrative, we should note that these new mestizo/a and mulatto/a Hispanic populations grew over time and spread out over the American territories that were incorporated into and controlled by the Spanish Empire, including large segments of North America. Spain managed to maintain tight economic, political, and cultural control over these territories and their inhabitants for approximately three centuries. But eventually Spain's rule over these territories and populations began to break down, as some of its colonies grew more independent, as movements and wars for independence ensued in different parts of the Americas, and as chinks within the Spanish Empire contributed to the weakening of its stronghold over the Americas. However, just as the Spanish Empire began to crumble in the 19th century, the United States commenced its ascension as a world force, buttressed by an expansionist ideology known as "manifest destiny." Through annexations, military conquest, and diplomatic maneuvering, the United States took control of areas that once belonged to Spain or had achieved their independence from Spain, including the northern half of Mexico and Puerto Rico. And just like that, the varied Hispanic/Latino(a) persons who had been living in these and other territories became part of the emerging United States due to shifting borders and U.S. imperialistic pursuits.

Over the centuries, this U.S. Hispanic/Latino(a) population has grown. As a result of the Spanish-American war; the U.S. restructuring of Puerto Rico's political, production, and economic systems in the early 20th century, and the ensuing economic insecurities, upheaval, and large waves of migration of Puerto Ricans to the mainland in the 1930s, 1940s, and 1950s; the 1959 socialist revolution in Cuba, and the waves of Cuban immigration into the United States that resulted from it; and the diverse forms of political unrest and economic insecurity experienced in countries such as Mexico, Argentina, Chile, Colombia, El Salvador, Guatemala, Nicaragua, Peru, and Venezuela over the past six decades, at times exacerbated by U.S. foreign policies and interests, Latin Americans have settled in the United States by the millions. At the same time, the resident U.S. Latino/a population has grown exponentially in part because of its overall young median age (26.4 years according to 2000 census tabulations). As a result of all these forces, the Hispanic/Latino(a) population has become the largest so-called minority group in the United States, with an estimated population of 41,926,302 by 2005 count, constituting 14% of the total U.S. population.

There is absolutely no homogeneity within this community of persons. And how could there be, given the racial and cultural hybridity that led to its existence in the first place? The internal distinctions found within this diversified community are made even greater by differences in socioeconomic standing and duration of U.S. residency, among other things. Adding to the diversity is also the rich incorporation of distinct nationalities into the group, along with the unique idiosyncrasies this implies. The fact is that Latino/as are, as Juan Flores puts it, "an ethnicity of ethnicities, an 'ethnic group' that does not exist but for the existence of its constituent 'subgroups.'"[4] Needless to say, this is a sizable and diverse ethnic community—diverse in its racial composition and physical appearance, and in national identities, cultures, and traditions.

Despite this diversity, the U.S. Hispanic/Latino population has managed to forge a fragile yet appreciable pan-Latino identity within the United States. Since the 1960s especially, the U.S. Latino/a communities have taken in an idea of wholeness or solidarity, rallying around a sense of collectivity and panethnicity when necessary, as is manifest in their growing identification with the umbrella terms "Hispanic" and "Latino." It is true that Hispanics/Latinos(as) generally identify primarily with the subgroup or nationality to which they belong, be it Mexican or Cuban or Puerto Rican or other. However, a panethnic consciousness or sense of partnership is in fact appreciable within this diverse community, perhaps especially among those Latino/as who have been living in the United States for a while. As Edna Acosta-Belen puts it, the shorthand label "Hispanic" or "Latino" is for some Latino/as turning into "a symbol of cultural affirmation and identity in an alienating society that traditionally has been hostile and prejudicial to cultural and racial differences, and unresponsive to the socioeconomic and educational needs of a large segment of the Hispanic population."[5]

Various other factors contribute to this sense of solidarity. These include the sharing of certain widespread cultural traits, varyingly manifested in the use of the Spanish language by many, though not all, Latino/as, and many other customs, rituals, and life sensibilities; an ubiquitous exilic sensibility that arises from the fact that the countries of origin of most Latino/as have at some point or another been annexed or colonized by the United States, and the fact that even those born in the United States (64% of all Latino/as) often feel marginalized in their own country of origin; a prevalent sense of being a hyphenated people, at once part of two or more counties, cultures, or nationalities; the commonplace encounters with racial discrimination; the widespread sense of cultural alienation that stems from living within a dominant society that seeks the victory of its own excluding Anglo culture; and the fact that Latino/as have mostly found themselves at the bottom of the economic ladder with a limited degree of freedom to improve their socioeconomic condition.

In any case, this is the complex history and complex amassment of experiences that U.S. Hispanic/Latino(a) theology reflects on, builds from, and responds to. Academic theological consideration of this broad history and set of experiences began in earnest in 1975, with the initiatory inflections of the Mexican American Catholic theologian Virgilio Elizondo, and has continued to the present. Over time, a growing number of Latino/a theologians has emerged, contributing to the flourishing of U.S. Latino/a theology.

Although Latino/a theological discourse may still seem to be a novel elaboration to some in the mainstream of U.S. theology, it is actually possible to speak of three historical folds or evolvements in the elaboration of U.S. Hispanic/Latino(a) theology. I refer to these simply as the inaugural unfolding of Latino/a theology, from 1975 to 1990; the second unfolding of Latino/a theology, from 1991 to 2000; and the third unfolding of Latino/a theology, from 2001 to the present.

The advent of Hispanic/Latino(a) theology as an intentional and self-defined academic discourse begins with the work of Elizondo. He has been active as a religious leader since the early 1960s, having served as founder and president of the Mexican American Cultural Center, as a contributing editor of the internationally known journal *Concilium*, as rector of the San Fernando Cathedral in San Antonio, as a professor at universities throughout the world, and as an internationally recognized lecturer on Mexican American culture and religion. At present he is professor of pastoral and Hispanic theology at the University of Notre Dame.

Although he was already writing essays that called for the inclusion of Hispanic cultural elements in Catholic religious practices in the late 1960s, Elizondo's first monograph appeared in 1975, with a book titled *Christianity and Culture*.[6] I trace the emergence of Latino/a theology to this book-length work. Here one finds evidence of Elizondo's first attempts to translate the lived *mestizaje*—the racial and cultural mixture—that characterizes the Mexican American and overall Latino/a heritage and experience. Elizondo's most renowned and important work, however, appeared in 1983, titled *Galilean Journey: The Mexican American Promise*.[7] In this book Elizondo puts forth three important formulations: a thorough tracing and interpretation of Mexican American *mestizaje*; a conception of the historical Jesus as a *mestizo*—as a kind of first-century "borderlands" Jew who stood at the margins of both Jewish and Gentile society because he came from an out-of-the-way and uninspiring peasant village in Galilee called Nazareth; and a comparison of Jesus' *mestizaje* or experience of marginality as a Galilean Jew and the condition of Mexican American cultural identity today. Being a Galilean Jew in first-century Palestine, Elizondo intimates, was very much like being a Mexican American in the United States today: just as the Galilean stood at the margins of two social worlds, the Mexican American person today is neither fully accepted as an "American" or U.S. citizen nor fully accepted as a Mexican. Yet, just as Jesus was divinely destined to generate new life or modalities of life from the margins of his society, and just as he was able to come to terms with his status as a borderlands Jew and to turn it into a stimulus for social good, Elizondo believes that, similarly, Mexican Americans now find themselves in a unique position to advance a liberating mission, not only for their own well-being but also for that of others in our current society.

Besides his pioneering work on the interpretation of *mestizaje* and the elaboration of a kind of "mestizo/a Christology," Elizondo has also considered the significance of Latino/a popular religious expression. That is, in some of his writings he has unearthed, analyzed, and interpreted the religious beliefs and practices that Latino/as give rise to independently of the consent of theologians, priests, religious professionals, or ecclesiastical offices.[8] As a whole, I suggest that Hispanic/Latino(a) theology's subsequent convergence on culture, on *mestizaje,* and on popular religion owes much to Elizondo's initial inflections in these areas.

As with Elizondo's contributions, those of Cuban American theologian Justo González cannot be overemphasized. Since he completed his doctoral studies in church history at Yale Divinity School in 1961, González has not ceased writing and editing books. Some of these have been written for an academic audience and others for a more popular or church audience. Overall, he has written over fifty books and three hundred articles, which have been translated into several languages.

Even before turning his attention to the articulation of a Latino/a theology, González was well known in Latin America, in this country, and around the world for his writings on the history of the church. But since the early 1980s he has increasingly been at work on the development of Hispanic/Latino(a) theology. Two of his important works in this area are titled *Mañana* and *Santa Biblia.*[9] The first of these, published in 1990, stands as the only full-fledged Latino/a systematic or constructive theology to this point. In this work, González offers a brief retelling of U.S. Latino/a history, an exploration into the sources and methods of Latino/a theology, and an interpretation of the meaning of Christian doctrines such as those concerning God, the Trinity, creation, the human being, Jesus Christ, and the Roman Catholic Church from the perspective of U.S. Latino(a) experience. The second of these works, published in 1996, looks into the enterprise of biblical hermeneutics or biblical interpretation through the lenses of five predominant Latino/a experiences or occurrences: the experience of marginality, the experience of poverty, the occurrence of *mestizaje* and *mulatez,* the experience or impressions of exilement and alienation, and the encountering of solidarity. González's other works in Latino/a theology or related to it include *Out of Every Tribe and Nation* and *Voces: Voices from the Hispanic Church.*[10]

González's contributions, however, go far beyond the publication of books. He has also founded many educational enterprises that have provided the means for scholars and church leaders to focus on the theology of U.S. Latino/as. These include the journal *Apuntes,* the Hispanic Summer Program, AETH (the Association for Hispanic Theological Education), and the Hispanic Theological Initiative. Through his work as author, organizer, teacher, and mentor, Justo González has bridged the gap between academic and pastoral concerns and greatly contributed to the shaping of Latino/a theology.

Cuban-born theologian Ada María Isasi-Díaz has also contributed importantly to the beginnings and foundations of Latino/a theology. Currently she is professor of ethics and theology at Drew University in Madison, New Jersey. Isasi-Díaz, the most published Latina theologian to date, is well known for her development of a distinctive form of Latina theological discourse which she has labeled "mujerista theology." Although she was already writing articles in the late-1970s and mid-1980s that spoke on issues of women's ordination and on the development of a theology from the perspective of Hispanic women, Isasi-Díaz labeled and defined her mujerista theology in 1989 in an article that she published in a journal called *Christian Century,* under the title of "Mujeristas: A Name of Our Own."[11] Noting that the naming process can be an act of self-determination, and believing that the volitional act of self-naming could lend distinctness to Latina theological articulation, Isasi-Díaz made use of the Spanish term most commonly employed by Latino/as to refer to women (i.e., *mujer*) to designate her proposed Latina theology of liberation. She more fully elaborated the elements of this theology in two later works—*En la Lucha/In the Struggle,* published in 1993, and in a book appropriately titled *Mujerista Theology,* published in 1996.[12] In brief, mujerista theology attempts to accomplish two important tasks: to enable Hispanic women to identify and understand the many oppressive structures that influence their lives and to help Hispanic women better define a future.

The development of Latino/a theology owes much to the writings and activities of these three pioneering and influential figures. But it must be acknowledged that the blossoming of Latino/a theology during this initial or early period of articulation is also attributable to the written contributions of other thinkers. One is Orlando Costas, a Puerto Rican–born Latino Protestant/Evangelical theologian who wrote various books that explored the topic of Christian mission from both a Latin American and a U.S. Hispanic liberationist viewpoint, including *Christ outside the Gate* and *Liberating News.*[13] Roberto Goizueta, a Cuban-born Catholic theologian who has been publishing since 1985, has contributed important works on theological method that have placed Hispanic theology in dialogue with Latin American liberation theology, such as *Liberation, Method, and Dialogue,* and also on theological aesthetics, as in his more recent *Caminemos con Jesus.*[14] Andres Guerrero, a Texan of Mexican descent and Roman Catholic persuasion, has provided a basic outline for a Chicano theology of liberation in a 1987 work titled *A*

Chicano Theology;[15] and Allan Figueroa-Deck, another well-published Mexican American priest, has developed a framework for understanding Hispanic ministry in the Catholic Church, as seen in his most discussed work to date, titled *The Second Wave: Hispanic Ministry and the Evangelization of Cultures.*[16] The writings of these figures contributed greatly to the early foundations of Hispanic/Latino(a) theology.

Since 1991, U.S. Hispanic/Latino(a) theology has burgeoned: the number of its written articulations has grown as a result of an increase in the number of its exponents. From 1992 to 1999, for instance, seven anthologies were published on Latino/a theology.[17] Besides these anthologies, many other individually authored books and articles appeared in the 1990s. These texts bear witness to the emergence of what could be called a second wave in the articulation of Latino/a theological thought, authored by thinkers such as Edwin Aponte, María Pilar Aquino, Arturo Bañuelas, Carlos Cardoza-Orlandi, Elizabeth Conde-Frazier, Orlando Espín, Sixto García, Francisco García-Treto, Ismael García, Alex García-Rivera, Pablo Jimenez, David Maldonado Jr., Loida Martell-Otero, Timothy Matovina, Luis N. Rivera Pagán, Luis Pedraja, Harold Recinos, Gary Riebe-Estrella, Luis Rivera, Jeanette Rodríguez-Holguin, José David Rodríguez, Jean-Pierre Ruiz, Teresa Chavez Sauceda, Fernando Segovia, Samuel Solivan, David Traverzo, Eldin Villafañe, and others.

Many of these thinkers took up topics or themes that some of the pioneering figures had previously emphasized, such as "mestizaje" and "popular religion." However, some of them expounded on and further developed these themes. Orlando Espín, for example, gave great impetus to the interpretation of forms of Latino/a popular Catholicism in a book titled *The Faith of the People.* Alex García-Rivera did the same by way of his wonderful book *St. Martin de Porres.* Jeannette Rodríguez-Holguin also contributed nicely to the interpretation of popular religious expression by delving into the spirituality of Mexican American women in two books: *Our Lady of Guadalupe* and *Stories We Live/Cuentos Que Vivimos.*[18]

At the same time, new subjects and new measures began to appear among Latino/a theologians in this central and "boom" period. For example, the writings of Fernando Segovia greatly advanced the development and clarity of Latino/a biblical interpretation by means of his sophisticated analyses of hermeneutical theory and postcolonial studies. His polished and distinguished hermeneutics and proposals are prominently displayed in essays such as "Two Places and No Place on Which to Stand" and "Reading the Bible as Hispanic Americans" and in books such as *Interpreting beyond Borders* and *Decolonizing Biblical Studies,* among others.[19] Ismael Garcia's *Dignidad* advanced the construction of a specifically Latino/a social ethic, by delineating the moral challenges that confront the Hispanic/Latino(a) community, Hispanic styles of moral reasoning, and the basis for a Latino/a Christian ethic.[20] Harold Recinos's works embrace the subject matter of the church's nature and mission. In books such as *Hear the Cry, Jesus Weeps,* and *Who Comes in the Name of the Lord?* Recinos can be seen challenging the church to immerse itself in the struggles of Latino/as and the poor and expounding on his idea of what constitutes a "barrio" or U.S. urban theology.[21]

David Maldonado Jr. has also contributed importantly to Latino/a theological study. Besides having been the first Latino/a president of a U.S. school of theology (Iliff School of Theology in Denver, Colorado), he has played a part in fostering a better understanding of the history, theology, experiences, and perspectives of Hispanic Protestants in the United States.[22] Timothy Matovina has done similarly, but in respect to the history and features of Latino/a Catholicism in the continental United States. His writings give a window onto the recorded rites and liturgy of U.S. Hispanic Catholics from colonial times to the present, especially of Mexican American Catholics living in the southwest regions of the United States.[23] In addition, the works of Eldin Villafañe and María Pilar Aquino bring to the discussion new insights into the comprehension of Latino/a Pentecostal Christianity and to the elaboration of a distinctively Latina feminist theology of liberation.[24] The writings of these and other authors contributed to the further unfolding of Latino/a theology in the 1990s.

I believe that at present we are beginning to witness a third unfolding of Latino/a theological expression, with the initial and distinctive writings of thinkers such as Efrain Agosto, Jorge Aquino, María Teresa Davila, Miguel De La Torre, Teresa Delgado, Miguel Díaz, Michelle González Maldonado, Jose Irizarry, Francisco Lozada Jr., Daisy Machado, Carmen Nanko-Fernández, Nancy Pineda-Madrid, Mayra Rivera, Christopher Tirres, and myself, Benjamín Valentín. The work of these and other more recent authors honors and builds on the thematic, interpretive, and methodological foundations put in place by earlier and still active Latino/a writers. But beyond this, I believe that the work of some of these authors has contributed to the broadening of the thematic range of Latino/a theology and to the promotion of a more critical acuteness or perception in this theology.

For example, Efrain Agosto has contributed to biblical scholarship and to the study of Christian origins by way of an analysis of leadership patterns given witness to in the public activity of Jesus and in the instructional methods of the Apostle Paul. Indeed, his writing in this area provides guidance for commendable Christian leadership today.[25] Miguel De La Torre, a Christian ethicist of Cuban heritage, has written many books that range over several previously unexplored or, at the very least, underexplored topics, such as sexuality, the role of the margins on Christian ethics, the beliefs and rituals of Santería, and the distinctive composition of Cuban and African American religions, among other things.[26] Teresa Delgado has brought to the theological discussion insights gleaned from the popular literature, especially novels, of Puerto Rican women writers in the United States.[27] Miguel Díaz and Michelle González Maldonado, both of whom are Cuban American theologians, have contributed importantly to the elaboration of a Latino/a theological anthropology.[28] González's work also explores questions related to the particularity of Afro-Cuban religion and contributes to the study of Latina popular religion and the development of a Latina feminist constructive theology.[29]

Francisco Lozada Jr. has contributed to the development of Latino/a biblical hermeneutics by way of the presentation and elucidation of different reading strategies and by relating biblical studies to matters of multiculturalism and globalization.[30] Daisy Machado's writings offer new insights into Latino/a church history and contribute toward the rethinking of ideas of justice and the mission of the church in light of the sufferings encountered by undocumented immigrants.[31] Mayra Rivera Rivera, a Puerto Rican–born Latina theologian, brings to the discussion critical insights from postcolonial thought and critical theory. The distinctive appeal of her work lies in its intellectual depth, sophisticated interdisciplinarity, and constructive or reconstructivist theological intent, as she tries to rethink the meanings of Christian doctrines and notions in light of current affairs and ideas.[32] Christopher Tirres's work places Latino/a theology in conversation with American pragmatism and contributes impressively to the work of theorizing liberation from a U.S. Latino standpoint.[33] As for my own work in Latino/a theology, I have attempted at once to diagnose and address the crisis of the American left from a Latino's point of view; to take inventory of, interpret, and assess the sensibilities and methods of Latino/a theology; and to put forth a conception of a liberationist Latino(a) public theology that is adequate to the justice demands of our age.[34]

Whether by expanding on previous categories, focusing on new themes and motifs, seeking to fill earlier gaps in thinking, or casting a critical eye on previous assumptions or tendencies, the writings of these newer thinkers provide insight into the continued unfolding of Latino/a theology in the 21st century.

Description

Various descriptive terms could probably be used to give an accounting of the kind of theological expressions found within the archives of Hispanic/Latino(a) theology. For example, one could classify these as expressions or examples of "contextual theology," or perhaps as demonstrations of an "inculturated" or "cultural theology." All of these are possible and may make for correct characterizations. However, I think that Hispanic/Latino theology could best be described as a distinctive expression of "liberation theology."

The term "liberation theology" began to be applied in the late 1960s to modalities of theological expression that appeared among Christian theologians in different parts of the Americas. Generally put, liberation theologies are modes of theological discourse that rethink the meaning and purpose of human existence, social life, faith, and religious thought and practice by paying attention to those ignored by history—that is, those who have generally been denied voice, positive identity, and an adequate material standard of living. In sum, these are theological colloquies that take the problem of injustice and oppression seriously and seek to advance enhancing self-images and communal images, enabling coping techniques and sociopolitical adjustments that could foster greater social justice as a whole. For that reason, these theologies ask and seek to find responses to questions about how we are to think and speak about God, about human achievement and limitation, about the saving example of Jesus Christ, about the challenge and promise of the church, and about Christian hope in the face of undeserved suffering, unjustified subjugation, inequity, and marginalization. But besides their characteristic concern with injustice and suffering, and besides their ameliorative impulse, liberation theologies are also generally marked by two other keynotes: first, the understanding that theological treatises are shaped by and should look to respond to the historical, sociocultural, and socioeconomic contexts from which they originate; second, the desire to reach into and draw from the particular experiences, life circumstances, and expressive cultures of a specific people, community, or social group.

All of these emphases can be identified in the writings of U.S. Latino/a theologians. In their writings, for instance, Latino/a theologians often inquire into and seek to respond to the particular experiences and situations that have marked their lives and those of Latino/as in the social milieu of the United States. This at times translates into writings that inquire into the history and cultures of Latino/as, into the history of the United States, and into the role and social location of Latino/as within it. Furthermore, the works of Latino/a theologians also make an effort to excavate and draw from "the stuff of Latino/a life": to delve into and build theologies from the particular experiences, life circumstances, and cultural practices of the Hispanic/ Latino(a) peoples. Thus and so, they aim to respond to, as well as to fashion, theological reflections that "embody" the cultural agency of Latino/as. In some cases this can be exemplified by way of the interpretation of scripture and of theological doctrines through the lenses of experiences or perceptions lived through in the Latino/a communities, such as those of marginality, poverty, exile, alienation, or estrangement. In others, this might take form through the use of the experience of *mestizaje* or *mulatez*—of being persons of mixed ancestry and cultural heritage—as a vantage point from which to explore and decipher the meanings of religious ideas. And in other cases this might also take place by the use of the cultural production of Latino/as in the construction of theological reflection (e.g., the language or idioms, literature, and other such artistic or cultural expressions of the Latino/a communities).

Finally, whether implicitly or explicitly, the works of Latino/a theologians also display a concern over injustice and a desire to better the lives of Latino/as and the civil and religious communities they live in or are a part of. Given the atmosphere of overt and covert discrimination and the disrespect of Hispanic cultures often experienced by Latinos and Latinas in the United States, Latino/a theologians have been inclined to an "identity politics," or a "cultural politics of recognition," that focuses on injustices rooted in social patterns of representation, interpretation, and communication. Examples of such cultural injustices include

> cultural domination (being subjected to patterns of interpretation and communication that are associated with another culture and are alien and/or hostile to one's own); non-recognition (being rendered invisible by means of the authoritative representational, communicative, and interpretative practices of one's culture); and disrespect (being routinely maligned or disparaged in stereotypic public cultural representations and/or in everyday life interactions).[35]

Latino/a theologians have generally shown great concern over these kinds of injustices. Although injustices that are related to political economy have not gone unnoticed by them, I believe that these theologians have thus far given more attention to injustices that are related to culture or "symbolic culture." Basically, they have come to realize that there may be sources of oppression other than political sources—for example, cultural imperialism, colonialism, ethnic prejudice, racism, and sexism—contributing to the sufferings of Latino/as. Thus, Latino/a theologians have been inclined to enfold their liberatory discourses in cultural terms in order to help counter U.S. efforts at cultural homogenization; to unearth, defend, and uplift certain beliefs and practices connected to U.S. Latino(a) peoples; to replace denigrating images of Latino/as with self-defined and affirming images; and to assist in the incorporation of Latino/as as full, equal, and participating citizens into the society in which we live.

Sources

By virtue of their predominantly Christian orientation, Latino/a theologians look to put into service insights gained from four sources or reservoirs of information and wisdom. These derive from scripture, tradition, culture, and experience.

In the case of Christian theology, "scripture" generally refers to the Bible—that is, the canonized Jewish and Christian scriptures, sometimes referred to as the Old Testament and New Testament. For Christian theologians the Bible is an important source or resource because it is the original document that bears witness to the initiatory events, testimonies, and beliefs on which the Christian faith is based. The term "tradition" refers to the many streams of interpretation that have come about, accrued, and been transmitted in the history of Christian thought and practice. This can include interpretation(s) of scripture, of Christian doctrines, and of Christian ritual or practice. Depending on the theologian who is using it, the term "culture" could refer specifically to the sphere devoted to the production, circulation, and use of meanings and identities, or more generally to all of the things that make up the social matrix in which religion occurs and in which theology gets done. In the grander sense of this last definition or usage, the term "culture" could include everything that characterizes a social location—that is, the philosophies, ideologies, systems of meaning, moral and social principles or values, laws, artistic styles and works of art, literature, popular creations and practices, and political systems that identify a people or a social context. Finally, the term "experience" refers at once to personal life experience and perception, including religious experience and perception, and to the collective historical experiences of a religious, national, ethnic, cultural, or social group.

The fact that Latino/a theologians make use of these general sources of data in their theological thinking process is not noteworthy in and of itself, especially since most if not all Christian theologians do so as well. What is notable is that Latino/a theology habitually manifests a different understanding of these sources and approaches them in some distinctive ways. First, Latino/a theologians generally gravitate toward what I call a dialogical or co-relational model of biblical interpretation. At the most basic level, this means that Latino/a theologians commonly aspire to put the message of the Bible in conversation with or in relation to the experience of Latinos and Latinas today and vice versa. Usually this is exemplified by a critical reading of the sociocultural situation of U.S. Latino/as and of the Bible in light of one to the other. At times this can also be illustrated through attempts at the reading or interpreting of biblical material through the lenses of the historical and current-day experiences of many Latino/as. In *Santa Biblia,* for example, Justo González strives to interpret biblical themes from the vantage point of five experiences, circumstances, or happenings that can be said to mark U.S. Latino/a life and history: the experience of marginality, the encountering of poverty, the happening and impression of *mestizaje* and *mulatez* (i.e., cultural mixture), the sense or feeling of exile and alienation, and the longing for and valuing of solidarity. But in using the terms "dialogical" and "co-relational" to describe Latino/a theology's hermeneutical or interpretive penchant, I also mean one other thing: that Latino/a theologians generally assume that each time we read the Bible it has or should have an effect of some kind on us; at the same time, we always contribute something to the continuing history of the Bible's meaning or influence. In this way, Latino/a theologians envision biblical interpretation as a "fusion of horizons," as a merging of the message of the Bible with the experience of its readers or interpreters—in this case, the experience of U.S. Latinos and Latinas.

Second, Latino/a theology inclines toward widening the meanings and contents of "tradition." What I mean is this. Often, other Christian theologians understand "tradition" as the pronouncements, interpretations, and renderings of "church professionals" from the past and present—that is, the theologians or official and authoritative leaders of the church. In other words, more often than not, it is the ideas of authoritative figures that are granted value and importance in theological reflection; the religious understanding of common persons is ordinarily left out of consideration. Latino/a theologians, however, depart from this way of doing theology. Not only do they reflect on the religious ideas and perceptions of important or official church leaders of the past and present, they also pay attention to the living witness and faithful intuitions of everyday people. In short, as many Latino/a theologians see it, the living intuition, witness, faith, and religious wisdom of the people are as inspired and valid as are the written pronouncements and texts of the church's magisterium. For this reason, they attend to and analyze and even draw on the popular religious expressions—the unique devotions, rites, practices, and celebrations—that can be found or observed in the Latino/a communities. These may include the following, for example:

1. Devotions to a host of *virgenes*, such as La Virgen de Guadalupe (Our Lady of Guadalupe) and La Virgen de la Caridad (Our Lady of Charity)
2. Devotions to patron saints such as San Martin de Porres and Santa Barbara
3. Festivities and practices that embody a religious dimension, such as Las Posadas (festivities in honor of the nine months that Mary carried Jesus in her womb), El Dia de los Muertos (the day of the dead, which involves the remembrance and honoring of ancestors and beloved persons); the Quincea-ñeras ceremonies celebrated during the fifteenth birthday of Latinas, which always include a religious blessing; Los Rosarios (the rosaries practiced during funerals), Las Fiestas Patronales (patron saints celebrations), and a host of Procesiones (processions practiced throughout the calendar year)
4. The *coritos* or short songs that are often sung in Latino/a Pentecostal churches and that are often composed by local parishioners themselves
5. Forms of non-Christian, or at least less explicitly Christian, Latino(a) popular religions such as Santería, Palo, Espiritismo (types of spiritism) and Curanderismo (types of native healing practices and rituals)

To the extent that they look to reflect on or draw on these sorts of popular, inborn, and everyday expressions of religion, Latino/a theologians are contributing to a widening of theological "tradition."

Finally, I note that Latino/a theology also tends to localize the meaning of culture and to widen the meaning of experience. I will explain what I mean by way of a general observation and comparison. I have noticed that when many European and North American theologians speak of "culture," they often are referring to the general conditions of life that mark a historical era or part of the world, or to the domain of social subjectivity, or to the living result of all the elements in the general organization of a society. In this sense the idea of culture meets with a more sweeping or generic and, therefore, less-specific meaning. It is really culture with a capital "C" that is being spoken of here, as in for instance, "Modern Western Culture" or "U.S. Culture," etcetera, etcetera.

Hispanic/Latino(a) theologians use this grander sense of culture, too, from time to time, when reflecting on the conditions of existence in the

"Modern or Late Modern Western World" or on the conditions of existence in the "United States of America." But, more often than not, they understand culture in a more localized and particular way, using it in reference to the range of practices and significations through which the Latino/a reality is constructed and maintained. In this usage the idea of culture meets with a narrower and therefore more localized or particular meaning: it is the practices, traditions, and agency of Latinos that is in mind here. This includes the complex of values, customs, beliefs, identity constructions, self-expressions, and practices that constitute the way of life of Latinos. It is this multiplex, but yet more circumscribed, local, or specific subjective world that Latino/a theologians inquire into and build from when doing theology.

Whereas their penchant is to localize and particularize the idea of culture, Latino/a theologians show a tendency to amplify the meanings of experience. The human experience referred to in Latino/a theology is not simply religious experience—the encountering of the sacred or experiencing of ultimate reality or ultimate concern—or simply personal experience, although these are not excluded. Rather, it includes the whole of Latino/a experience, including the common dimensions of life—*lo cotidiano,* or the everyday events of life—the vicissitudes, and the accumulated wisdom or impressions of the Latino/a community.

Theoretical and Methodological Considerations

I have already noted that Latino/a theology has been influenced by the principles and practices of liberation theology. These include a concern with oppression and the achievement of justice, an emphasis on the contextual character and accountability of theological reflection, and the desire to reach into and draw on the specific experiences and expressive cultures of a people or community. I have also already alluded to some of the ways in which this influence appears in Latino/a theology. Even so, I think it might be useful to illuminate a number of recurring patterns that provide examples of Latino/a theology's use of the methodology of liberation theology.

I suggest that the following "liberationist-informed" and "liberationist-driven" methodological patterns or techniques recur in Latino/a theology. The first involves a critical reading or analysis of the sociohistorical and sociocultural situation of the U.S. Latino/a experience. Latino/a theologians strive to interpret the historical and present-day circumstances of Latino/a peoples within the context of the United States. For this purpose, they employ the means of historical study, anthropology, sociology, and cultural study in an attempt to situate the U.S. Latino/a experience. They use the tools of these modes of analysis in order to better understand the history of Latino/as; in order to better apprehend the issues, pressures, and hindrances that Latino/as have commonly faced; in order to better discover and tap into the repository of subversive activities and life-affirming formations that have come about among Latino/as; and in order to better learn how to transform U.S. society for the benefit not only of Latino/as but of all.

The second is the incorporation of the concrete voices of people in the development of a theological outlook. This means that Latino/a theologians sometimes try to provide an opportunity in their theologies for the voices of Hispanic women and men to be heard. Although other representative illustrations can be pointed to, I believe that the works of Ada María Isasi-Díaz and Harold Recinos offer good examples of this technique. In two of her books—*Hispanic Women* and *En la Lucha*—Isasi-Díaz uses interview-like colloquies with lay Hispanic women in her theological reflections. Similarly, Harold Recinos includes the declarations and affirmations of Hispanic men and women in some of the chapters of his book *Who Comes in the Name of the Lord?* and in an essay "Popular Religion, Political Identity, and Life-Story Testimony in an Hispanic Community."[36] In this way, they and other Latino/a theologians hope to "adopt" the views of people in distinct Latino/a communities and to present not only their own experience but also the experience of other Latino/as. The deeper hope is that this kind of conversational method will lead to a "fusion of horizons" between the experience, concern, worldview, faith, and hope of Latino/a peoples and that of religious thinkers and theologians.

Third, related to the second, is the use of the personal story or autobiography. This is uncommon or distinctive because the longing to take account of who we are by way of personal narrative has rarely commanded high regard in modern theological scholarship. Obviously, this has not always been the case. After all, as his *Confessions* show, Augustine thought that theological reflection could be incorporated into and illustrated by telling one's own story. Some Latino/a theologians would agree. Virgilio Elizondo, for one, has used the genre of autobiography quite nicely. His book *The Future Is Mestizo* offers an example of a theological autobiography that takes the form of a quest narrative. Here Elizondo traces and elucidates his own process of social and theological awakening—a process that results in a theological viewpoint that recognizes and denounces the evils of "American" bigotry and inequality on the one hand and aims toward the realization of self-and-communal affirmation and cultural, religious, and social change on the other.[37]

Fourth, one finds throughout Latino/a theology, as with the Jewish prophets of old, a clear use of critical denunciation. This includes the criticism and indictment (1) of social, political, and economic systems that create and bolster inequality; (2) of cultural traditions and practices that bring about and sustain patterns of discrimination, nonrecognition, and disrespect; (3) of an ecclesiastical establishment that often remains unresponsive to the social, economic, and cultural dilemmas of our age and at times espouses religious convictions and ideologies that undermine the struggle for human rights and earthly justice; and (4) of a theological or academic establishment that fails to take seriously and to address long-standing issues of inclusion and exclusion, of underrepresentation, and of gender-based, sexual, and racial-ethnic injustice that have existed within it. In this way Latino/a theology issues a critical and challenging address to academia, church, and general society.

Finally, I submit that Latino/a theologians often bring to the doing of theology a utopian vision. Using Christian parlance, we can say that their writings and speeches exude a belief in the biblical notion of the "kingdom" or, in Ada María Isasi-Díaz's words, the "kin-dom of God."[38] As a persistent theme in the message and mission of Jesus, the notion of the kingdom of God served to point Jewish people of the first century toward an alternative rendering of the world—a world in which justice flourishes, compassion abounds, and concern for the poor, oppressed, and marginalized carries weight. The writings and speeches of Latino/a theologians call on persons and institutions of the 21st century to do the same—they call on them to think of and work toward a U.S. society that allows justice to flourish, compassion to abound, and care for the poor, oppressed, and marginalized to carry the day.

Ongoing Issues

Since its appearance, Hispanic/Latino(a) theology has gone on to grow in its variety of expressions, all the while developing its own conceptual motifs and emphases and establishing its own identity as a unique liberationist theological expression. Among its characteristics one can count the turn to cultural memory as a theological source; the theological theorization of the concepts of *mestizaje/mulatez* and popular religion; the comparison of Jesus' sociohistorical identity with that of current-day Latinos and Latinas; the elaboration of a distinctive expression of Latina feminist and mujerista theology of liberation; the depiction of a Christian mission that emanates from the context of the margins and the barrio; the undertaking of biblical interpretation from the vantage point of Hispanic/Latino experience; the elucidation of the promise of postcolonial studies for biblical interpretation; the development of a distinctive Christian ethics based on Latino/a notions of *dignidad* (dignity); the mapping of a "public theology" from a Latino/a liberationist perspective; and many other innovative developments. This long and yet still selective and incomplete list shows that Latino/a theology has flourished, and indeed it continues to grow and evolve in ways that reflect new theological and religious curiosities and the changing nature of Latino/a communities themselves. Still, there are some issues that will require further attention and solution within Hispanic/Latino(a) theology. I speak to three such points at issue.

The first issue pertains to my observation that Latino/a theologians have thus far tended to shy away from the task of systematically interpreting, scrutinizing, and extending the meanings of Christian doctrines. This means that the effort to interpret, question, and reformulate the meanings of themes or doctrines such as God, creation, human being, sin, Christ, the church, pneumatology, and eschatology has received limited consideration in the works of these theologians. Although some of this sort of theological work can be found within it, the archives of Latino/a theology are not exactly replete with this kind of formal, systematic, and reconstructive pursuit. To date, the only representative illustration of a full-fledged Latino "systematic theology" one can point to is found in Justo González's book *Manana*. This book was published in 1990, and yet it is still the *only* thorough work in systematic theology written by a Latino or Latina author.

Two anthologies, *Teologia en conjunto* (1997) and *From the Hearts of Our People* (1999) have attempted to fill this void. However, being limited by their very nature as anthologies or as collections of short essays, these two works offer more of a digest's view, a prefatory treatment, or a synopsized handling of these doctrines rather than a careful and thorough analysis of them. One would not be wrong in saying that what these two volumes offer us are pointed and abridged commentaries on the possible significance of certain Christian doctrines from a Latino/a Protestant or Catholic point of view rather than a more thorough analysis of these doctrines, complete with an exploration of their historical emergence and development, their underlying and varying meanings, and the present-age conditions that call for and allow for a reformulation of their meanings from a uniquely Latino/a point of view.

And although one can find within the annals of Latino/a theology single-authored monographs that look into individual doctrines in more length, these are neither plenteous nor, in some cases, thoroughgoing in their doctrinal analysis. Two monographs, *On Being Human* and *Created in God's Image*, written by Miguel Díaz and Michelle González Maldonado, respectively, offer a thorough and well-defined view of theological anthropology from a Latino/a viewpoint. Yet these are the only two single-authored books dedicated to this subject thus far. Virgilio Elizondo, in his *Galilean Journey*, and Luis Pedraja, in his book *Jesus Is My Uncle*,[39] deal creatively and splendidly with matters tied to the subject of Christology, but neither of these works presents a full-fledged Christology. In fact, Christology is a multifaceted undertaking: it requires us to deliberate over the obscure and elusive history or life story of Jesus of Nazareth, the testimony of the past regarding his religious significance, and the questions and challenges of our time in order not only to interpret but also to extend the meanings of Jesus' life, message, and purposeful public activity for religious thought and practice today. It can be argued that to date no single-authored monograph in Latino/a theology has followed the trail of this more comprehensive venture. Similarly, the works of Latino/a authors such as Orlando Costas, Harold Recinos, and Roberto Goizueta deal impressively with topics that are related to ecclesiology, but the truth is that we still await the first full-fledged presentation of a distinctively Latino/a ecclesiology. And doctrines or subject matters such as the doctrine of creation, pneumatology, eschatology, and the work of a Christian theology of religions have yet to be taken up in any substantive manner.

This is all to say that I believe there is still much work to be done within Latino/a theology in the area of a more systematic and constructive treatment of the Christian doctrines. As I see it, it is important that we take up this charge—that we take up the task of interpreting, scrutinizing, and reformulating the meanings of doctrines—because the pursuit of theology not only calls for it but is to a certain extent defined by it. Moreover, it is my belief that we Latino/a theologians can make a great contribution to the field of theology by way of the interpretation, evaluation, and reconstruction of the various Christian doctrines from a uniquely Latino/a point of view.

The second issue has to do with what I describe as a constrained exploration and use of Latino/a experience and expression. As I noted earlier, a distinctive mark of liberation theologies is their turning to the realm of individual and collective or group experience to carry out theological reflection that is immersed in and responds to the particularity of that experience. Latino/a theology, as an expression of liberation theology looks to carry out this goal by delving into the specificity of Latino/a identity and culture. However, my bone of contention is that it has thus far limited this immersion to a small slice of Latino/a life. It has, for instance, done well in poring over matters of Latino/a history and identity such as *mestizaje* and *mulatez* and in inquiring into forms of popular religious expression that appear within the different Latino/a communities. A few Latino/a theologians have even taken stock of forms of Latino/a literary expression, particularly of Latino/a novels in their theological reflections. But there are many other dimensions of Latino/a culture that have escaped our review. For example, little has been done with the music, art, drama, fashion, cuisine, comedy, movies, and television shows generated by Latino/as in the past and present. I believe that these other dimensions and expressions of Latino/a life and culture can and even should be explored in our theologies. Immersion in these repositories of Latino/a culture and agency could lead to a deeper level of contextuality, of specificity, of corporality, or a more palpable level of "Latinidad" in our theologies.

The third issue concerns the political vision of Latino/a theology. Given its underlying desire to be of consequence in a liberating way, Latino/a theology has from its inception been marked by a moral sensibility and ameliorative impulse. In other words, this theological tradition has always been concerned with issues of injustice, and it has always, whether explicitly or implicitly, aspired to the furtherance of justice. However, I believe that Latino/a theology has tended to focus predominantly on issues of cultural or symbolic injustice and given too little attention to issues of socioeconomic or material injustice. So, for instance, one finds that injustices having to do with cultural imperialism or domination—with the disparagement of Latino/a cultures, with assimilatory pressures faced by Latino/as in the United States, with the nonrecognition of or the rendering of Latino/as as invisible in the wider U.S. social realm, and with disparaging stereotypic representations of Latino/as found in U.S. culture—receive prominent mention and scrutiny in the writings of Latino/a theologians.

One finds that these theologians have in general been less inclined to scrutinize and address injustices that have to do with the maldistributive effects of American capitalism, with economic inequity and material inequality, with the exploitation of and the economic marginalization of Latino/as, with the denial of access to dignified housing, educational, and health care opportunities, and the like. To be sure, we encounter brief statements here and there that mention and denounce poverty and other such socioeconomic injustices. But it is one thing to mention or denounce these social and economic conditions in passing or in vague form. It is quite another to devote a good deal of attention to them by way of careful and sustained analysis of their causes, conditions, and prospects for remediation.

I suggest that Latino/a theologians should connect their concerns and demands for cultural change to an equally resolute, principled, and well-reasoned concern and demand for socioeconomic change. And we must do so in good part because the reality is that Latino/as suffer injustices that are traceable to both political economy and culture simultaneously. In fact, as theologians who aim to promote social justice, we should seek to acknowledge, analyze, and oppose all of the many crosscutting inequities that afflict not only Latino/as but also many other suffering persons and groups in our society.

To close, I want to stress that my mentioning of these unresolved issues should not lead us to think any less of Latino/a theology. The fact is that every tradition of theology or thought, and every human enterprise in general, will always be found to be limited in some way or another. This is simply a fact of life and a consequence of human finiteness. Hence, it should not surprise us that there are problems that still require solutions in Latino/a theology. The bigger picture is this, however: Latino/a theology has already achieved a mature level of articulation and developed deep foundations of thought and practice. Moreover, given its growth and its continued unfolding, I have no doubts that Latino/a theology will not only resolve my charges but also that it will accomplish many other realizations. That's why perhaps the most appropriate words of advice that I can offer in closing are these: "Stay tuned to it," "Stay tuned to us."

NOTES

1. Although their linguistic background differs, the terms "Hispanic" and "Latino" or "Latina" are commonly used interchangeably and synonymously in the parlance of the United States. These "ethnic labels" or identifying constructs are used within the United States to refer to citizens and residents of the United States who in some way or another can trace their ancestry to the different countries that make up Spanish-speaking Latin America. Spanish-speaking Latin America is comprised of Cuba, Puerto Rico (which is a U.S. commonwealth), the Dominican Republic, Mexico, Nicaragua, Costa Rica, Guatemala, El Salvador, Honduras, Panama, Venezuela, Colombia, Ecuador, Peru, Bolivia, Chile, Argentina, Uruguay, and Paraguay. All citizens and residents of the United States who originated from these countries or from the commonwealth of Puerto Rico, or whose ancestors did, are known as Hispanics or Latino/as. These words or labels have currency in the United States, but in Latin America people do not ordinarily refer to themselves as Hispanic or Latino. And even within the United States, the use and validity of these coalescing ethnic labels can be debated. Some in the Hispanic/Latino(a) community prefer not to use them at all, while others may prefer one term to the other. Because certain Latino/a theologians prefer the term "Latino" or "Latina," while others prefer to use the term "Hispanic," to encompass the U.S. experiences of peoples with Spanish-speaking

ancestry and to refer to their theologies, I generally use the signifier "Hispanic/Latino(a)" when referring to the theological works of this community of theologians. For a sophisticated and critical study on the history and current debates surrounding the use of the "Hispanic" and "Latino" label within the Latino/a community, see Jorge J. E. Gracia, *Hispanic/Latino Identity* (Malden, MA: Blackwell, 2000), esp. 1–26; and Suzanne Oboler, *Ethnic Labels, Latino Lives: Identity and the Politics of (Re)presentation in the United States* (Minneapolis: University of Minnesota Press, 1995).

2. To be sure, in this essay I focus on the writings of Latino/a academic theologians—of thinkers, in other words, who identify with the discipline of theology more generally; this includes biblical scholars, Christian historians, systematic or constructive theologians, ethicists, and folk working in the domain of practical theology or ministerial studies. I do not, therefore, include an overview of the important and interesting work being done by a fine and growing body of Latino/a scholars of religion, including those operating within the domain of the history of religions, the sociology of religion, the anthropology of religion, and other such realms of religious study. Moreover, here I limit myself to a consideration of the theological writings of Latino/a academics living within the United States of America.

3. For example, Charles Gibson, *Spain in America* (New York: Harper and Row, 1966), esp. 1–47, 112–135; Leslie Bethell, ed., *The Cambridge History of Latin America*, 11 vols. (Cambridge: Cambridge University Press, 1984–1995), esp. 1:149–388, 2:67–149; Alfredo Jimenez, ed., *Handbook of Hispanic Cultures in the United States* (Houston: Arte Publico, 1994), esp. 2:23–183; and Herbert S. Klein, *African Slavery in Latin America and the Caribbean* (Oxford: Oxford University Press, 1986).

4. Juan Flores, "Pan-Latino/Trans-Latino: Puerto Ricans in the New Nueva York," in *Centro: Journal of the Center for Puerto Rican Studies* 8, nos. 1–2 (1996): 176.

5. Edna Acosta-Belen, "From Settlers to Newcomers: The Hispanic Legacy in the United States," in *The Hispanic Experience in the United States: Contemporary Issues and Perspectives,* ed. Edna Acosta-Belen and Barbara R. Sjostrom (New York: Praeger, 1988), 103–104.

6. Virgilio Elizondo, *Christianity and Culture: An Introduction to Pastoral Theology and Ministry for the Bicultural Community* (Huntington, IN: Our Sunday Visitor, 1975).

7. Virgilio Elizondo, *Galilean Journey: The Mexican-American Promise* (Maryknoll, NY: Orbis, 1983).

8. For instance, Virgilio Elizondo, "Popular Religion as the Core of Cultural Identity in the Mexican American Experience," in *An Enduring Flame: Studies on Latino Popular Religiosity,* ed. Anthony Stevens-Arroyo and Ana María Díaz-Stevens (New York: PARAL, 1984), 113–132; and Elizondo, *Guadalupe: Mother of the New Creation* (Maryknoll, NY: Orbis, 1997).

9. Justo González, *Mañana: Christian Theology from a Hispanic Perspective* (Nashville, TN: Abingdon, 1990); and González, *Santa Biblia: The Bible through Hispanic Eyes* (Nashville, TN: Abingdon, 1996).

10. Justo González, *Out of Every Tribe and Nation: Christian Theology at the Ethnic Roundtable* (Nashville, TN: Abingdon, 1992); and González, *Voces: Voices from the Hispanic Church* (Nashville, TN: Abingdon, 1992).

11. Ada María Isasi-Díaz, "Mujeristas: A Name of Our Own," *Christian Century* (May 24–31, 1989): 550–562.

12. Ada María Isasi-Díaz, *En la Lucha/In the Struggle* (Minneapolis: Fortress, 1993); and Isasi-Díaz, *Mujerista Theology: A Theology for the Twenty-First Century* (Maryknoll, NY: Orbis, 1996).

13. Orlando E. Costas, *Christ outside the Gate: Mission beyond Christendom* (Maryknoll, NY: Orbis, 1982); and Costas, *Liberating News: A Theology of Contextual Evangelization* (Grand Rapids, MI: Eerdmans, 1989).

14. Roberto S. Goizueta, *Liberation, Method, and Dialogue* (Atlanta: Scholars, 1988); and Goizueta, *Caminemos con Jesus: Toward a Hispanic/Latino Theology of Accompaniment* (Maryknoll, NY: Orbis, 1995).

15. Andres G. Guerrero, *A Chicano Theology* (Maryknoll, NY: Orbis, 1987).

16. Allan Figueroa-Deck, *The Second Wave: Hispanic Ministry and the Evangelization of Cultures* (Mahwah, NJ: Paulist, 1989).

17. I am referring here to the following anthologies: (1) Roberto S. Goizueta, ed., *We Are a People: Initiatives in Hispanic American Theology* (Minneapolis: Fortress, 1992); (2) González, *Voces: Voices from the Hispanic Church* (1992); (3) Allan Figueroa-Deck, ed., *Frontiers of Hispanic Theology in the United States* (Maryknoll, NY: Orbis, 1992); (4) Arturo Bañuelas, ed., *Mestizo Christianity: Theology from the Latino Perspective* (Maryknoll, NY: Orbis, 1995); (5) Ada María Isasi-Díaz and Fernando Segovia, eds., *Hispanic/Latino Theology: Challenge and Promise* (Minneapolis: Fortress, 1996); (6) José David Rodríguez and Loida I. Martell-Otero, eds., *Teologia en conjunto: A Collaborative Hispanic Protestant Theology* (Louisville, KY: Westminster John Knox, 1997); and (7) Orlando O. Espín and Miguel H. Díaz, eds., *From the Heart of Our People: Latino/a Explorations in Catholic Systematic Theology* (Maryknoll, NY: Orbis, 1999).

18. Orlando O. Espín, *The Faith of the People: Theological Reflections on Popular Catholicism* (Maryknoll, NY: Orbis, 1997); Alex García-Rivera, *St. Martin de Porres: The "Little Stories" and the Semiotics of Culture* (Maryknoll, NY: Orbis, 1995); Jeannette Rodríguez[-Holguin], *Our Lady of Guadalupe: Faith and Empowerment among Mexican-American Women* (Austin: University of Texas Press, 1994); and Rodríguez[-Holguin], *Stories We Live/Cuentos Que Vivimos: Hispanic Women's Spirituality* (Mahwah, NJ: Paulist, 1996).

19. Fernando F. Segovia, "Two Places and No Place on Which to Stand: Mixture and Otherness in Hispanic American Theology," in *Listening: Journal of Religion and Culture* 27, no. 1 (1992): 26–40; Segovia, "Reading the Bible as Hispanic Americans," in *The New Interpreter's Bible* (Nashville, TN: Abingdon, 1994), 1:167–173; Segovia, *Interpreting beyond Borders: Bible and Postcolonialism* (London: Sheffield Academic Press, 2000); and Segovia, *Decolonizing Biblical Studies: A View from the Margins* (Maryknoll, NY: Orbis, 2000).

20. Ismael Garcia, *Dignidad: Ethics through Hispanic Eyes* (Nashville, TN: Abingdon, 1997).

21. Harold Recinos, *Hear the Cry! A Latino Pastor Challenges the Church* (Louisville, KY: Westminster John Knox, 1989); Recinos, *Jesus Weeps: Global Encounters on Our Doorsteps* (Nashville, TN: Abingdon, 1992); and Recinos, *Who Comes in the Name of the Lord?* (Nashville, TN: Abingdon, 1997).

22. David Maldonado Jr., "Hispanic Protestant Clergy: A Profile of Experience and Perspectives," in *Protestantes/Protestants: Hispanic Christianity within Mainline Traditions,* ed. David Maldonado Jr. (Nashville, TN: Abingdon, 1999); and Maldonado, *Crossing Guadalupe Street: Growing Up Hispanic and Protestant* (Albuquerque: University of New Mexico Press, 2001).

23. Especially Timothy M. Matovina, "Our Lady of Guadalupe Celebrations in San Antonio, Texas, 1840–1841," "Liturgy, Popular Rites, and Popular Spirituality," and "Marriage Celebrations in Mexican-American Communities," all in *Mestizo Worship: A Pastoral Approach to Liturgical Ministry* (Collegeville, MN: Liturgical, 1998), 49–67, 81–91, and 93–102; and Timothy Matovina and Gerald E. Poyo, eds., *Presente!: U.S. Latino Catholics from Colonial Origins to the Present* (Maryknoll, NY: Orbis, 2000).

24. Eldin Villafane, *The Liberating Spirit: Toward an Hispanic American Pentecostal Social Ethic* (Grand Rapids, MI: Eerdmans, 1994); María Pilar Aquino, "Perspectives on a Latina's Feminist Liberation Theology," in *Frontiers of Hispanic Theology in the United States*, ed. Allan Figueroa-Deck (Maryknoll, NY: Orbis, 1992), 23–40; Aquino, "Directions and Foundations of Hispanic/Latino Theology: Toward a *Mestiza* Theology of Liberation," *Journal of Hispanic/Latino Theology* 1, no. 1 (1993): 5–21; and Aquino, "Theological Method in U.S. Latino/a Theology: Toward an Intercultural Theology for the Third Millennium," in *From the Heart of Our People: Latino/a Explorations in Catholic Systematic Theology*, ed. Orlando O. Espín and Miguel H. Díaz (Maryknoll, NY: Orbis, 1999), 6–48.

25. Efrain Agosto, *Servant Leadership: Jesus and Paul* (St. Louis, MO: Chalice, 2005).

26. Miguel A. De La Torre, *A Lily among the Thorns: Imagining a New Christian Sexuality* (San Francisco: Jossey-Bass, 2007); De La Torre, *Doing Christian Ethics from the Margins* (Maryknoll, NY: Orbis, 2004); De La Torre, *Santeria: The Beliefs and Rituals of a Growing Religion in America* (Grand Rapids, MI: Eerdmans, 2004); and De La Torre, *The Quest for the Cuban Christ: A Historical Search* (Gainesville: University Press of Florida, 2002).

27. Teresa Delgado, "Prophesy Freedom: Puerto Rican Women's Literature as a Source for Latina Feminist Theology," in *A Reader in Latina Feminist Theology: Religion and Justice*, ed. María Pilar Aquino, Daisy Machado, and Jeanette Rodríguez (Austin: University of Texas Press, 2002), 23–52.

28. For example, Miguel Díaz, *On Being Human: U.S. Hispanic and Rahnerian Perspectives* (Maryknoll, NY: Orbis, 2001); and Michelle A. González [Maldonado], *Created in God's Image: An Introduction to Feminist Theological Anthropology* (Maryknoll, NY: Orbis, 2007).

29. Michelle A. González [Maldonado], *Afro-Cuban Theology: Religion, Race, and Identity* (Gainesville: University Press of Florida, 2006); and González, *Sor Juana: Beauty and Justice in the Americas* (Maryknoll, NY: Orbis, 2003).

30. Francisco Lozada Jr., "Encountering the Bible in an Age of Diversity and Globalization: Teaching toward Intercultural Criticism," in *New Horizons in Hispanic/Latino(a) Theology*, ed. Benjamín Valentín (Cleveland: Pilgrim, 2003), 13–34; Lozada, "Reinventing the Biblical Tradition: An Exploration of Social Location Hermeneutics," in *Futuring Our Past: Explorations in the Theology of Tradition*, ed. Orlando O. Espín and Gary Macy (Maryknoll, NY: Orbis, 2006), 113–140; and Lozada, *A Literary Reading of John 5: Text as Construction* (New York: Peter Lang, 2000).

31. Daisy L. Machado, "The Unnamed Woman: Justice, Feminists, and the Undocumented Woman," in *A Reader in Latina Feminist Theology: Religion and Justice*, ed. María Pilar Aquino, Daisy Machado, and Jeanette Rodríguez (Austin: University of Texas Press, 2002), 161–176; and Machado, *Of Borders and Margins: Hispanic Disciples in Texas, 1888–1945* (New York: Oxford University Press, 2003).

32. Mayra Rivera, "En-Gendered Territory: U.S. Missionaries' Discourse in Puerto Rico (1898–1920)," in *New Horizons in Hispanic/Latino(a) Theology*, ed. Benjamín Valentín

(Cleveland: Pilgrim, 2003), 79–97; and Rivera, *The Touch of Transcendence: A Postcolonial Theology of God* (Louisville, KY: Westminster John Knox, 2007).

33. Christopher Tirres, "'Liberation' in the Latino(a) Context: Retrospect and Prospect," in *New Horizons in Hispanic/Latino(a) Theology,* ed. Benjamín Valentín (Cleveland: Pilgrim, 2003), 138–162.

34. For example, Benjamín Valentín, *Mapping Public Theology: Beyond Culture, Identity, and Difference* (Harrisburg, PA: Trinity Press International, 2002); Valentín, "Oye, y ahora que?/Say, Now What? Prospective Lines of Development for U.S. Hispanic/Latino(a) Theology," in *New Horizons in Hispanic/Latino(a) Theology,* ed. Benjamín Valentín (Cleveland: Pilgrim, 2003), 101–118; and Valentín, "Strangers No More: An Introduction to, and an Interpretation of, U.S. Hispanic/Latino(a) Theology," in *The Ties That Bind: African American and Hispanic American/Latino(a) Theologies in Dialogue,* ed. Anthony B. Pinn and Benjamín Valentín (New York: Continuum, 2001), 38–53.

35. Nancy Fraser, *Justice Interruptus: Critical Reflections on the "PostSocialist" Condition* (New York: Routledge, 1997), 14.

36. Ada María Isasi-Díaz and Yolanda Tarango, *Hispanic Women: Prophetic Voice in the Church* (Minneapolis: Fortress, 1992); Ada María Isasi-Díaz, *En la Lucha/In the Struggle: Elaborating a Mujerista Theology* (Minneapolis: Fortress, 1993); Harold J. Recinos, *Who Comes in the Name of the Lord? Jesus at the Margins* (Nashville, TN: Abingdon, 1997), esp. 105–137; and Recinos "Popular Religion, Political Identity, and Life-Story Testimony in an Hispanic Community," in *The Ties That Bind: African American and Hispanic American/Latino(a) Theologies in Dialogue,* ed. Anthony B. Pinn and Benjamín Valentín (New York: Continuum, 2001), 116–128.

37. Virgilio Elizondo, *The Future Is Mestizo: Life Where Cultures Meet* (Bloomington, IN: Meyer Stone, 1988).

38. Isasi-Díaz suggests the use of the expression "kin-dom of God" as a way of avoiding the sexist and hierarchical presumptions that come with the notions of "kingdom." See *En la Lucha/In the Struggle,* esp. xi and 35.

39. Luis Pedraja, *Jesus Is My Uncle: Christology from a Hispanic Perspective* (Nashville, TN: Abingdon, 1999).

FURTHER STUDY

Bañuelas, Arturo, ed. *Mestizo Christianity: Theology from the Latino Perspective.* Maryknoll, NY: Orbis, 1995.

De La Torre, Miguel A., and Edwin David Aponte. *Introducing Latino/a Theologies.* Maryknoll, NY: Orbis, 2001.

De La Torre, Miguel A., and Gaston Espinosa, eds. *Rethinking Latino/a Religion and Identity.* Cleveland: Pilgrim, 2006.

Fernandez, Eduardo C. *La Cosecha: Harvesting Contemporary United States HispanicTheology.* Collegeville, MN: Liturgical, 2000.

Goizueta, Roberto S., ed. *We Are a People: Initiatives in Hispanic American Theology.* Minneapolis: Fortress, 1992.

González, Justo, ed. *Voces: Voices from the Hispanic Church.* Nashville, TN: Abingdon, 1992.

Isasi-Díaz, Ada María. *En la Lucha/In the Struggle: A Hispanic Women's Liberation Theology.* Minneapolis: Fortress, 1993.

Isasi-Díaz, Ada María, and Fernando F. Segovia, eds. *Hispanic/Latino Theology: Challenge and Promise*. Minneapolis: Fortress, 1996.

Pedraja, Luis G. *Teologia: An Introduction to Hispanic Theology*. Nashville, TN: Abingdon, 2003.

Valentín, Benjamín. *Mapping Public Theology: Beyond Culture, Identity, and Difference*. Harrisburg, PA: Trinity Press International, 2002.

———, ed. *New Horizons in Hispanic/Latino(a) Theology*. Cleveland: Pilgrim, 2003.

5

Asian American Theology

ANDREW SUNG PARK

Historical Backdrop

Asian American life is marked by memory of trauma and discrimination: the Chinese Exclusion Act of 1882; the Immigration Act of 1924, including the Asian Exclusion Act; and the Japanese American Internment during World War II. Activism and liberation movements, such as the civil rights movement and the feminist movement of the 1960s and 1970s, would begin to crack the structures of oppression. However, signs of progress were not indicative of racial harmony among minoritized and marginalized groups. In 1992, as but one example, the Los Angeles South Central eruptions targeted and completely burned down over two thousand Korean American and other Asian American small business shops.

It was in light of both violent conflict and moments of progress that Asian American theology emerged. Clear markers of this new theological discourse include the establishment of the Pacific and Asian American Center for Theology and Strategies (PACTS) in Berkeley in 1972, the Center for Pacific and Asian American Ministries in 1976, and the formation of the PANA Institute (Institute for Leadership Development and Study of Pacific and Asian North American Religion) in 2002.

Several other Asian American centers and programs have emerged and actively served Asian American academic and ecclesial communities: the Asian-American Ministries Center at Garrett Evangelical Seminary (1984); the Center for Asian American Ministry at McCormick Theological Seminary, Institute for the Study of Asian American Christianity (ISAAC) (2005); and programs for Asian American ministries and theology hosted by major theological seminaries such as Princeton Theological Seminary and Brite Divinity School.

Description

Situated in multicultural soil, Asian American theologians have reflected on their experiences of racial and cultural discrimination and have critically analyzed discrimination encountered to construct their own theologies. These life experiences motivated them to commit themselves to transforming the oppressive structures of society and the church and led them into the construction of their sociocultural and personal identities that were characterized by their contested negotiations of the complex and difficult relationships among their Christian faith, culture, ethnicity, and personhood.[1]

Generally speaking, Asian American theology may be divided into two stages: the first stage began in the early 1970s through the 1980s. The active theologians of this stage were males and Protestants, consisting of Japanese, Korean, and Chinese Americans. Facing considerable challenges from their own churches, communities, and society, they endeavored to unravel and change entrenched racist prejudices and discriminations of Christian institutions and beyond.[2] The second stage of Asian American theology emerged during the 1990s. It used interdisciplinary perspectives and treated a variety of issues such as ethnic identity, feminism, marginality, multiculturalism, diasporic experience, racial reconciliation, community transformation, evangelism, and faith journey. Whereas the Asian American theologians of the first stage were critical of external social structures but paid little attention to the negative aspects of their own ethnic communities, the Asian American theologians of the second stage have reflected on intracommunal oppression and repression, including the issues of internal ethnocentrism, racism, and gender relations.

Sources

Most male Asian American scholars have used multiple sources to construct their theologies, heavily drawing on their personal and communal experiences and theologies of liberation such as *minjung* (the downtrodden);[3] Black and Latin American theology; sociocultural studies; Asian religions such as Taoism, Buddhism, and Confucianism; their own Asiatic spiritual, cultural, and ethnic heritages; and Diasporic, racial relations, and Asian American studies. An effective way to present these source materials is to provide an overview of the manner in which the work of certain theologians has developed. I begin with Roy Sano.

Scripture: Prophetic Tradition

Sano expressed his apocalyptic theology through several articles in the 1970s.[4] Apocalyptic theology refers to the overthrow of existing unjust social and political systems through God's drastic acts. Sano contrasted an apocalyptic vision with a prophetic tradition that rose to prominence when Israel established its nationhood and when they gained the ear of rulers. He believed that Euro-American theologians were more concerned with the ideas of prophecy, whereas theologians of color were interested in apocalyptic visions. In the world of the "two-category system" where Euro-Americans dominate over other peoples of color and their values supersede values of other groups, simple reshufflings of social orders do not help the situation fundamentally.[5] Sano finds a colonial pattern in the relationship between Euro-Americans and peoples of color in the United States and rejects a wholesale integration of the lower category into the upper category in the two-category system. He does not reject reconciliation between the two levels, but he aspires to see peoples of color obtain liberation from the dominance of the upper group.

Drawing on biblical sources, Sano elaborates on the importance of Moses, Esther, and the books of Daniel and Revelation for illustrating his apocalyptic theology. Moses represents the liberator: Moses led his people out of slavery rather than just changing a few problems in the system of slavery. Sano also features Esther's story in his theology, highlighting the differences from Ruth's story. Ruth is a Moabite woman who well assimilated herself into the Jewish culture, losing her ethnic identity, while Esther tried to hide her ethnic identity for her own safety in the beginning but later disclosed her identity to save her own people because of the plea from her uncle Mordecai. By highlighting the story of Esther, Sano offers a warning to rather light-skinned Asian Americans who attempt to identify themselves with Euro-Americans, hoping that the melting pot theory comes true for them and their children in this country. Sano reminds them of the case of American Indians who have lived in this land from the beginning yet have been severely discriminated against. According to Sano, Esther is a better role model than Ruth.

Sano also holds that the books of Daniel and Revelation support apocalyptic visions of radical transformations rather than revision as change. He opposes any imperialistic systems that make colonies and vassals wherever they go. Sano envisages an apocalyptic transformation in such a situation. He points out biculturalism in the Bible, such as David, who has a Moabite and Hebrew ancestry, and Esther and Daniel in their bicultural contexts. Accordingly, Asian American Christians need to use their bicultural values to follow Jesus Christ. Some of the Asian cultural values that Asian Americans need to preserve are virtues of filial piety, the Taoist heritage of living harmoniously with nature, and the balance between yin and yang. He also advises us "to address a long-standing rejection of syncretism."[6]

Asian American Experience

In the late 1990s, Peter Phan starts his Asian American theology with a "betwixt and between" theme. To be betwixt and between means to be neither here nor there; it is to dwell at the periphery or at boundaries spatially. It means politically existing outside the center of power and abiding in the dangerous and narrow margins of social conflict and domination. However, the advantage of being betwixt and between involves an ability to envision personal and social transformation and enrichment.

When doing theology "betwixt and between," two matters are indispensable: "imagination and memory": "Memory anchors the theologian in the ocean of history and tradition, the Church's and one's own." Phan uses the 19th-century German historian Leopold von Ranke's "remembering" as a way to avoid reproducing reality as it took place but, instead, to re-create it through a process of imagination. Such imagination is the act of re-collecting divergent fragments of the past and forging them together into a new reality in light of present experiences with a view to form a possible future. The imagination "empowers the theologians to break out of the limits of the past and bring human potentialities to full flourishing." For Phan, memory and imagination are like a pair of wings helping theologians soar to the level of "linking past and future, east and west, north and south, earth and heaven."[7] They are indispensable tools for theologians. Theology would be empty if absent of memory, and it would be blind if lacking imagination.

Phan also is aware of the danger of doing theology with imagination and memory alone, which can lead us to solipsism if not involved with suffering people. He sides with the oppressed, using hermeneutics of suspicion, retrieval, and reconstruction to unmask the social and ecclesial structures that exploit them. For him, Christian discipleship needs to have personal solidarity with victims of injustice and oppression.

Theology becomes useless and even pernicious unless it transforms a society of oppression into a community of liberation, justice, peace, and compassion.[8] For example, Phan's article "The Dragon and the Eagle: Toward A Vietnamese American Theology" depicts how Vietnamese American Catholics undergo the pain of leaving their old country and facing hardships in their new country, oscillating betwixt and between two cultures and two churches. Phan holds that Vietnamese Americans can develop a theology that represents harmony between the dragon (the symbol of traditional Vietnamese cultural and religious traditions) and the eagle (the symbol of the contemporary United States Christianity), the cross and the bamboo.[9]

In *Christianity with an Asian Face: Asian American Theology in the Making,* Phan offers several essential theological themes for a Vietnamese American theology. First, a Vietnamese American theology must make use of the Vietnamese worldview of *triet Ly tam tai* (heaven, Earth, and humanity). Second, Jesus Christ is understood as "the immigrant par excellence, the marginalized one living in the *both-and* and *beyond* situation." Furthermore, from the Vietnamese religious experience, Jesus would also be regarded as the elder brother and the paradigmatic ancestor. Third, a Vietnamese theology should understand the church's mission as the threefold task of inculturation, interreligious dialogue, and liberation. Fourth, it is necessary for Vietnamese American theology to initiate liturgical inculturation by considering Vietnamese cultural heritages. Fifth, Vietnamese American theology incorporates Asian values as "love of silence and contemplation, closeness to nature, simplicity, detachment, frugality, harmony, nonviolence, love for learning, respect for the elders, filial piety, compassion, and attachment to the family."[10] Harmonizing heaven, Earth, and humanity, Vietnamese American theology develops the ethics and spirituality of Asian, particularly Vietnamese, values.

Within this discussion one must also take note of the work of Fumitaka Matsuoka. He seeks "to articulate alternative faith paradigms rooted in Asian American dispositions, including multiracial, multicultural ways of being religious and the impact that historical injuries have had on the ways Asian American Christians construct theology."[11] His primary concern is race relations. His first book *Out of Silence* treats the nature of human relations across racial and ethnic lines in the United States. Regarding this he offers five premises related to the meaning of Asian American Christian life. The first premise is that "for Asian American Christians faith plays a determinative role in our attempt to respond to these questions." The second is "a call to acknowledge the historical character of all theologies." The third is that "the primary hermeneutical approach used by Asian American Christians is to discover the questions arising out of an intersection of the saga of faith and our lives of today, and to name the theological clues out of such an interaction between the two." The fourth is that "Christianity is primarily a matter of practice within a particular historical setting and that it is in practice that the key theological issues are found." The fifth is that "Christian faith that transcends all histories is stated communally in terms of each particular history."[12] By means of these five premises, he points out the mosaic and unfolding character of Christian faith.

His overall thesis is that Asian American churches are a primary setting for the emergence of a new culture that surpasses its previous one. For

Matsuoka, human diversity is not a problem but is "the supreme expression of the creative spirit that under girds the whole of humanity."[13] Each ethnic group is an image of God that should have its self-determination. By means of theology, he wants to make sure that every ethnic group, particularly long-silenced cultures of color, lifts its voice and contributes to the shaping of a mutually interactive new America.

In *The Color of Faith*, Matsuoka continues examining the interrelationship between race and the faith community. He treats the issue of a theological articulation of the U.S. racial plurality, ways of addressing the issue of race and the persistent public embarrassment of racial pluralism, racism as the monopolistic powers of collective imaginations, and some signs of peoples' coming together in spite of opposing forces. He concludes that those who are involved in God's suffering love can glimpse the glory of God, a God who is in solidarity with people experiencing the deep pain of racial pluralism. He is convinced that Christian churches continually witness to the vision of human community that bridges the walls of hostility in a racially and eth-nically divided nation. Beyond fostering and affirming the racial identity of peoples, the churches seek after the "ultimate justice of things."[14] However, when a church exclusively gratifies one group while overlooking others, it loses its spiritual integrity and falls into a social club. Race matters for the health of society and for the wellness of the church.

Matsuoka reminds us of the legacy of engagement and commitment to racial justice by our forebears, and he suggests that we pursue possibilities of racial equality however slim they may be. The cross is the symbol of such reality "that insists that possibilities are given only through the experience of limits; that the way to victory lies through exposure to decay and per-haps death."[15] In his introduction to the volume *Realizing the America of Our Hearts,* Matsuoka specifically illustrates his point by discussing the intern-ment experiences of Japanese Americans. In spite of the fact that Japanese Americans are willing to forgive and move forward, "this society has not been able to value their generosity."[16] To him, America can become the country of our hearts by taking this challenge responsibly. The celebration of racial and ethnic diversity and plurality in Christ is Matsuoka's theological focus.

In ways related to the above, Anselm Min, as a Korean American theolo-gian, names several challenges for Korean American theology. First, it is "the task of retrieving both the Western and the Korean tradition for the need of the Korean communities in America, whose needs are new, complicated ones born of new circumstances." Second, the task of Korean American the-ology is to reflect on the theological significance of the Korean American experience such as separation, ambiguity, diversity, and love of the stranger. The third task is "to elaborate a political theology appropriate to Korean Americans as citizens of the United States who have both domestic responsibilities toward the common good and international responsibilities as the sole surviving superpower in an increasingly globalizing world." Related to these tasks, according to Min, "God is the universal creator of all reality and Christ died and was raised for all."[17] On this theological foundation, he proposes a theological model of "solidarity of others," which is dialectical. Although opposing all particularism and tribalism, he does not reject particularity. As solidarity of particular theologies in their complementarity and tension makes a universal theology possible, so does the communion of local churches and the universal church.

Min intentionally does not use the expression "solidarity with others" and selects the phrase "solidarity of others":

> [On the one hand,] solidarity with others still implies a privileged center or normative perspective that regards the liberation of one's own group as the overriding concern and selects the relevant others with whom to enter into solidarity precisely for the sake of and around one's own agenda and goal. . . . Solidarity of others, on the other hand, implies mutual solidarity of others who are truly other to one another yet actively cooperate as subjects of a common destiny.[18]

As he advocates solidarity of others, ethnic theology cannot cease to be Christian in its particularity. Solidarity of others provides not only the Christian integrity of each ethnic theology but also the liberation of a particular group. No particular group can liberate itself from our globally connected world in isolation. For example, Min believes that blacks in Los Angeles are not truly liberated unless whites and Asian Americans are liberated from their dominations and are willing to be in solidarity with blacks and unless blacks are ready to accept their conversions.

According to Min, theology can be in part autobiographical, but theology should not be reduced to autobiography—personal or collective. Autobiography expresses the particularity of a theology but shows no dialectic of that concrete particularity in interaction with other particularities in a gradually more universalizing and interwoven world. Autobiography is subjective, and global solidarity of others increasingly demands the objective social, global dialectic of reality. Min desires to keep a dialectical balance between subjective autobiographical theology and objective universal theology. Developing an ethnic theology requires difficult tasks. For a Korean American theology, it is necessary to reflect on the theological traditions of the West and the indigenous Korean traditions of Confucianism, Buddhism, and shamanism as sources of theology. Then "it must address the needs of Korean communities in the United States, reflect on the theological implications of the Korean American experience, and enter into the solidarity of others with other ethnic groups and their theologies."[19] Min eloquently defines the boundary of and points out the direction of Korean American theology.

Theoretical and Methodological Considerations

In terms of methodological approaches, Asian American theologies employ social analyses, autobiography, storytelling, apocalyptic hermeneutics, anthropological approaches, eschatological imagination, sociotheological hermeneutics, paradoxical dialectics, and "hybridized Asian American biblical hermeneutics that are attentive to the issue of re-envisioning Asian American ethnic-racial identities within their Diasporic existence in the United States."[20] As was the case with the discussion of sources, I take this as an opportunity to discuss theoretical and methodological issues by turning to the work of particular theologians, beginning with Sang Lee.

Introducing pilgrimage as a theological paradigm, Sang Lee stresses that the experience of Korean immigrants is marginality, a sign of a "sacred calling." As God called Abraham into the land of Canaan through the wilderness, so God calls Koreans into this new country through the experience of marginality—our wilderness. Using American sociologist Everett Stonequist's *The Marginal Man*, Lee notes that the marginal person is "on the boundary" or "in between" two cultures without belonging to either.[21] Multicultural studies historian Ronald Takaki expresses it as an ambiguous "betwixt and between" situation.[22] In Lee's theology, marginality experience is not all negative but also positive in terms of providing creative opportunities for pilgrimage, and he finds the ultimate paradigm for the marginal in Jesus. The Crucified represents the pioneer and perfecter of the Asian American's pilgrim faith on Earth. This calling to the pilgrim of marginality is sacred in the sense of its divine providence for new creation.

The pilgrimage does not allow us to permanently settle at any location but exhorts us to move forward to a better country or toward a heavenly one. It does not mean, however, to escape or withdraw from this world but to participate in "building houses," "plant[ing] gardens," and "bear[ing] sons and daughters" in this land (Jeremiah 29:1–7).[23] His emphasis is on our *sojourn-*

ing through this world to work for God's kingdom. Lee's pilgrim theology is paradoxical: although Korean American Christians live in the United States, they can find a true home neither in this country nor in Korea. They are meant to wander through this wilderness, only yearning for a better home in God's city. As long as they sojourn in this world, the tension and paradox of their identity will follow them all the days of their lives. Pilgrims' faith is always looking for the ultimate not the relative. By detaching themselves from their earthly desires, these people paradoxically take part in the life of society more fully. Detachment does not denote a withdrawal or escapism from the world but unselfish genuine participation in the world of God. They take their responsibility seriously as God calls them into this journey.

Within his theology, Lee introduces a new concept, "liminality." Borrowing cultural anthropologist Victor Turner's idea, he outlines three salient points of the creative powers of the *in-betweenness*: "openness to the new," "the emergence of *communitas*" (a genuine human community and a generic bond transcending to particular cultural definitions and normative ordering of social ties), and "the creative space for the prophetic, knowledge, and action" (the negative capacity to be critical and subversive about what is wrong with the structure, the center, and the positive and transformative capacity). To Asian Americans, marginality is coerced liminality. Because of racism, Asian Americans may experience the potential of their liminal conditions in a negative way. Lee suggests that "self-consciously liminal Asian Americans gather together" to promote liminality.[24] Although Asian Americans are coerced into marginality, they are able to develop a potential creativity of liminality in their communitas.

In the mid-1990s, Jung Young Lee picked up the theme of marginality and developed it further. For him, theology is autobiographical. With such a background of experience, he articulated the meaning of marginality. From a perspective of center or dominant groups, marginality means negative in-between, belonging to neither. From a perspective of marginalized or ethnic groups, marginality denotes positive in-between, belonging to both. This positive "in-between" is "in-both" for Jung Lee. Applied to Asian Americans, the self-affirming marginality signifies: *"I am more than an Asian because I am an American, and I am more than an American because I am an Asian."*[25]

Marginality is being at the edge that connects both worlds. The *in-beyond* people are the creative core. Lee says, "The marginal and the creative core are inseparable in new marginality."[26] The new marginal can be reconcilers and wounded healers in the broken and two-category system world. Using the yin and yang paradigm, Lee rejects the paradigms of either/or and neither/

nor. In light of new marginality, he contends that marginality needs to be the focal point of Christian theology. He reads Jesus' incarnation as divine marginalization and Jesus' life as a paradigm of new marginalization. Marginality is God's opting for loving humanity. Rejected and crucified by the people, Jesus loved them, affirming their humanity and living a life of the in-beyond paradigm.

The themes of Jesus, God, creation, the Fall, and the church are treated through his new marginality paradigm. Lee stresses overcoming marginality through marginality—overcoming all structural and personal marginalized experiences that come from love and patience in Jesus. The marginal work together toward the goal of creating such a community of new marginality, even inviting centralist people to the cause:

> No matter how much I have committed myself to marginality or to the Christian faith, my personal experience of marginality cannot be fully overcome without my solidarity with the community of marginality. . . . When centralist people understand that the center they seek is not real, they will be liberated from centrality and seek the creative center. When this transformation happens, centrality changes to marginality, and marginality changes to new marginality, and all people become marginal. Marginality is overcome through marginality, and all are marginal to God manifest in Jesus-Christ. When all of us are marginal, love becomes the norm of our lives, and service becomes the highest aspiration of our creativity. We then become servants to one another in love.[27]

When the marginal discover their authentic self-identity, they become creative minorities and catalysts that transform the world. When people become the new marginality—whether they are Asian Americans or centralists—they became the subject of salvation history. Lee suggests that all Christians and their organizations form a community of marginality that lives up to servanthood, transforming the centralist world with a holistic in-beyond approach.

During the early 1990s, Andrew Sung Park developed his transmutation theology. To resolve interracial and interethnic conflict and problems, sociologists have provided three major theories: assimilation, melting pot (amalgamation), and cultural pluralism. Presently, the ideas of cultural pluralism and assimilation prevail. Park contends that, although espousing a society of diversity in unity and unity in diversity, the idea of cultural pluralism has fostered the separation and isolation of ethnic groups, as they are lacking in the interactive unity of diverse groups (mutual understanding) and mutual challenges that has resulted in racial conflicts and tensions such as the 1992 Los Angeles racial eruptions. Park endeavors to develop a Christian model of social interactions. In the model, he suggests that Korean Americans and other oppressed groups change their *han* (the deeply accumulated pain that has festered in victims for a long time) into constructive energy to establish a community of Christ.[28]

Although both terms refer to internal and external change, Park's use of "transmutation" stresses its natural, biological, and internal aspect, whereas "transformation" underscores its external and structural aspect. The way of transmutation is the way of Tao: changing an object not by force but by cogency. Park uses a metaphor of a huge rock in flowing water. Water carves and rounds the rock tenderly and slowly, but surely. Like water, the way of transmutation changes social injustice and evil by persuasion without violent coercion.[29] His transmutation idea does not seek unity in diversity and diversity in unity. In this view, unity is not a goal but an outcome of moving toward a community of Christ through working together for the change of unfair customs and tradition in each culture and unjust social systems such as racism, ethnocentrism, sexism, classism, ageism, and humanocentrism. In this model, we respect other cultures enough to celebrate their strengths and care for them enough to challenge their weak points.

Diversity takes place when each group tries to pursue its own identity and change its own shortcomings. Diversity transpires not only in confirming what each culture is but also in affirming what each culture can be. His model underpins both unity and diversity in transmutation. Transmutation dialectically interweaves them. Without transmutation, diversity turns into separation and unity turns into uniformity:

- Mutual enhancement involves mutual enrichment and mutual challenge.[30] Mutual enrichment concerns the promulgation of each ethnic culture and tradition. Diverse ethnic groups accept, encourage, and appreciate each other's culture, tradition, and custom.
- Mutual challenge involves three movements: respect (recognizing others' values, capacity, and potential), care (considering others' situations and to attend their needs), and confrontation (coming face to face with others' problem in honesty).[31]

One might wonder what spiritual and cultural ethos Korean Americans should work toward. Park answers this question by explaining two kinds of ethos: existential and essential. The existential ethos is *han,* the ineffable agony of the downtrodden; the essential ethos can be said to be *hahn* (paradoxical inclusiveness), *jung* (affectionate attachment), and *mut* (graceful elegance).[32] By promoting the essential ethos of Koreanness, one can contribute to the whole society. That is, Park proposes to transmute the *han* and sin of the society into its *hahn, jung,* and *mut.*[33] Unlike a violent revolution model, his transmutation works like water, gently but surely, intending to change unjust social structures by mutual challenge and mutual enrichment in the strength of truth, reasoning, and persuasion.

For Park, Korean theology has at least a fourfold task: self-transmutation (incessant self-critical reflection and change by the renewal of the heart in the Spirit), the transmutation of the Korean American church (the transmutation of patriarchal, hierarchical, and exclusively ethnocentric Korean American churches), the transmutation of Korean American communities (the conversion of sexist, economically exploitative and racist community practices), and the transmutation of U.S. cultures (the conversion of sexism, racism, economic injustice, intolerance, media monopoly, violence, rugged individualism, global domination, the culture of transnational corporation, and neoimperialism).[34]

Ongoing Issues

In this section I again present ongoing themes in Asian American theology by turning to the work of a particular theologian, in this case Eleazar S. Fernandez.

The Nature of Liberation

Fernandez discusses an unfinished dream for racial and ethnic people as a theological stance and thus problematizes the nature and meaning of liberation in *A Dream Unfinished,* coedited by Fernandez and Fernando Segovia. God is not finished with history yet, in spite of the strong presence of the forces of death. There àre several points he makes regarding unfinished dreams.

First, he suggests that we name our unfinished dreams as our ultimate defiance and hopeful realism. Our full accountability enables us to name our unfinished dreams and nightmares. Second, unfinished dreams are eschatological imagination and vision. Facing suffering and alienation, ethnic people may become cynical and fatalistic. They can, however, come to foster eschatological vision and imagination by naming unfinished dreams. To spell out unfinished dreams is not only to denounce social wrongs but also to announce our imagination to alternative tomorrows. The imagination and vision that address alternative tomorrows are eschatological. Third, unfinished dreams remember the dismembered. To exhume the pains of the past is not to reside in the past but to forgive them and move forward. This act of remembering is "to make whole those who have experienced brokenness." Fourth, unfinished dreams involve living between memory and hope. To live between them is to live in the tension of memory and hope. It is not a life of either/or but of both-and: both "a life laden with pain" and "a creative and grace-filled life." Fifth, an unfinished dream is waiting in hope. Only those who have hope can wait. Waiting in hope redeems the in-between time and offers significance to the time being. For the waiting people in hope, the in-between time is a precious and historic time, a time to be creative and actualizing.[35]

The ethnic in the United States are "children of unfinished dreams and children of promise." Some ethnic and racial persons have broken through the glass ceiling only because some others have courageously broken their silence and have employed their stammering tongues. Those trailblazers deserve our gratitude, but more important is the fact that we also transform the monuments of the past into movements of transformation and movement of the incorporation of scattered voices and visions today. Our dreams are still unfinished, and a tomorrow awaits our work.[36]

Like Black theologian James Cone, Fernandez believes that sin involves desiring to be white by internalizing the colonial values of whites. For example, constructing an image of God according to European Americans is giving away a positive self-image. It is necessary to encounter God in one's own ethnicity. Borrowing from United Methodist pastor Elizabeth Tay, Fernandez holds that we are led to see who God is when God encounters us in our ethnicity and race. It is the theological and anthropological character of our understanding of God and self-identity. Fernandez stresses Filipino American subjecthood in a globalized world. The plight of Filipino Americans in the United States is a microcosm of the plight of third world people. Their presence in the United States results in the globalization phenomenon that has led them to economic, political, and cultural marginalization in comparison with peoples from affluent countries. Social justice issues concerned Fernandez most while he was in the Philippines, but both social justice issues and the politics of identity call his commitment in this country. First, Filipino American theology needs to interweave the global and the local. Second, it seeks to forge the postcolonial subjecthood of Filipino Americans in the wakefulness of transformative praxis. This requires the long journey of exorcising colonial selfhood and "the visionary praxis of articulating a new social self."[37] It is "our time" to dare to be postcolonial subjects.

NOTES

1. Jonathan Y. Tan, "Asian American Theologies," in *Global Dictionary of Theology*, ed. William A. Dyrness and Veli-Matti Kärkkäinen (Downers Grove, IL: InterVarsity, 2008).

2. Ibid. To Tan, some prominent Asian American theologians in this stage were Roy Sano, Paul Nagano, Jitsuo Morikawa, Sang Hyun Lee, and David Ng.

3. *Minjung* is a Korean term to describe those who are politically oppressed, economically exploited, socially alienated, or culturally despised. *Minjung* theology is for the liberation of these downtrodden.

4. Roy Sano, comp., *The Theologies of Asian Americans and Pacific Peoples: A Reader*, (Berkeley, CA: Asian Center for Theology and Strategies, Pacific School of Religion, 1976).

5. Roger Daniels and Harry Kitano outline this "two-category" system in their book *American Racism* (Englewood Cliffs, NJ: Prentice Hall, 1970).

6. Sano, *Theologies of Asian Americans*, 125.

7. Peter C. Phan, "Betwixt and Between: Doing Theology with Memory and Imagination," in *Journeys at the Margin*, ed. Peter Phan and Jung Young Lee (Collegeville, MN: Liturgical, 1999), 127, 114, 115.

8. Ibid., 131.

9. Peter C. Phan, "The Dragon and the Eagle: Toward A Vietnamese American Theology," *Theology Digest* 43, no. 3 (2001): 203–218.

10. Peter C. Phan, *Christianity with an Asian Face: Asian American Theology in the Making* (Maryknoll, NY: Orbis, 2003), 246–247.

11. At http://www.psr.edu/page.cfm?1=131.

12. Fumitaka Matsuoka, *Out of Silence: Emerging Themes in Asian American Churches* (Cleveland: United Church Press, 1995), 2–7.

13. Ibid., 10, 139.

14. Fumitaka Matsuoka, *The Color of Faith* (Cleveland: United Church Press, 1998), vii, 125.

15. Ibid., 127.

16. Fumitaka Matsuoka, introduction to *Realizing the America of Our Hearts: Theological Voices of Asian Americans*, ed. Fumitaka Matsuoka and Eleazar S. Fernandez (St. Louis, MO: Chalice, 2003), 3.

17. Anselm Min, "From Autobiography to Fellowship of Others: Reflections on Doing Ethnic Theology Today," in *Journeys at the Margin*, ed. Peter C. Phan and Jung Young Lee (Collegeville, MN: Liturgical, 1999), 146–153.

18. Ibid., 157.

19. Ibid., 158.

20. Ibid.

21. Sang Hyun Lee, "Called to Be Pilgrims," in *Korean American Ministry: A Resource Book*, ed. Sang Hyun Lee (Princeton, N.J.: Consulting Committee on Korean American Ministry, Presbyterian Church, 1987), 97, 92.

22. Ronald Takaki, *Strangers from a Different Shore* (New York: Penguin, 1989).

23. Sang Lee, "Called to Be Pilgrims," 107.

24. Ibid., 60.

25. *Jung Young Lee, Marginality: The Key to Multicultural Theology (Minneapolis: Fortress, 1995)*, 58; italics in original.

26. Ibid., 60.

27. Ibid., 170.

28. For Park, "community of Christ" is a concrete community of God's presence, the eschatological community of economic, cultural, and political democracy in tolerance, equity, freedom, affection, gusto, and peace.

29. Andrew Sung Park, *Racial Conflict and Healing: An Asian-American Theological Perspective* (Maryknoll, NY: Orbis, 1996), 100.

30. The term "mutual enrichment" is the expression used for describing the aim of life experience in John Cobb, *Beyond Dialogue: Toward a Mutual Transformation of Christianity and Buddhism* (Philadelphia: Fortress, 1982). I use it in a different context.

31. Andrew Sung Park, "A Theology of Transmutation," in *A Dream Unfinished: Theological Reflections on America from the Margins*, ed. Eleazar S. Fernandez and Fernando F. Segovia (Maryknoll, NY: Orbis, 2001), 157–158.

32. To avoid confusion between the *han* of woundedness and the *han* of greatness, Park uses "hahn" for the latter. In Korean, they are the same word. Some scholars use the Romanization *jeong* instead of *jung*.

33. Park, *Racial Conflict and Healing*, 107–117.

34. Ibid., 101–102.

35. Eleazar Fernandez, "On Unfinished Dreams, Defiant Hopes, and Historical Projects," in *A Dream Unfinished: Theological Reflections on America from the Margins*, ed. Eleazar S. Fernandez and Fernando F. Segovia (Maryknoll, NY: Orbis, 2001), 275–276.

36. Ibid., 278.

37. Eleazar Fernandez, "Postcolonial Exorcism and Reconstruction: Filipino Americans' Search for Postcolonial Subjecthood," in *Realizing the America of Our Hearts: Theological Voices of Asian Americans*, ed. Fumitaka Matsuoka and Eleazar S. Fernandez (St. Louis, MO: Chalice, 2003), 95.

FURTHER STUDY

Fernandez, Eleazar, and Segovia, Fernando, eds. *A Dream Unfinished: Theological Reflections on America from the Margins*. Maryknoll, NY: Orbis, 2001.

Lee, Jung Young, *Marginality: The Key to Multicultural Theology*. Minneapolis: Fortress, 1995.

Lee, Sang Hyun, ed. *Korean American Ministry: A Resource Book*. Princeton, NJ: Consulting Committee on Korean American Ministry, Presbyterian Church, 1987.

Matsuoka, Fumitaka. *The Color of Faith*. Cleveland: United Church Press, 1998.

———. *Out of Silence: Emerging Themes in Asian American Churches*. Cleveland: United Church Press, 1995.

Matsuoka, Fumitaka, and Eleazar Fernandez, eds. *Realizing the America of Our Hearts: Theological Voices of Asian Americans*. St. Louis, MO: Chalice, 2003.

Min, Anselm. *The Solidarity of Others in a Divided World: A Postmodern Theology after Postmodernism*. New York : T and T Clark International, 2004.

Ng, David, ed. *People on the Way: Asian North Americans Discovering Christ, Culture, and Community.* Valley Forge, PA: Judson, 1996.

Park, Andrew Sung. *Racial Conflict and Healing: An Asian-American Theological Perspective.* Maryknoll, NY: Orbis, 1996.

———. *The Wounded Heart of God: The Asian Concept of Han and the Christian Doctrine of Sin.* Nashville, TN: Abingdon, 1993.

Phan, Peter C. *Christianity with an Asian Face: Asian American Theology in the Making.* Maryknoll, NY: Orbis, 2003.

———. *Vietnamese-American Catholics.* New York: Paulist, 2005.

Phan, Peter C., and Lee, Jung Young, eds. *Journeys at the Margin: Toward an Autobiographical Theology in American-Asian Perspective.* Collegeville, MN: Liturgical, 1999.

Sano, Roy I., ed. *The Theologies of Asian Americans and Pacific Peoples: A Reader.* Berkeley, CA: Asian Center for Theology and Strategies, Pacific School of Religion, 1976.

6

Asian American Feminist Theology

GRACE JI-SUN KIM

Historical Backdrop

Asian American women's theology is nascent and emerges in the aftermath of Christianity's involvement in colonialism, which altered the spirit of Asian American women in many ways. This political and cultural configuration made these women deny their own traditions and regard their multireligious traditions and wisdom as demonic. It also devalued their physical appearance and forced them to accept Western notions of "beauty" as superior. Hence, Asian cultural resources have often been written with the gaze of colonialism, "orientalism," and racism.[1]

Maxine Hong Kingston's story "No Name Woman" in her book *The Woman Warrior: Memoirs of a Girlhood among Ghosts* illustrates how quickly a woman's life and existence can be eliminated from our memory and consciousness. The narrator tells the story of her aunt, who committed suicide after giving birth to a girl, conceived not with her husband who was away at Gold Mountain but with another man. This aunt, this "no name woman," like all other "no name women," existed on the margins of a patriarchal Asian culture that held that "it was better to raise geese than girls." Even in death she was punished by being deliberately forgotten, unconnected to the living—the descent line—and became a "wandering ghost," who was "always hungry, always needing," begging or stealing food from other ghosts, who had living kin to give them gifts of food and money. This no name woman was expunged from the family record, "as if she had never been born," and even her name was erased from memory, like all the countless other no name women who fail to appear in the pages of history books "as if they had never been born." Her illegitimate child, who died with her, could not have been included within the circle of kin, because she posed a severe critique of male dominance, having been conceived out of either rape or defiance of "female chastity."[2] This story is a reminder of a recurring event within a patriarchal society as women's actions are interpreted by men and, in turn, their consequences are defined and determined by men. Like the no name woman, there are countless other women whose identity and existence have been extinguished.

During Korea's Yi dynasty (1392–1910), women had no names of their own and were identified relative to men: so-and-so's daughter, so-and-so's wife, and so-and-so's mother. When she married, only her family name was entered into her husband's family registry, and her name was removed from her own family registry, where only the name of her husband was recorded.[3] Having no name thus meant being defined in relation to men, and having no name meant erasure and ostracism. This omission served to bolster a system of male dominance, a system of privilege and oppression.[4] Some remnants of this practice still exist as many Asian women's names are not used after they are married. They are only referred to by their marital status with children or by their nonmarital status. It is this sociocultural history that Asian American women have come to bear and inherit. They are primarily viewed as childbearers who will continue the husband's family line by bearing a son. Many women who wanted to be free from this burden sought to leave Asia and go to America, where they believed they would have a better life outside of a patriarchal society. However, as women left their Asian context and moved to the West, further barriers and burdens came their way.

Since the early 19th century, Asians have been migrating worldwide but especially to the United States and Canada. At the height of the westward expansion in the United States (across the American Indian lands and Mexican territory to a new Pacific frontier) and the building of its economy, Asians provided cheap and abundant labor. Their first area of destination was Hawaii, and over 300,000 Asians entered the islands between 1850 and 1920. The U.S. government and private companies ordered Asian labor as if it was a commodity, and the Chinese were among the first as they worked in the sugar industry in Hawaii. These laborers helped transform the sugar industry into a "King" industry and earned income, while at the same time displacing Native Hawaiian laborers.[5]

The annexation of California in 1848 opened the floodgates for Asian laborers. Aaron Palmer, a U.S. policy maker, recommended the importation of Chinese labor for the construction of the Transcontinental Railroad with the idea of cultivating the fertile lands of California and making San Francisco the "great emporium of our commerce on the Pacific."[6] Other Asians also arrived in response to the need for laborers to build America: Japanese (1880s), Filipinos (1900), Koreans (1903), and Indians (1907).

Korean immigration patterns were not the same as other Asian groups as many Koreans initially did not want to immigrate to the United States. Missionaries played an active role, and Koreans eventually overcame the initial resistance to the idea of immigration. A number of missionaries persuaded members of their congregations to go to Hawaii, a Christian land. As a result of the active role missionaries played, an estimated 40% of the seven thousand emigrants who left the country between December 1902 and May 1905 were converts. Moreover, unlike the Chinese and Japanese who came from geographically confined areas, Korean emigrants originated from many places, especially seaports and their vicinities. Furthermore, fewer of the Korean emigrants than Chinese or Japanese came from agricultural backgrounds. Of the seven thousand Koreans taken to Hawaii, about one thousand eventually returned home, and another one thousand continued on to the U.S. mainland.[7]

Asian women's immigration to the United States was at times prompted by a desire for freedom, and often their migration was induced and orchestrated by men for profit and exploitation.[8] Many women were misinformed about their expectations and life in the United States. Many were not ready for the hardships that immigrant life was going to deliver. Once they arrived, there was little chance of returning to their country of origin. They had to live in the United States and attend to work daily while raising their children.

On the plantations of Hawaii and on the farms of the western United States, these women cooked, washed, and cleaned, not only for their own families; often, for a small fee, they did these chores for bachelors and married men who had come without their wives. Those who cooked for the unattached men had to get up at 3 or 4 A.M. to cook breakfast for as many as forty persons and to pack an equal number of lunch boxes in primitive kitchens with no modern conveniences.[9] Others who worked in the fields for wages spent a full day under the sun, sometimes with babies strapped to their backs, before returning home to fix supper. In the evenings, they washed, ironed, and mended. Those who bore children did all this work even while pregnant.[10]

In addition to the physical hardships, Asian American women experienced psychological and legal hardships in the form of racism, prejudice, and discrimination. Beginning in the 1850s, a series of restrictive laws against Asians were enacted. In 1870, Congress passed a law that made Asian immigrants the only racial group barred from naturalization. In 1882, the Chinese Exclusion Act was passed. This suspended the immigration of Chinese laborers for ten years, but this was later extended indefinitely, eventually being lifted only in 1943. The 1917 Immigration Act further limited Asian immigration, banning immigration from all countries in the Asia-Pacific Triangle except for the Philippines (a U.S. territory) and Japan. Japanese immigration, however, was subsequently limited by the 1924 Exclusionary Immigration Act, which literally halted new immigration from Asia. In addition, Asians were segregated in public facilities including schools, were heavily taxed, were prohibited from owning land and from intermarriage with whites, and so on. The most visible incident in the country's history of discrimination against Asian Americans was probably the internment of Japanese Americans during World War II.[11] It was not until the passage of sweeping civil rights legislation in 1965 that state-supported discrimination ended.

Description

Theology never occurs in a vacuum but always within a specific context. Thus one needs to carefully examine the different historical, social, and political contexts within which we are developing our theology. Theology that intentionally relates itself to a particular time and place has been given the name "contextual theology." Contextual theology has its social roots in the experience of third world Christians as they recognized that the theology they received was not a-historical, a-social, or a-cultural but was "contextual" in an unconscious way. In considering the relationship of context to theology, these third world Christians realized it was not that one's theological conclusions were necessarily different from place to place but, rather, that the context determined the kinds of questions to be raised.[12] Contextuality (as distinct from contemporaneity) means the discovery of the place-dimension of the human condition.[13]

This means that Asian American women's context will bring forth expectations and understandings of theology that are distinct from those of the majority in both North America and Asia. That is, their context of patriarchy, prejudice, and hardship gave birth to the need for Asian American women to examine the questions of theology and to further develop theology that frees them to a more meaningful and liberating life.

It is important to recognize that the terms "Asian" and "Asian American" are social and cultural constructs, arising out of particular historical stages of political struggles.[14] These terms have been useful for creating a space for theological discourse and should not be essentialized or homogenized so as to hinder critical reflections on diversity within the community.[15] When Asian theologians call themselves Asian, the term signifies the consciousness of belonging to the history of particular groups of people. It means that they are inheriting the myths, languages, and cuisines of certain cultures. Use of that designation also encompasses a commitment to looking at the world and themselves from particular vantage points. In addition, identification as an *Asian* theologian suggests solidarity with the struggles and destiny of specific peoples.

In a word, the term "Asian" has an identifiable set of meanings: shared colonial history, multiple religious traditions, rich and diverse cultures, immense suffering and poverty, and a long history of patriarchal control and present political struggles. Therefore, one must keep all these identifiable sets in mind as one engages in Asian American women's theology as "Asian" is an integral part of the development and emergence of this theology.[16] Asian American women theologians need to lift up the multivocal nature of Asian traditions and begin new lines of theological inquiry by rearticulating theology through the liberating language of myths, stories, and the rituals of women.[17]

Asian American feminist theologians join other Asian theologians in their tendency to highlight the effect of entrenched cultural myths, rituals, and traditions on women's roles in society and the cultural and religious dimensions of oppression that result. They are interested in assessing Christianity's role in supporting colonialism and patriarchy because political independence for many of them happened only a generation ago.[18]

Theology that is not in touch with their life experience cannot be a living theology.[19] Chung Hyun Kyung suggests that Asian women's theology is a "cry, plea and invocation" to God in search of justice and healing.[20] It is an embodied and critical reflection on Asian American women's experiences, and it is aimed at bringing about a community of harmony, peace, and love.

Sources

Wisdom

The concept of wisdom deeply affects the lives of Asian women through their various religious and cultural traditions. Wisdom is an important concept in Buddhism, in that it manifests hope and liberation. It is generally believed that wisdom is the absolute knowledge through which enlightenment is attained. Since absolute knowledge is compassionate in its nature, the Enlightened One (Buddha) leads people to their emancipation. It is the essential virtue without which no being may claim to be an Enlightened One (Buddha).[21]

Wisdom is also central to Confucianism, and links can be made here also to biblical wisdom. Wisdom is closely related to the "Way" to live, a concept found in most religions, including the three Semitic religions: Judaism, Christianity, and Islam. Confucianism views wisdom mainly through sageliness or sagehood.[22] Confucianists held that the learning of human ethical relations was the true "orthodox" learning and that acquiring moral purity is the way to become a sage. The Confucianist emphasis on wisdom as essential to practical, moral life closely resembles the Hokmah of biblical wisdom, especially as found in Proverbs.

When comparing these various wisdom figures, it is important to note the many similarities in deed and character to biblical wisdom. Wisdom in the Old Testament is portrayed as a feminine image with feminine characteristics and roles; these attributes are then carried into the New Testament and linked with Christ, which consequently provides a feminine understanding of God.[23] It is possible to syncretize these various wisdom figures into a Christian understanding of wisdom to develop a hybrid wisdom Christology.

As we turn to pneumatology and examine the role and understanding of the Holy Spirit within the church, an inculturated perspective of spirit from the Asian concept of *chi* is a helpful tool for Asian American women. The Chinese character *chi* originated in the concept of cloud or vapor, which was regarded as the primordial vitality for prosperity and productivity. Western-language translations of *chi* include air, wind, vapor, breath, gas, vital spirit, anger, appearance, intelligence, vital fluid, energy, material force, vital force, and subtle spirits.[24] *Chi* is what makes one alive, as it is the life force energy that makes one a living being. Every living thing has *chi*. It is the central, animating element of our overall energy system, giving power and strength.[25] It is a vital, dynamic, original power that permeates the entire universe and leads to an ultimate unity.[26] The Spirit becomes the essence of all things as all things exist because of the Spirit as *chi*. *Chi* is the ultimate reality and is immanent in all things; and all things in the universe consist of *chi*, which means no being can exist apart from *chi*.[27] This notion of the Spirit as *chi* assists us in reaffirming the idea of divine immanence or Immanuel, God is with us.[28] This makes one move toward a panentheistic understanding of God: God is in all things.[29]

The Old Testament *ruach* and the New Testament *pneuma* carry the same ambiguity of multiple meanings, as *chi* does, such as breath, air, wind, or soul. The word *ruach* has its etymological origin in air, which manifests itself in two distinctive forms: that of wind in nature and that of breath in living things. Because God as the Spirit manifests herself as wind or *ruach*, she is also chi. Wind symbolizes the power of life in nature, while breath symbolizes the power of life in the living. Without chi, life does not exist;[30] similarly, if there is no Spirit, nothing living can exist. God as the life-giving spirit is the proper source of life and strength; in a derivative sense, *ruach* also denotes the life force of the individual (Judges 15:19) and of the group (Numbers 16:22).[31]

Hence, Spirit/*chi*[32] is essentially what keeps humanity alive as it is the life-giving force within us that sustains and keeps us in harmony with nature and the world. Spirit/*chi* embraces life and makes it full. Spirit/*chi* is crucial to Asian American women's theology as it emphasizes the Spirit/*chi* power within all of us to make a difference in this world. Spirit/*chi* is salvific and negotiates a space to save those who are living in the liminal spaces between us.

Context/Experience

Asian American feminist theology is inductive, and it does not begin with the Bible or Christian doctrines but with the stories of women: "The text of God's revelation was, is, will be written in our bodies and our peoples' everyday struggle for survival and liberation."[33] Therefore, it is necessary to listen to the women's stories and experiences to begin to do theology as they come to know God through experience. This is a dynamic and experiential way of doing theology much closer to the Bible, in which people did not come to know God by discussion or argument but by experiencing God.[34] This is an alternative to a typical Western method based on analysis and debate.[35]

Regarding the nature of experience, Koreans have articulated *han* as a mode of responding to the tragic situation of the oppressed. In terms of its etymology, *han* is a psychological term that denotes repressed feelings of suffering through the oppression of others or through natural calamities or illness. Sometimes translated as "just indignation," *han* is deep spiritual pain that rises out of the unjust experience of the people. *Han* appears inevitably in the biographies of Asian American women in their stories. Asian American people embody this *han* as they experience oppression and suffering in their daily lives.[36] *Han* is "the suppressed, amassed and condensed experience of oppression caused by mischief or misfortune, so that it forms a kind of 'lump' in one's spirit."[37]

Han is the brokenheartedness but also the raw energy for the struggle for liberation. Because Asian American women face issues of prejudice, discrimination, alienation, exclusion, and shame in this society, their experiences can be called *han*—the deep pain of a victim. *Han* has emotive and transrational aspects and is quite a useful term for theological discourse.[38] *Han* has three levels: individual, collective, and structural. At its individual level, *han* is the will to avenge, the will to resign, bitterness, and helplessness; it is a reaction to individualistic oppression, which is often connected to collective and structural oppression. At its collective level, *han* is the collective consciousness and unconsciousness of victims such as the ethos of cultural inferiority complex, racial melancholy, racial resentment, the sense of physical inadequacy, and national shame. At the structural level, sin is unjust and evil systems that perpetuate racism, sexism, exclusiveness, and monopolistic capitalism.[39]

Therefore, if it is to have any impact on their lives, Asian American women's theology needs to work toward this goal of releasing *han*. There needs to be a praxis component within their theology to help release this *han*, which can be destructive and damaging if it is left to sit within them. But many Asian American women do not have the public channels that men have to express their *han*, which has led to a sense of helplessness in their lives. They have been enclosed within the home to take care of the family and household. Women have been discouraged from taking on leadership positions and play only a minimal role in society.[40] Thus a major goal of doing theology is to release this *han* in the sense of *won-han*. *Won-han* is the refusal to accept *han* as their being but to fight it so that they can actively work toward releasing it. The process that untangles and resolves accumulated *han* is called *han-pu-ri*. The term originally came from the Korean shamanistic tradition as the shamans played the role of the priest/ess of *han-pu-ri* in his or her community.[41]

One group that lives with *han* is the *minjung*. *Minjung* means oppressed, alienated, exploited, and despised "people of God." *Min* means "people," and *jung* signifies "the mass." Hence *minjung* literally means "the mass of people."[42] In Korean, women are the *minjung* of the *minjung*. The concept of *minjung* is opposite to the concept of power and different from the middle-class intelligent strata. Political power originates from addressing the concerns of *minjung*. As political power becomes institutionalized, it changes into the oppression of *minjung*. In the process of history, *minjung* rebelled against this power by returning it to its original place and restoring public righteousness. Kim Chi-Ha argues that when the powerful betray justice and become anti-*minjung*, it is righteous to take the side of the *minjung* and unrighteous to take the side of the power.[43] As Asian American women struggle to exorcise the evils of imperialism, globalization, racism, and patriarchy, their *han* needs to be realized to prevent them from embodying the life of a *minjung*.

Theoretical and Methodological Considerations

There is concern among theologians about the interpretation of the Bible, and some turn to "context" to help them understand the meaning of particular passages for "here and now." Biblical texts will make sense only if they are read with insight into the social, political, and religious context of their own time.[44] Due to the patriarchal bias, one needs to read the biblical words with a critical eye and be aware of their origin and intent.

Multifaith hermeneutics can be described as the task of relating Christian biblical interpretation positively to other religious texts and traditions. Multifaith hermeneutics assumes the willingness to look at one's own traditions from other perspectives, the maturity to discern both similarities and differences in various traditions, and the humility to learn from other partners in the conversation. Multifaith hermeneutics requires us to affirm that other religious traditions have as much right to exist as Christianity.[45] The interaction between Asian scriptures and Christian scriptures is not meant to prove that they are compatible, or incompatible, but aims at a "wider intertextuality" and a fruitful and continuous cross-cultural dialogue.[46]

Kwok Pui Lan suggests that a "dialogical imagination" must become operative in biblical interpretation. This approach invites more dialogue partners by shifting the emphasis from one scripture (the Bible) to many scriptures, from responding to one religious narrative to many possible narratives. It shifts from a single-axis framework of analysis to a multiaxial interpretation, taking into serious consideration the issues of race, class, gender, culture, and history. Dialogical imagination uses Asian cultural and religious traditions and sacred texts as dialogical partners in biblical reflection and "the social biography of the people" as hermeneutical keys for biblical interpretation.[47]

Asian cultural roots are embedded in nondualistic metaphysics and religions that express their understandings of life and reality in terms of fluidity, flexibility, and multiplicity. The sacred is embedded in life's ambiguities, and the margins and centers shift constantly. An understanding of reality as fluid, transitional, and impermanent connects meaningfully with many Asian American women's struggles to live a transcultural, and marginalized existence.[48] Their impermanent location leads to a hybrid identity that seeks to find a home in between realities.

The term "hybridity" needs further elaboration and is an essential tool that Asian American feminist theologians are turning to to help describe this situation of instability and create new spaces and places of discourse. Essentially, hybridization is a mixture of two things as it brings together and fuses but also maintains separation. Hybridity makes difference into sameness and sameness into difference, but in a way that makes the same no longer the same, the different no longer simply different.[49] Hybridity is a way to conceptualize porous religious, ethnic, and cultural boundaries. What hybridity does is shift the conceptualization of identity in that identity is no longer a stable reference point. Hybridity is not about the dissolution of differences but about renegotiating the structure of power built on difference.[50]

Ongoing Issues

Asian American feminist theology is growing and changing. In this section, I explore continuing concerns within this form of liberation theology. I am interested in providing readers with a sense of future direction of this theological approach by presenting the experiential framework that must be addressed. Recalling the link between experience and theology, readers will see how this approach corresponds with a sense of ongoing issues.

Sexuality

There is much concern about footbinding in China as it was painful, oppressive, and inhumane. This practice, among certain classes and ethnicities of Chinese women, secured their dependence on men and served to confine them within the household gates. Although Chinese men depicted Chinese woman as weak, timid, and sexually available, they also saw them as dangerous, powerful, and sexually insatiable. The cults of footbinding, chastity, and virginity and the rules that oppressed women were the reactions of men to women's resistance.[51]

Men are socialized into and reinforced in their behaviors and attitudes through the cult of hypermasculine culture. Men are concentrated away from women for periods of time and taught appropriate masculine behavior, which usually includes some form of control of the body and repression of sexuality through celibacy or the periodic sexual exploitation of women. Women are objectified and eroticized, and men are expected to fit into a power hierarchy that stresses obedience and loyalty to higher authorities. Throughout these systems, women are forced to be the "gatekeepers" of male sexual activity even as they are exploited by it and demonized by the sexual projections and obsessions of men. The sexual use of women is tied to men's power to control and dominate those with less power. This sense of entitlement extends to those perceived as vulnerable to domination such as younger males and children. In an extension of this sense of entitlement, men may molest girls and boys. Legal and religious systems categorize women and children as under male authority and ownership. Nowhere in this system of male entitlement is a woman fully human, nor is there an understanding of the basic bodily integrity and right to safety of women and children.[52]

Orientalism: The Other

Unlike Europeans, who can assimilate after they lose any trace of a foreign accent, Asian Americans continue to be regarded as "exotic" foreigners. The dominant North American culture continues to think Asian Americans are interchangeable with Asians, whose cultures may be as unfamiliar to Asian Americans as European cultures are to many white Americans. Some Americans view Asian Americans through the lens of exoticized, colonialist constructions of race and gender, captured by the term "Oriental."[53]

Orientalism has been used by Europeans and North Americans as a way of dominating the East and having self-ascribed authority over it. European culture gained in strength and identity by setting itself off against the Orient as a sort of surrogate and even underground self.[54] Furthermore, the Orient has become feminized by Europeans as the Orient is viewed as the weaker, the exotic, and the less intelligent.[55] Europe's feminization of Asia was preceded and paralleled by Asian men's subjugation of Asian women. Europe's intellect and vigor in contrast to Asia's sensuality and softness were the counterparts of the Asian "yang" or male attributes of light, strength, agency, and the endowments of the "firm nature of heaven," as opposed to "yin" or female traits of dark, weak, passive, and the "yielding nature of the earth."[56]

As objects and people become feminized, a natural progression of domination occurs as women have generally been understood to be dominated by men. As a place becomes feminized, the entire concept becomes romanticized and understood as the subject who exists for the master. Thus with the notion of Orientalism came many adversities that Asia had to overcome. The relationship between Occident and Orient is a relationship of power, of domination, in varying degrees of a complex hegemony. The Orient was Orientalized not only because it was discovered to be "Oriental" in all those ways considered commonplace by an average 19th-century European but also because it could be made Oriental.[57] Orientalism is constructed by white Euro-American power over the Orient. Edward Said's *Orientalism* has opened a space for many thinkers, for it talks back to the Western authorities by demystifying their cultural representations of the Orient.[58]

There are certainly power differentials between Asian immigrant and nonimmigrant women. It is important to recognize this unequal power and conflicting interests while not giving up on community or solidarity or sisterhood.[59] As Asian American women experience oppression through racism, discrimination, and multiculturalism, they also have to endure the consequences of Orientalism and the experience of being treated as the Other. While Asian feminist theology has successfully established itself as a countermovement to the prevalent dominance of Western Christian traditions, Asian feminist theologians are being caught in the polemics of East versus West, and they "allow" Asia to remain as "Other" to the West.[60] In many ways, Asian women immigrants have become the Other. The Other is viewed as inferior and powerless. The Other is weaker, less intelligent, or a nuisance to society. Furthermore, the Other has become essentialized as they are imagined to possess inherently "Oriental" characteristics and traits that are supposedly universally valid but in fact are not. One of the central consequences of the essentialization of the Other is that the Other becomes an object for manipulation.[61] If the Other becomes an object, it is easily dominated or is open to domination.

The Other never becomes equal to but is incorporated as marginal and as such fulfills a useful role.[62] European culture has gained strength by setting itself against the Other. In characterizing and defining the Other, the West has characterized and defined itself as a superior culture in comparison with all the non-European peoples and cultures.[63] Therefore the Other is a necessary and useful commodity for those who are the majority and the dominators; we need to dispel the category of the Other and continue to dialogue so that Asian American women are not placed in that role.

In striving to use multicultural, interdisciplinary methods, the myriad forms of knowledge being created by new voices attuned to power, identity, history, and liberatory ideas and practices need to be embraced.[64] Asian American women's theological journey involves construction of a fluid and relational social self, a communal understanding of existence, and an embodied way of knowing and practicing religious life. Asian American women's identity involves interstitial integrity and hybridity. It is important to note that interstitial integrity deals with the complex cross-cultural identities that include subordination and draws from fluid, multilayered, and transversal experiences. It is not passive, an acceptance of abuse, but is how Asian American women cope with marginality and struggle to live amid transcultural forces in that it allows the making of meaning out of multiple worlds. And it does so by holding in creative tension the various spaces or worlds of meaning that Asian American women occupy rather than forcing them to restrict themselves to one set of social relationships and arrangements. It allows space for the multiple social locations of identity in a multicultural context. Asian American women live in the interstices and should engage in solidarity with others who also live there.[65] In short, through the use of the interstitial concept in theology, Asian American women consciously and carefully seek to hybridize religious commitments, practices, and beliefs with those of the "reluctant other."[66]

Racism

Racism promotes domination of the vulnerable by a privileged group in the economic, social, cultural, and intellectual spheres.[67] We live in a society in which racism has been internalized and institutionalized and is woven deeply into a culture from whose inception racial discrimination has been a regulative force for maintaining stability and growth and for maximizing other cultural values. Racism is the manifestation of the deeply entrenched determination to maintain the existing dominant culture and group. Only a full awareness of this disturbing reality leads to a new insight into what is possible: "The nation cannot redeem what has not been established."[68]

Asian American women's lives intersect with racism. Racism is prejudice and discrimination and is the *han* of our communities. Asian American women need to challenge and transform the structure of the *han* of racism in the society.[69] Assimilation into the dominant culture has been seen as a source both of alienation from Asian identity and of freedom from the constraints of traditional culture.[70] There appears to be an invisible boundary that prevents Asian American women from becoming part of the mainstream white culture. Problems of racism and culturism have set up walls that Asian American women cannot seem to climb. This has become a constant struggle and will remain one as long as racism and culturism persists. Therefore it is necessary to work toward removing these barriers.

Marginality

Asian immigrants experience a betwixt-and-between predicament, which, while a source of much soul-searching and suffering, can also serve as an incentive and resource for a creative rethinking of cultural traditions, the native and the foreign. Being in-between is being neither this nor that but also being both this and that. Immigrants belong fully to neither their native culture nor to the host culture. They belong to both, though not fully. Since they dwell in the interstices between the two cultures, they are in a position to see more clearly and to appreciate more objectively.[71] Socially to be in-between is to be part of a minority, a member of a marginalized group. Culturally, it means not being fully integrated into and accepted by either cultural system, being a mestizo, a member of a marginalized group. Psychologically and spiritually, the person does not possess a well-defined and secure self-identity and is often marked with excessive impressionableness, rootlessness, and an inordinate desire for belonging.[72] Therefore there are many limitations to those living in-between two groups and cultures.[73]

These ongoing issues of sexuality, being the Other, racism, and marginality are crucial and need to be addressed daily and seriously as they affect the means of survival. These pressing issues encompass the being of Asian American women and, in turn, affect how they perceive themselves and the divine. As Asian American women work to liberate themselves from sexism, Orientalism, racism, and marginality, they will continue to work toward building a theology that is truly authentic to their being and liberating to their souls.

NOTES

1. Rita Nakashima Brock, "Pacific and Asian Women's Theologies," in *Feminist Theologies: Legacy and Prospect,* ed. Rosemary Radford Ruether (Minneapolis: Fortress, 2007), 46.

2. Gary Y. Okihiro, *Margins and Mainstreams: Asian in American History and Culture* (Seattle: University of Washington Press, 1994), 64, 65.

3. Grace Ji-Sun Kim, *The Grace of Sophia: A Korean North American Women's Christology* (Cleveland: Pilgrim, 2002), 55.

4. Okihiro, *Margins and Mainstreams,* 64, 65.

5. Eleazar S. Fernandez, "American from the Hearts of a Diasporized People," in *Realizing the America of Our Hearts: Theological Voices of Asian Americans,* ed. Fumitaka Matsuoka and Eleazar S. Fernandez (St. Louis, MO: Chalice, 2003), 256.

6. Quoted in Ronald Takaki, *Strangers from a Different Shore: A History of Asian Americans* (New York: Penguin, 1989), 22.

7. Sucheng Chan, *Asian Americans: An Interpretive History* (New York: Twayne, 1991), 15.

8. Okihiro, *Margins and Mainstreams,* 77.

9. Kim, *Grace of Sophia,* 66.

10. Mary Paik Lee, *Quiet Odyssey: A Pioneer Korean Woman in America,* ed. and intro. Sucheng Chan (Seattle: University of Washington Press, 1990), lvi, lvii. There are many painful stories of Asian immigrant women's lives as they struggled to survive as laborers, cooks, and domestic workers. A second-generation Korean American woman recalls her childhood experience in Hawaii: "My mother had many maids in Korea, but at Kipahulu [*sic*] plantation she worked in the canefields with my older brother and his wife. I remember her hands, so blistered and raw that she had to wrap them in clothes [*sic*]. One morn-

ing she overslept and failed to hear the work whistle. We were all asleep—my brother and his wife, my older sister and myself. I was seven years old at the time. Suddenly the door swung open, and a big burly luna burst in, screaming and cursing, 'Get up, get to work.' The luna ran around the room, ripping off the covers, not caring whether my family was dressed or not. I'll never forget it." Quoted in Fumitaka Matsuoka, *The Color of Faith: Building Community in a Multiracial Society* (Cleveland: United Church Press, 1998), 14.

11. Seung Ai Yang, "Asian Americans," in *Handbook of U.S. Theologies of Liberation*, ed. Miguel A. De La Torre (St. Louis, MO: Chalice) (2004), 174.

12. Christopher J. L. Lind, "An Invitation to Canadian Theology," *Toronto Journal of Theology* 1 (1985): 17.

13. Douglas Hall, "On Contextuality in Christian Theology," *Toronto Journal of Theology* 1 (1985): 10.

14. The term "Asia" has different and complex trajectories in North America. During the civil rights era, in order to indicate inter-Asian group relationships, to identify this grow-ing hybridity, and to mobilize a political movement for justice, people of Asian descent came to call themselves "Asian Americans." Thus the term "Asian American" arose out of a particular historical moment to signify a visible racial group and had profound political implications. Kwok Pui Lan and Rachel A. R. Bundang, "PANAAWTM Lives!" *Journal of Feminist Studies in Religion* 21 no. 2 (2005): 149.

15. Kwok Pui Lan, Seung Ai Yang, and Rita Nakashima Brock, "The Future of PANAAWTM Theology," July 2004, available at www.panaawtm.org, as cited by Rita Nakashima Brock, "Pacific and Asian Women's Theologies," in *Feminist Theologies: Legacy and Prospect,* ed. Rosemary Radford Ruether (Minneapolis: Fortress, 2007), 46. There is an overarching question of what it means to be an Asian woman living across the ocean from her motherland in a multicultural society. Certainly, not all women share the same experience of "being a woman." Even if all women are oppressed by sexism, we can-not automatically conclude that the sexism all women experience is the same. Elizabeth Spelman, *Inessential Women: Problems of Exclusion in Feminist Thought* (Boston: Beacon, 1988), 14. This is a significant realization that undermines any reductionist, essential-izing definition of "women's oppression" as a universal female experience. Ien Ang, "I'm a Feminist but . . . 'Other' women and Postnational Feminism," in *Feminist Postcolonial Theory: A Reader,* ed. Reina Lewis and Sara Mills (New York: Routledge, 2003), 191.

16. Kwok Pui Lan, *Postcolonial Imagination and Feminist Theology* (Louisville, KY: West-minster John Knox, 2005), 24.

17. Kwok Pui Lan, *Introducing Asian Feminist Theology* (Cleveland: Pilgrim, 2000), 35.

18. Kwok, *Postcolonial Imagination and Feminist Theology,* 152.

19. Jung Young Lee, *Marginality: The Key to Multicultural Theology* (Minneapolis: Fortress , 1995), 1.

20. Chung Hyun Kyung, *Struggle to Be the Sun Again: Introducing Asian Women's Theology* (Maryknoll, NY: Orbis, 1991).

21. Genryu Tsutsumi, "Karuna (Compassion) and Prajna (Wisdom): A Note of Seizan-Sect Doctrine," *Japanese Religions* 4 (1966): 45, 46. Wisdom can be found in almost every culture and religion. Wisdom appears in the Christian scriptures as Hokmah (Hebrew) and Sophia (Greek), both clearly feminine. It also appears in Buddhism as *prajna,* which is a grammatically feminine noun in Sanskrit. Wisdom (sagehood) can also be found in the Confucian tradition. Wisdom is very much a part of Asian religion, culture, and society.

22. Leonard Swidler, "A Christian Historical Perspective on Wisdom as a Basis for Dialogue with Judaism and Chinese Religion," *Journal of Ecumenical Studies* 33 (1996): 558, 559.

23. Old Testament: Solomon 7:7–12; and Proverbs 1:20–21; 3:18, 8:1–4, 9:1–5. New Testament: I Corinthians 1:17, 1:23–24, 3:19, 10:1–4; and Matthew 11:1–14:13a, 11:28–30. For further and Old Testament and New Testament references to Jesus as wisdom, see Kim, *Grace of Sophia.*

24. Lee Rainey, 'The Concept of *Ch'i* in the Thought of Wang Ch'ung," *Journal of Chinese Philosophy* 19 (1992): 263.

25. Sue Benton and Drew Denbaum, *Chi Fitness: A Workout for Body, Mind, and Spirit* (New York: HarperCollins, 2001), 1, 11.

26. Hans Kung and Julia Ching, *Christianity and Chinese Religions* (London: SCM, 1988), 266.

27. Jumsik Ahn, "Korean Contextual Theology as Related to Ch'i: An Assessment on the Theology of Jung Young Lee," Ph.D. diss., Trinity Evangelical Divinity School, Deerfield, MI, 2002, 162, 305.

28. Jung Young Lee, *The Trinity in Asian Perspective* (Nashville, TN: Abingdon, 1996), 98.

29. Rob Cook, "Alternative and Complementary Theologies: The Case of Cosmic Energy with Special reference to Chi," *Studies in World Christianity* 6 (2000): 182.

30. Lee, *Trinity in Asian Perspective*, 96, 97.

31. Veli-Matti Kärkkäinen, *Pneumatology: The Holy Spirit in Ecumenical, International and Contextual Perspective* (Grand Rapids, MI: Baker Academic, 2002), 26.

32. Due to the similarity between chi and Spirit, it seems appropriate to combine the words to write Spirit/chi.

33. Kyung, *Struggle to Be the Sun Again*, 111.

34. Masao Takenaka, *God Is Rice: Asian Cultures and Christian Faith* (Geneva: World Council of Churches, 1986), 9.

35. Veli-Matti Kärkkäinen, "A Mapping of Asian Liberative Theology in Quest for the Mystery of God amidst the Minjung Reality and World Religions," in *Asian Contextual Theology for the Third Millennium: Theology of Minjung in Fourth-Eye Formation*, ed. Paul S. Chung, Veli-Matti Kärkkäinen, and Kim Kyoung Jae (Eugene, OR: Pickwick, 2007), 109.

36. Kim, *Grace of Sophia*, 56.

37. Chung Hyun Kyung, "Han-pu-ri: Doing Theology from Korean Women's Perspective," cited inKim, *Grace of Sophia*, 57.

38. The early Christians used cultural terms and words to help in theological discourse, and it is only appropriate for Asian American women theologians to do likewise. For example, although the synoptic gospel authors did not employ the term "Logos" in describing Jesus' incarnation or mission, the Johannine author adopted this Greek term to help the people of the Hellenistic civilization understand the nature of Jesus' coming. The gospel of John turned the Jewish concept of wisdom into the Greek notion of logos. Had the Johannine author lived in Asia, he or she would have used the term "Tao" instead of Logos for his or her apologetic work. Andrew Sung Park, "A Theology of Tao (Way): Han, Sin and Evil," in *Realizing the America of Our Hearts: Theological Voices of Asian Americans*, ed. Fumitaka Matsuoka and Eleazar S. Fernandez (St. Louis, MO: Chalice, 2003), 41, 43.

39. Andrew Sung Park, "Sin," in *Handbook of U.S. Theologies of Liberation*, ed. Miguel A. De La Torre (St. Louis, MO: Chalice) (2004), 116.

40. Chung, *Struggle to Be the Sun Again*, 39.

41. Kim, *Grace of Sophia*, 60.

42. Koo D. Yun, "Minjung and Asian Pentecostals," in *Asian Contextual Theology for the Third Millennium: Theology of Minjung in Fourth-Eye Formation*, ed. Paul S. Chung, Veli-Matti Kärkkäinen, and Kim Kyoung Jae (Eugene, OR: Pickwick, 2007), 87.

43. Quoted in Suh Nam-Dong, "Missio Dei and Two Stories in Coalescence," in *Asian Contextual Theology for the Third Millennium: Theology of Minjung in Fourth-Eye Formation*, ed. Paul S. Chung, Veli-Matti Kärkkäinen, and Kim Kyoung Jae (Eugene, OR: Pickwick, 2007), 51.

44. Letty M. Russell, "Exploring the Context of Our Faith," in *Changing Contexts of Our Faith*, ed. Letty M. Russell (Philadelphia: Fortress, 1985), 22.

45. Kwok Pui Lan, *Discovering the Bible in the Non-Biblical World* (Maryknoll, NY: Orbis, 1995), 57, 58.

46. Ibid., 63.

47. Ibid., 36.

48. Rita Nakashima Brock, "Interstitial Integrity: Reflections toward an Asian American Women's Theology," in *Introduction to Christian Theology*, ed. Roger Badham (Louisville, KY: Westminster John Knox, 1998), 188.

49. Robert J. C. Young, *Colonial Desire: Hybridity in Theory, Culture and Race* (London: Routledge, 1995), 22, 26.

50. R. S. Sugirtharajah, *Asian Biblical Hermeneutics and Postcolonialism: Contesting the Interpretations* (Maryknoll, NY: Orbis, 1998), 125, 126.

51. Okihiro, *Margins and Mainstreams*, 70.

52. Rita Nakashima Brock, "Facing Sexual Exploitation: Understanding Prostitution in Asia and the United States," *Journal of Asian and Asian American Theology* 2 (1997): 13.

53. Brock, "Interstitial Integrity," 185.

54. Edward W. Said, *Orientalism* (New York: Vintage, 1979), 3.

55. Edward W. Said, *Power, Politics and Culture* (New York: Vintage, 2001), 217. Feminization is a key to legitimize domination. Nature has been feminized, and thus nature can be dominated. Horrific acts of domination have been and will continue to be committed against nature.

56. Okihiro, *Margins and Mainstreams*, 68.

57. Said, *Orientalism*, 5. Parts of this section on "Orientalism: The Other" are excerpts from Grace Ji-Sun Kim, "What Forms Us: Multiculturalism, the Other and Theology," in *Feminist Theology with a Canadian Accent: Canadian Perspectives on Contextual Theology*, ed. Mary Ann Beavis, Elaine Guillemin, and Barbara Pell (Ottawa: Novalis, 2008), 78–99.

58. Kwok, *Postcolonial Imagination and Feminist Theology*, 3.

59. Jan Pettman, *Living in the Margins* (Sydney: Allen and Unwin, 1992), 158.

60. Wong Wai-Ching, "Asian Theologians between East and West: A Postcolonial Self-Understanding," *Jian Dao* 8 (1997): 91.

61. Bain-Selbo, "Understanding the Other: The Challenge of Post-Colonial Theory to the Comparative Study of Religion," *Religious Studies and Theology* 1 (1999): 64.

62. Marcella María Althaus-Reid, "Grace and the Other: A Postcolonial Reflection on Ideology and Doctrinal Systems," in *The Bright Side of Life*, ed. Ellen van Wolde (London: SCM, 2000), 67.

63. R. S. Sugirtharajah, *Asian Biblical Hermeneutics and Postcolonialism: Contesting the Interpretations* (Sheffield: Sheffield Academic, 1999), 102.

64. Brock, "Pacific and Asian Women's Theologies," 47.

65. Brock, "Interstitial Integrity," 190, 192.

66. Tinu Ruparell, "The Dialogue Party: Dialogue, Hybridity, and the Reluctant Other," in *Theology and the Religions: A Dialogue*, ed. Viggo Mortensen (Grand Rapids, MI: Eerdmans, 2003), 244.

67. Fumitaka Matsuoka, *The Color of Faith: Building Community in a Multiracial Society* (Cleveland: United Church Press, 1998), 3.

68. Ibid., 95.

69. Andrew Sung Park, "Church and Theology: My Theological Journey," in *Journeys at the Margin: Toward an Autobiographical Theology in American-Asian Perspective*, ed. Peter C. Phan and Jung Young Lee (Collegeville, MN: Liturgical, 1999), 171.

70. Brock, "Interstitial Integrity,"189.

71. Peter C. Phan, *Christianity with an Asian Face: Asian American Theology in the Making* (Maryknoll, NY: Orbis, 2003), 9.

72. Peter C. Phan, "The Dragon and the Eagle: Toward a Vietnamese American Theology," in *Realizing the America of Our Hearts: Theological Voices of Asian Americans*, ed. Fumitaka Matsuoka and Eleazar S. Fernandez (St. Louis, MO: Chalice, 2003), 165.

73. Yang, "Asian Americans," 176.

FURTHER STUDY

Brock, Rita Nakashima. "Interstitial Integrity: Reflections toward an Asian American Women's Theology." In *Introduction to Christian Theology: Contemporary North American Perspectives*, ed. Roger A. Badham. Louisville, KY: Westminster John Knox, 1998.

———. *Journeys by Heart: A Christology of Erotic Power*. New York: Crossroad, 1998.

———. "Pacific and Asian Women's Theologies." In *Feminist Theologies: Legacy and Prospect*, ed. Rosemary Radford Ruether. Minneapolis: Fortress, 2007.

Chan, Sucheng. *Asian Americans: An Interpretive History*. New York: Twayne, 1991.

Chung, Hyun Kyung. *Struggle to Be the Sun Again: Introducing Asian Women's Theology*. Maryknoll, NY: Orbis, 1990.

Jones, Serene, and Paul Lakeland, eds. *Constructive Theology: A Contemporary Approach to Classical Themes*. Minneapolis: Fortress, 2005.

Kim, Grace Ji-Sun. *The Grace of Sophia: A Korean North American Women's Christology*. Cleveland: Pilgrim, 2002.

Kung, Hans, and Julia Ching. *Christianity and Chinese Religions*. London: SCM, 1988.

Kwok, Pu Lan. *Introducing Asian Feminist Theology*. Cleveland: Pilgrim, 2000.

———. *Postcolonial Imagination and Feminist Theology*. Louisville, KY: Westminster John Knox, 2005.

Lee, Jung Young. *The Trinity in Asian Perspective*. Nashville, TN: Abingdon, 1996.

Lee, Mary Paik. *Quiet Odyssey: A Pioneer Korean Woman in America*. Ed. Sucheng Chan. Seattle: University of Washington Press, 1990.

Matsuoka, Fumitaka. *The Color of Faith: Building Community in a Multiracial Society*. Cleveland: United Church Press, 1998.

Okihiro, Gary Y. *Margins and Mainstreams: Asian in American History and Culture*. Seattle: University of Washington Press, 1994.

7

Native Feminist Theology

ANDREA SMITH

Historical Backdrop

While liberation theologies rooted in diverse communities of color have proliferated, the development of Native liberation theology, particularly Native women's theology, has been a slow process.[1] Nonetheless, Native women's perspectives on spirituality and social justice have much to contribute to the field of liberation theology.

There are a number of reasons for the reluctance of many Native religious scholars to embrace theology. First, theology's generally traditional emphasis on proscribing proper doctrines and beliefs often runs counter to indigenous spiritual practices. Jace Weaver argues that theology is inconsonant with indigenous worldviews, which hold that systematic study of God is both presumptuous and impossible. "Traditional Native religions are integrated totally into daily activity," Weaver argues. "They are ways of life and not sets of principles or creedal formulation. . . . Native 'religion' does not concern itself—does not try to know or explain—'what happens in the other world.'"[2]

Vine Deloria Jr., whose work became the foundation for almost all Native scholars in the field of religion or theology, argues that even liberation theology is grounded on a western European epistemological framework that is no less oppressive to Native communities than is mainstream theology. "Liberation theology," Deloria cynically contends, "was an absolute necessity if the establishment was going to continue to control the minds of minorities. If a person of a minority group had not invented it, the liberal establishment most certainly would have created it."[3] According to Deloria, Native liberation must be grounded in indigenous epistemologies—epistemologies that are inconsistent with western epistemologies, of which liberation theology is a part: "If we are then to talk seriously about the necessity of liberation, we are talking about the destruction of the whole complex of Western theories of knowledge and the construction of a new and more comprehensive synthesis of human knowledge and experience."[4] Even if we distinguish the "liberation" church from mainstream churches, the challenge brought forth by Native scholars and activists to other liberation theologians would be, Can a "liberation" church escape complicity in Christian imperialism? Deloria in particular raises the challenge that Christianity, because it is a temporally rather than a spatially based tradition (that is, it is not tied to a particular landbase but can seek converts from any landbase), is necessarily a religion tied to imperialism because it will never be content to remain within a particular place or community: "Once religion becomes specific to a group, its nature also appears to change, being directed to the internal mechanics of the group, not to grandiose schemes of world conquest."[5] Hence, all Christian theology, even liberation theology, remains complicit in the missionization and genocide of Native peoples in the Americas.

Despite the fact that Deloria disavowed the usefulness of a Native liberation theological project, his work has been foundational for the development of Native theology. In his work, he posited an absolute difference between Native spirituality and Christianity. While many Native Christians may clearly disagree with this dichotomy, they have had to respond to Deloria's challenge of how seemingly incommensurate epistemologies can be harmonized. They have also had to fundamentally address the complicity of Christianization in the genocide of Native peoples.

Robert Warrior's germinal essay, "Canaanites, Cowboys, and Indians," furthers Deloria's analysis by again troubling liberatory potential in many of the theological assumptions of liberation theology. In this essay, Warrior argues that the Bible is not a liberatory text for Native peoples, especially considering the fact that the liberation motif commonly adopted by liberation theologians—the Exodus—is premised on the genocide of the indigenous people occupying the Promised Land: the Canaanites. Warrior does not argue for the historical veracity of the conquest of the Canaanites. Rather, the Exodus operates as a narrative of conquest, a narrative that was foundational to the European conquest of the Americas. Warrior's essay points not only to the problems with the Exodus motif but also to liberation theology's conceptualization of a God of deliverance. He contends that "as long as people believe in the Yahweh of deliverance, the world will not be safe from Yahweh the conqueror." That is, by conceptualizing ourselves as oppressed peoples who are to be delivered at all costs, we necessarily become complicit in oppressing those who stand in the way of our deliverance. Instead, Warrior argues, we need to reconceptualize ourselves as "a society of people delivered from oppression who are not so afraid of becoming victims again that they become oppressors themselves."[6]

Other theologians take a less oppositional view toward Christianity. George Tinker's *Missionary Conquest,* for instance, takes up Deloria's charge to center genocide in his analysis of the missionization of Native peoples. He argues that, despite even the best of intentions of some Christian missionaries, the overall effect of their work was to facilitate the cultural, spiritual, and physical genocide of Native peoples. He argues that this genocide happened because missionaries could not separate out the gospel message from European culture. Hence, Tinker takes a different stance from Deloria, who contends that the gospel message itself is already tied into an epistemology of conquest by suggesting that a liberating gospel can be separated from the colonial culture that promotes it. In his later work, Tinker continues to maintain that the problem with Christianity is not Jesus but the religious tradition itself. He rereads biblical scripture to critique colonial concepts within Christianity, such as the "kingdom of God." He also harmonizes some Native traditions with Christian narratives. For instance, he draws parallels between the Cherokee story of Corn Mother with that of Jesus. One could argue that this approach—similar to that of theologian Steve Charleston arguing that Native traditions are the Native "Old Testament" of the Gospel—does not allow Native traditions to stand on their own apart from Christianity. However, Tinker is careful to argue that Native traditions have "inherent spiritual power."[7] He also concludes that, while it may be possible to harmonize Native spiritualities with Christianity to some extent, it may be the case that for many Native peoples, Christianity will continue to be irredeemable in light of its complicity in genocide.

Description

Since Tinker, in chapter 8 in this volume, focuses on the development of Native theologies, here I provide a brief context mentioning only a few pivotal thinkers in order to set the context for Native feminist theologies.

Suffice to say, if Native liberation theology is less developed as a field compared with other theologies, then it is perhaps not a surprise that Native feminist theology is almost nonexistent. The previously described thinkers do not stress a gender analysis in their work (as of yet). Both Jace Weaver and James Treat have edited anthologies on Native peoples and Christianity, which feature Native women authors,[8] but almost none of those selections engage the academic field of theology per se.

The development of Native women's theology has also been hindered by a lack of feminist analysis in Native studies generally speaking. One of the most prominent writings on Native American women and feminism is Annette Jaimes (Guerrero) and Theresa Halsey's (Hunkpapa Lakota) early 1990s article, "American Indian Women: At the Center of Indigenous Resistance in North America." Here they argue that Native women activists, except those who are "assimilated," do not consider themselves feminists. Feminism, according to Jaimes and Halsey, is an imperial project that assumes the givenness of a U.S. colonial stranglehold on indigenous nations. Thus, to support sovereignty, Native women activists reject feminist politics:

> Those who have most openly identified themselves [as feminists] have tended to be among the more assimilated of Indian women activists, generally accepting of the colonialist ideology that indigenous nations are now legitimate sub-parts of the U.S. geopolitical corpus rather than separate nations, that Indian people are now a minority with the overall population rather than the citizenry of their own distinct nations. Such Indian women activists are therefore usually more devoted to "civil rights" than to liberation per se. . . . Native American women who are more genuinely sovereigntist in their outlook have proven themselves far more dubious about the potentials offered by feminist politics and alliances.[9]

According to Jaimes and Halsey, all Native women reject feminist analysis, as typified by these quotations from one of the founders of Women of All Red Nations (WARN), Lorelei DeCora Means:

> We are *American Indian* women, in that order. We are oppressed, first and foremost, as American Indians, as peoples colonized by the United States of America, *not* as women. As Indians, we can never forget that. Our survival, the survival of every one of us—man, woman and child—*as Indians* depends on it. Decolonization is the agenda, the whole agenda, and until it is accomplished, it is the *only* agenda that counts for American Indians. . . . You start to get the idea maybe all this feminism business is just another extension of the same old racist, colonialist mentality.[10]

The critique and rejection of the label of feminism made by Jaimes and Halsey is important and shared by many Native women activists. However, it has also been uncritically cited as the Native stance on the issue of feminism. (In addition, scholars have failed to notice that Jaimes herself has shifted in her analysis.) The mantra "Native women can't be feminist" has occluded the work of Native women activists and scholars who do see themselves as feminists. Native women activists' theories about feminism, about the struggle against sexism within both Native communities and the society at large, and about the importance of working in coalition with non-Native women, are complex and varied. These theories are not monolithic and cannot simply be reduced to the dichotomy of feminist versus nonfeminist. Furthermore, there is not necessarily a relationship between the extent to which Native women call themselves feminists, the extent to which they work in coalition with non-Native feminists or value those coalitions, whether they are urban or reservation-based, and the extent to which they are "genuinely sovereigntist." In addition, the very simplified manner in which Native women's activism is theorized straightjackets Native women from articulating political projects that both address sexism and promote indigenous sovereignty simultaneously.

Thus, given the reluctance of most scholars to combine an analysis of Native studies with feminist thought or to engage the field of theology from the vantage point of Native studies, it becomes challenging to locate scholars who would describe themselves as Native feminist theologians.

The scholar who most closely fits this bill would be Michelene Pesantubbee, who recently published *Choctaw Women in a Chaotic World*. In it, she challenges previously held notions that Choctaw women did not hold positions of power in precolonial Choctaw society through a process of creative historiography. She notes that Choctaws have been subjected to a double missionization process, so the written historical record is not a trustworthy account of Choctaw women's status. Based on what we know about Choctaw spiritual traditions, she argues that it is quite likely that Choctaw women did hold positions of power, positions that become eroded through colonialism. She further investigates how the church was not simply a site of assimilation but also a site of resistance to cultural genocide whereby Choctaw spiritual practices, particularly those under the domain of women, could continue under the unsuspecting eye of missionaries.[11] Her creative imagining as a tool for feminist historiography is certainly a helpful model for those who would want to do Native feminist theology.

Sources

Rather than replacing totalizing traditional systematic theologies with equally totalizing liberation theologies that trap Native peoples within a primitivist politic of cultural essentialism, our task becomes to identify resources within the context of communal struggle. However, given the shortage of Native women who would explicitly define themselves as liberation theologians, it becomes necessary to be creative in developing Native feminist theologies. The perspective on source material found in womanist and mujerista theologies offers possibilities for uncovering Native women's perspectives on liberation theology. Feminist theologians often focus on the experiences of women as a starting point for theology.

To get at the voices of women in their communities, many womanist and mujerista theologians use stories to represent Black and Latina women's voices. Because enslaved Africans were not allowed to read the Bible and learned it by word of mouth, Black communities have tended to experience the Bible through the flexibility of an aural culture. According to womanist biblical scholar Renita Weems, the protean nature of oral tradition has given Black communities the freedom to modify and retell stories from the Bible to suit their changing needs. Womanist theologian Delores Williams, for example, uses this freedom to tell the story of Hagar in a manner she thinks will speak to African American women today. But storytelling is not limited to biblical stories. M. Shawn Copeland uses slave narratives to analyze Black women's experiences of suffering. Katie Cannon claims that Black women's literature is a crucial link to the oral traditions of the past as a mode of ethical instruction and cultural dissemination.

Like African American culture, Native cultures are orally based. Consequently, storytelling is a critical resource for uncovering Native women's experiences. The burgeoning literary tradition of Native women provides a window into how story maintains community. Such literature is generally more accessible and more likely to be written with Native people in mind, unlike theological texts, which are written for a non-Indian audience. Consequently, Native women's literature, as well as the more academic writings of Native women, even by women who are not professional theologians, can be a helpful theological resource.

However, while feminist, womanist, or mujerista theologians often use a variety of resources to give voice to the communities they represent, they often do not emphasize the perspectives of activists and organizers in their work. The problem that this approach presents for a theology of liberation is that most people, even most women, are not activists or organizers for social change. Therefore, to identify Native women's liberation theology, it is also important to highlight the spiritual and political perspectives of Native women activists specifically. Based on these sources, one can detect some central themes emergent in Native women's theology. These themes may not be based on standard Christian theological terms. First, to address Deloria's charge that Christianity is implicated in genocide against Native peoples, it is important to center indigenous beliefs and practices rather than Christian doctrines in theological formations. In addition, because Native religions, like Native cultures in general, are orally based, they are quite flexible. Indians give less weight to orthodoxy of religious belief than to spiritual centeredness and ethical behavior—what Native people call "walking in balance." Second, Indian spiritualities tend to be more centered on practice than on belief; that is, what makes one Indian is not simply holding the proper set of core beliefs but how one relates to one's community through concrete praxis. Of course, this should not be taken to mean either that Indian religions have no content or that anyone gets to be an Indian who "decides" to "behave like one." These points suggest that in looking at Native women's activism as a source for liberation theology, standard theological categories may have less relevance than they do for other communities.

If we understand that Native spiritualities are fundamentally communal, then it makes sense to locate sources for a Native women's liberation theology within the context of communal struggle. Thus, while there is a shortage of Native feminist theologians, there is no shortage of Native women who engage in praxis of liberation from a spiritually grounded framework. Native women involved in liberation struggles often do so from a sense of divine purpose. Whether or not they call themselves Christian, they are theologizing because they are articulating what they perceive to be the relationship between spirituality, liberation, and the vision of the world they hope to co-create. Their theologies may not be concerned with definitive statements about faith and belief but, rather, with exploring the possibilities about thinking about spirituality in light of our current political context.

Theoretical and Methodological Considerations

If we expand our understanding of theology beyond that of an academic discipline, then we can identify some of the theoretical and methodological considerations for developing Native women's theology both inside and outside academia.

Biblical scholar Justine Smith's work on indigenous biblical criticism suggests that our approach to developing a Native feminist theology should rely on a framework of performativity. Smith critiques the prevalent project within Native studies of replacing western epistemologies and knowledges with indigenous epistemologies as a project unwittingly implicated in a pro-capitalist and western hegemonic framework. She argues that the framework of "epistemology" is based on the notion that knowledge can be separated from context and praxis and can thus be fixed. She contends that a preferable approach is to look at indigenous studies through the framework of performativity: that is, indigenous studies focused on Native communities as bounded by practices that are always in excess but ultimately constitutive of the very being of Native peoples themselves.[12] The framework of performativity is not static and resists any essentializing discourse about Native peoples because performances by definition are never static.

Today, much of Native studies is content-driven, which leads to essentialized notions of "what are Native knowledges" or "what is Native identity, and the like.[13] This approach contributes to the previously mentioned problem of scholars always directing their energy toward "knowing" more about Native peoples. Furthermore, as anthropologist Micaela di Leonardo argues: there is a tendency among academics to study "Native people" as a means for those in the dominant culture to learn more about themselves. Either Native communities have "ancient wisdom" to bestow on others, or they represent the "savage," which proves the superiority of the dominant society: "Primitives are ourselves, or our worse or best selves, or our former selves, undressed: human nature in the buff."[14] A framework of performativity intervenes in this primitivist discourse, argues Smith, because it demonstrates that Native nations are distinguished less by an essential essence and more by what she refers to as "ontopraxy." That is, Native peoples are fundamentally constituted by relationality and praxis.[15]

As the proliferation of Black, womanist, mujerista, Asian, and other theologies indicate, liberation theologians in the United States have often relied on a politics of representation. That is, these theologies seek to represent the theological concerns of the communities from which theologians emerge. As theologian Kwok Pui Lan argues, this strategy is not without its merits in a context where peoples from oppressed communities are denied a voice within mainstream theological discourse.[16] Unfortunately, however, this representational strategy can lend itself to totalizing and essentializing discourses about the communities theologians seek to represent. As theologian Namsoon Kang argues, this "trap of essentialized identity" discursively restricts our political imaginary.[17] This politics of recognition does not allow us to look at tensions and oppressive dynamics within communities, particularly homophobia, sexism, ableism, and class oppression. We also often create litmus tests for cultural authenticity that restrict the kinds of intellectual and political creativity we need to challenge the status quo. In Native struggles, this can be exemplified by the oft-stated mantras, "Traditional Native peoples cannot be Christian" and "Native women can't be feminists."

As biblical scholar Elizabeth Povinelli notes, this politics of representation relies on assertions of absolute cultural difference in order to gain recognition from the liberal multicultural state. Thus, we see some of the negative consequences of Deloria's work that dichotomizes Native spirituality from Christianity. In order to gain recognition as a true "Native," one must always demonstrate her or his complete rejection of all things European or Christian. But since, of course, all Native peoples have been affected by colonialism, Native peoples are trapped in performances that necessarily fail. These failed performances then disqualify almost all Native peoples from gaining recognition. For instance, in almost all land rights struggles, white people accuse the Native peoples in question of not being "really" Native, and hence not deserving of land rights.

What goes unquestioned, as political theorist Glen Coulthard points out, is why we are seeking recognition in the first place, whether from the state or from academia. How does liberation come to mean having one's political, legal, social, or cultural claims recognized by a white settler society?[18] As Povinelli demonstrates, assertions of cultural difference unwittingly recapitulate capitalist and colonial imperatives. The liberal state depends on a politics of multicultural recognition that includes "social difference without social consequence." She further argues: "These state, public, and capital multicultural discourses, apparatuses, and imaginaries defuse struggles for liberation waged against the modern liberal state and recuperate these struggles as moments in which the future of the nation and its core institutions and values are ensured rather than shaken."[19] Kwok similarly notes that multiculturalist rhetoric is used to erase the structures of domination within U.S. society.[20] Theologian Fumitaka Matsuoka sheds further light onto this problem. He notes that the important struggle to be fought is not cultural validation. The dominant culture is prepared to accommodate a little "multiculturalism"—a pow-wow here, a pipe ceremony there—as long as the structures of power are not challenged. Matsuoka states: "The central problems . . . have to do, ultimately, not with ethnic groupings or the distinctness of our cultural heritages as such, but with racism and its manifestations in American economic policy, social rule and class relations."[21]

Thus, we can be entrapped into the project of doing theological work primarily for academic recognition rather than through the praxis of actual liberation struggles. In our efforts to have our theological contributions recognized within the context of academia, we often do not question the political effects of this recognition. Louis Althusser argued that educational systems are an "ideological state apparatus" by which the capitalist system reproduces itself ideologically. "Education" is not innocent or neutral; it is designed to teach peoples to be subject to colonial and capitalist structures.[22] Similarly, as Pierre Bourdieu elaborates, dominating classes assure their position through domination not only over economic capital but also over cultural capital, a form of domination that enables them to secure the terms of discourse and knowledge to their benefit.

The educational system is particularly important in the reproduction of symbolic capital under capitalism. The standardization of academic qualifications—a given amount of labor and time in academic apprenticeship is exchanged for a given amount of cultural capital, the degree— enables a differentiation in power ascribed to permanent positions in society and hence to the biological agents who inhabit these positions.[23] Such standardization encourages a system of power and domination between institutions through "socially guaranteed qualifications and sociologically defined positions" rather than directly through individuals.[24] Thus, according to Bourdieu, what is significant about the educational system is not just the set of ideologies that it promotes but the set of tacitly unequal institutional power relations it ensures through the fiction of equal access to education.[25] Good intentions on the part of academics do not render them innocent of reinscribing prevailing power relations in society.

Thus, racism and sexism in universities are not products of racist or sexist individuals in the system; they are endemic to the system itself. Our work of legitimating liberation theologies within academia can have the unintended effect of simply multiculturalizing the political and economic status quo and distracting us from engaging in actual liberation struggles. If we develop liberation theologies not grounded in politics of representation and recognition, we do not have to follow Deloria's mandate to represent the distinctness of indigenous spiritualities in our theologizing. Rather, we can focus on the material conditions of white supremacy, capitalism, patriarchy, and colonialism under which Native women live and theologically reflect from this space of struggle against these conditions. Thus, it is important to turn to some of the issues of concern in the development of Native feminist theology as they relate to Native women's struggles for social justice.

Ongoing Issues
Christianity and Native Traditions

Native activists often engage in what they call "cowboys and Indians coalitions." That is, in order to secure political goals, they have had to develop political coalitions in contexts where the only available coalition partners were those who did not support Native sovereignty struggles. The irony here is that rural-based Native women activists initiated some of the most successful organizing campaigns against multinational corporations by developing coalitions with urban-based non-Native people whose politics otherwise reflected an anti-Indian bias. This model of rearticulation allows us to complicate views of religious and political identity that may presume a simple and unchanging relationship between religion and politics, and it enables us to see new possibilities for alliance-building for social change. If we have a capitalist system in which 5% of the population controls 90% of the wealth, then it is clear that most people would benefit from a change in the system and hence are our political allies. And as one Native activist puts it, "When you have an us versus them attitude, you united them against you."

To create new alliances, however, we need to be more flexible in how we understand religious and political configurations and how they could potentially operate. As feminist theologian Catherine Keller notes, liberation theologies offer equally rigid models of liberation as does Christian orthodoxy. As theologian Itumeleng Mosala argues, the Bible and other forms of theological discourse are never fixed and are always subject to contestation: "It is not enough to recognize text as ideology. Interpretations of texts do alter the texts . . . texts are signifying practices and therefore they exist ideologically and permanently problematically."[26] Mosala's approach suggests that theological discourse is never simply liberatory or oppressive but that oppressed groups can shift theological discourse to further liberatory struggles.

Justine Smith's work demonstrates that indigenous peoples have engaged the biblical text in complicated ways that go beyond a simple paradigm of "assimilation." Her essay demonstrates that when the Bible is translated into different languages (in this case, Cherokee), the very meanings of the texts change. Hence, the Cherokee Bible (which was translated directly from the Greek and Hebrew) can be read as a counternarrative to the English text rather than simply a mimicry of it. We cannot assume that indigenous peoples have the same reading strategies as do those of the dominant culture. Smith demonstrates how indigenous reading strategies and performances disrupt the colonial narrative of the Bible. As anthropologist Dorinne Kondo notes, assimilation is always unfinished business: "Even when colonized peoples imitate the colonizer, the mimesis is never complete, for the specter of the 'not quite, not white' haunts the colonizer, a dis-ease that always contains an implicit threat to the colonizer's hegemony."[27] In other words, groups that seemingly attempt to replicate the dominant culture or religious practice never fully do so, and the very act of mimesis challenges the hegemonic claims of colonizers. In any case, oppositional practices are never free from reinscribing that which they contest. Thus, rather than simply arguing that Christianity is either oppressive or liberatory, theologians might be able to think about (1) what areas of resistance are possible in any site and (2) how all of these options for resistance continue to reinscribe colonial paradigms.

Native feminists critique the manner in which Native traditions can also be used as a weapon to maintain systems of domination. In *Gender Trouble*, Judith Butler critiques theorists such as Jacques Lacan, Luce Irigaray, and Monique Wittig, who posit a naturalized prediscursive sexed body as the foundation by which to critique contemporary heteropatriarchal practices. She argues that theorizing a prediscursive body necessarily means that the body cannot be prediscursive and hence its account cannot be made outside of prevailing power relations within its discursive economy. But positing it as prediscursive allows the theorist to disavow her or his political investments because the theorist is supposedly rendering an account of the body prior to power relations. Butler's critique could then be more broadly applied to a critique of "origin stories." That is, when we critique a contemporary context through an appeal to a prior state before "the fall," we are necessarily masking power relations through the evocation of lost origins. Within the context of theology, Mary McClintock Fulkerson notes that feminist appeals to feminist origins within Christianity (i.e., Jesus was a feminist) rest on a "natural, prediscursive reality" which becomes the basis for a feminist politic that cannot be interrogated for its complicity in prevailing power relations.[28] Within Native feminist theologies, this analysis is helpful in interrogating how "tradition" often serves as the origin story that buttresses heteropatriarchy and other forms of oppression with Native communities while disavowing its political investments. That is, Native women are often told (even by other Native women) that Native feminism is not "traditional." This mantra speaks to the politics of who defines what is tradition. As Native rights activist Lakota Harden describes:

In trying to piece together our history, and our stories, and our legends, it seems that much of what we remember has actually been tainted and changed by colonization. We do not actually remember what happened before colonization because we were not there. So we have to ask ourselves, how much of what we think is tradition was really originally ours; and how much of it is Christian-influenced? Knowing how powerful Native women are now, how could we have ever accepted anything less then? How could we have let ourselves be ignored or degraded? I'm not saying that I know, because I don't. But those questions have brought me to wonder how much of the tradition is really ours, and how much does that even matter?

I remember at our school, all of us were preparing a sweat lodge in our backyard. Our backyard was huge, the plains. And I remember one of the boys saying, "Women can never carry the pipe." "Women never used to do this or that." (Now I realize that all comes from Christianity.) And I remember feeling very devastated because I was very young then. I was trying to learn these traditions. I was quite the drama queen and going to the trailer and my aunt was making bread or something. "Auntie, this is what they're saying!" She said, "Well you know, tradition, we talk about being traditional. What we're doing now is different. When we talk about trying to follow the traditions of say our ancestors from 100 years ago, it's probably different from 300 years ago. If when the horses came, what would have happened had we said, "Oh we don't ride the four-legged, they are our brother. We respect them; we don't ride them?" Where would we be? Hey man, we found those horses and we became the best horse riders there ever were, and we were having good winters. So tradition is keeping those principles, the original principles about honoring life all around you. Walk in beauty is another interpretation. Respecting everything around you. Leave the place better than you found it. Those were the kind of traditions that we followed. But they change as we go along."

And in a few minutes [after talking to my Auntie], then I went back to the room. Now, being a pipe carrier means that you don't drink alcohol, you don't smoke marijuana, you don't take drugs, you don't fight with people, and you don't abuse anyone. And I was really trying to follow that because that's what my uncle taught me. So I went to the middle of the room, and I said to the guys in the room, "I want everybody here who is following the tradition, who has given up the things I just named to stand here in the circle with me." And no one did. I said that until this circle is filled with men, when it's filled with men, I'll do something else like learn to cook. But until then, there has to be someone standing here doing this, and if you're not going to do it, I will. And no one ever said anything to me, or anything about women not doing these things ever, at least from that group.[29]

Navajo scholar Jennifer Denetdale's work deconstructs tradition as origin story, going so far as to argue that Native communities reproduce a heteronormative, Christian Right agenda in the name of "tradition." She also critically interrogates the gendered politics of remembering "tradition" in her germinal analysis of the office of Miss Navajo Nation. Denetdale notes that this office is strictly monitored by the Navajo nation to ensure that Miss Navajo models "'traditional' Navajo women's purity, mothering and nurturing qualities, and morality which are evoked by the Navajo Nation to extol Navajo honor and are claimed on behalf of the modernizing project of nationalism." Denetdale notes that "when Miss Navajo Nation does not conform to the dictates of ideal Navajo womanhood, she is subjected to harsh criticism intended to reinforce cultural boundaries. Her body literally becomes a site of surveillance that symbolically conveys notions about racial purity, morality, and chastity." Meanwhile, male leaders, who may be guilty of everything from domestic violence to embezzlement, are rarely brought before any tribal committees. She argues that the ideals that Navajo women are supposed to represent are not simply "traditional" Navajo values but unacknowledged European Victorian ideals of womanhood. She asserts that Navajo leaders, who are primarily men, reproduce Navajo nationalist ideology to reinscribe gender roles based on Western concepts even as they claim that they operate under traditional Navajo philosophy.[30]

At the same time, as theologian Katherine Tanner notes, "tradition" can also be a weapon against oppression. At the 2005 World Liberation Theology Forum held in Porto Alegre, Brazil, indigenous peoples from Bolivia stated that they know another world is possible because they see that world whenever they do their ceremonies. Native ceremonies can be a place where the present, past, and future become co-present, thereby allowing us to engage in what Native Hawaiian scholar Manu Meyer calls a racial remembering of the future. Before colonization, Native communities were not structured on the basis of hierarchy, oppression, or patriarchy. We will not re-create these communities as they existed before colonization because Native nations are and always have been nations that change and adapt to the surrounding circumstances. However, our understanding that it was possible to order society without structures of oppression in the past tells us that our current political and economic system is anything but natural and inevitable. If we lived differently before, we can live differently in the future. Thus, the past can serve as a radical critique of the present. Armed with a feminist analysis, many indigenous groups are using the past in a critical way to denaturalize the present, to show that different ways of living are possible.

Heteropatriarchy and the Nation-State

Native feminist theologies fundamentally challenge the givenness of the United States as empire and the nation-state form of governance. They further theologize possibilities of alternative forms of governance for the world. This theologizing also challenges male-dominated sovereignty and racial justice struggles because they demonstrate that the building block of the nation-state is the heteropatriarchal family.

That is, social justice activists as well as the U.S.-based liberation theologians often criticize U.S. policies, but they do not critically interrogate the contradictions between the United States articulating itself as a democratic country on one hand, while simultaneously founding itself on the past and current genocide of Native peoples on the other. Even progressives tend to articulate racism as a policy to be addressed within the constraints of the U.S. nation-state rather than understanding racism and genocide as constitutive of the United States. However, since the United States could not exist without the genocide of Native peoples, Native feminist interventions call us to question why we should presume the givenness of the United States in our long-range vision of social justice. These interventions provide a starting point for theological reflection on what exactly is a just form of governance, not only for Native peoples but also for the rest of the world. Native women activists have begun articulating spiritually based visions of nation and sovereignty that are separate from nation-states. Whereas nation-states are governed through domination and coercion, indigenous sovereignty and nationhood is predicated on interrelatedness and responsibility. As Native activist Crystal Ecohawk states: "Sovereignty is an active, living process. From that knot of relationships is born our histories, our identity, the traditional ways in which we govern ourselves, our beliefs, our relationship to the land, and how we feed, clothe, house and take care of our families, communities and Nations."[31] These models of sovereignty are not based on a narrow definition of nation that would entail a closely bounded community and ethnic cleansing.

In turn, spiritually based alternative visions of sovereignty challenge the heteronormative basis of nation building. That is, patriarchy is the logic that naturalizes social hierarchy. Under patriarchy, just as men are supposed to naturally dominate women on the basis of biology, so, too, should the social elites of a society naturally rule everyone else through a nation-state form of governance that is constructed through domination, violence, and control. Patriarchy, in turn, presumes a heteronormative gender binary system. Thus, as Christian Right scholar Ann Burlein argues in *Lift High the Cross*, it may be a mistake to argue that the goal of Christian Right politics is to create a theocracy in the United States. Rather, Christian Right politics work through private family (which is coded as white, patriarchal, and middle class) to create a "Christian America." She notes that the investment in the private family makes it difficult for people to invest in more public forms of social connection. In addition, investment in the suburban private family serves to mask the public disinvestment in urban areas that makes the suburban lifestyle possible. The social decay in urban areas that results from this disinvestment is then construed as the result of deviance from the Christian family ideal rather than as the result of political and economic forces. As former head of the Christian Coalition Ralph Reed states: "The only true solution to crime is to restore the family," and "Family break-up causes poverty."[32] Concludes Burlein: "'The family' is no mere metaphor but a crucial technology by which modern power is produced and exercised."[33]

Unfortunately, as Denetdale points out, the Native response to a heteronormative white, Christian America is often an equally heteronormative Native nationalism. In her critique of the Navajo tribal council's passage of a ban on same-sex marriage, Denetdale argues that Native nations are furthering a Christian Right agenda in the name of "Indian tradition." This trend is also equally apparent within racial justice struggles in other communities of color. As political scientist Cathy Cohen contends, heteronormative sovereignty or racial justice struggles will maintain rather than challenge colonialism and white supremacy because they are premised on a politics of secondary marginalization whereby the most elite class of these groups further their aspiration on the backs of those most marginalized within the community.[34] Through this process of secondary marginalization, the national or racial justice struggle takes on either implicitly or explicitly a nation-state model as the end point of its struggle: a model of governance in which the elites govern the rest through violence and domination, as well as exclude those that are not members of "the nation." However, as the articulations of Native women suggest, there are other models of nationhood we can envision, nations that are not based on exclusion and which are not based on secondary marginalization—nations that do not have the heteronormative, patriarchal nuclear family as their building block.

These issues and concerns are only a few that could be discussed within the context of Native feminist theology. If we take seriously the "liberation" within liberation theology, then our first concern must be theological approaches that further social justice, not academic legitimacy or recognition. But because the terrain of struggle constantly changes, our theoretical formulations must be in a constant state of flux. At the same time that we humbly work together, sharing our successes and our failures, we are also armed with a vision of a past that demonstrates it is possible to structure a society *not* based on the logics of white supremacy, heteropatriarchy, or colonialism. These past visions must always be interrogated in the present; they do not offer a simple blueprint for liberation, but they do show us that another world is indeed possible.

NOTES

1. Doing theology, thinking theologically, is a decidedly non-Indian thing to do. When I talk about Native American theology to many of my Indian friends, most of them just smile and act as if I hadn't said anything. And I am pretty sure that, as far as they are concerned, I truly hadn't said anything.

2. Jace Weaver, *That the People Might Live* (Oxford: Oxford University Press, 1997), vii.

3. Vine Deloria Jr., *For This Land* (New York: Routledge, 1999), 100.

4. Ibid., 106.

5. Vine Deloria Jr., *God Is Red* (Golden, CO: North American, 1992), 296–297.

6. Robert Warrior, "Canaanites, Cowboys, and Indians," in *Natives and Christians,* ed. James Treat (New York: Routledge, 1996), 99.

7. George Tinker, *Missionary Conquest* (Minneapolis: Fortress, 1993), 153.

8. James Treat, ed., *Native and Christian* (Oxford: Oxford University Press, 1996); and Jace Weaver, ed., *Native American Religious Identity: Unforgotten Gods* (Maryknoll, NY: Orbis, 1998).

9. M. Annette Jaimes and Theresa Halsey, "American Indian Women: At the Center of Indigenous Resistance in North America," in *State of Native American,* ed. M. Annette Jaimes (Boston: South End, 1992), 330–331.

10. Ibid., 314, 332. Women of All Red Nations was established in 1974 as a sister organization to the American Indian Movement.

11. Michelene Pesantubbee, *Choctaw Women in a Chaotic World* (Albuquerque: University of New Mexico Press, 2005).

12. Justine Smith, "Indigenous Performance and Aporetic Texts," *Union Seminary Quarterly Review* 59, no. 1–2 (2005): 114–124.

13. Dale Turner, *This Is Not a Peace Pipe* (Toronto: University of Toronto Press, 2006).

14. Micaela di Leonardo, *Exotics at Home* (Chicago: University of Chicago Press, 1998), 147.

15. Smith, "Indigenous Performance and Aporetic Texts," 117.

16. Kwok Pui Lan, *Postcolonial Imagination and Feminist Theology* (Louisville, KY: Westminster John Knox, 2005), 36.

17. Namsoon Kang, "Who/What Is Asian?" in *Postcolonial Theologies,* ed. Catherine Keller, Michael Nasuner, and Mayra Rivera (St. Louis, MO: Chalice, 2004), 104.

18. Glen Coulthard, "Indigenous Peoples and the 'Politics of Recognition' in Colonial Contexts," paper presented at the Cultural Studies Now Conference, University of East London, London, England, July 22, 2007.

19. Elizabeth Povinelli, *The Cunning of Recognition* (Durham, NC: Duke University Press, 2002), 16.

20. Kwok, *Postcolonial Imagination and Feminist Theology,* 42.

21. Fumitaka Matsuoka, *Out of Silence* (Cleveland: United Church Press, 1995), 93.

22. Louis Althusser, *Lenin and Philosophy and Other Essays* (New York: Monthly Review, 1971).

23. Pierre Bourdieu, *Outline of a Theory of Practice,* trans. Richard Nice (Cambridge: Cambridge University Press, 1998), 187.

24. Ibid.

25. Ibid.

26. Itumeleng Mosala, "Why Apartheid Was Right about the Unliberated Bible," *Voices from the Third World* 17, no. 1 (1994): 158.

27. Dorinne Kondo, *About Face* (New York: Routledge, 1997), 10.

28. Mary McClintock Fulkerson, *Changing the Subject* (Minneapolis: Fortress, 1994), 129.

29. Quoted in Andrea Smith, "Bible, Gender and Nationalism in American Indian and Christian Right Activism," Ph.D. diss., University of California—Santa Cruz, 2002, 303.

30. Jennifer Denetdale, "Chairmen, Presidents, and Princesses: The Navajo Nation, Gender, and the Politics of Tradition," *Wicazo Sa Review* 20 (Spring 2006): 18.

31. Crystal Echohawk, "Reflections on Sovereignty," *Indigenous Woman* 3, no. 1 (1999): 21–22.

32. Ralph Reed, *After the Revolution* (Dallas: Word, 1990), 231.

33. Ann Burlein, *Lift High the Cross* (Durham, NC: Duke University Press, 2002), 190.

34. Cathy Cohen, *The Boundaries of Blackness* (Chicago: University of Chicago Press, 1999).

FURTHER STUDY

Baldridge, William. "Toward a Native American Theology." *American Baptist Quarterly* 8 (December 1989): 227–238.

Deloria, Vine, Jr. *For This Land.* New York: Routledge, 1999.

———. *God Is Red.* Golden, CO: North American, 1992.

Denetdale, Jennifer. "Chairmen, Presidents, and Princesses: The Navajo Nation, Gender, and the Politics of Tradition." *Wicazo Sa Review* 20 (Spring 2006): 9–28.

Di Leonardo, Micaela. *Exotics at Home.* Chicago: University of Chicago Press, 1998.

Jaimes, M. Annette, and Theresa Halsey, "American Indian Women: At the Center of Indigenous Resistance in North America," in *State of Native American,* ed. M. Annette Jaimes, 330–331. Boston: South End, 1992.

Kondo, Dorinne. *About Face.* New York: Routledge, 1997.

Pesantubbee, Michelene. *Choctaw Women in a Chaotic World*. Albuquerque: University of New Mexico Press, 2005.

Smith, Justine. "Indigenous Performance and Aporetic Texts." *Union Seminary Quarterly Review* 59, no. 1–2 (2005): 114–124.

Tinker, George. *Missionary Conquest*. Minneapolis: Fortress, 1993.

Treat, James, ed. *Native and Christian*. Oxford: Oxford University Press, 1996.

Turner, Dale. *This Is Not a Peace Pipe*. Toronto: University of Toronto Press, 2006.

Warrior, Robert. "Canaanites, Cowboys, and Indians." In *Natives and Christians*, ed. James Treat, 93–100. New York: Routledge, 1996.

Weaver, Jace, ed. *Native American Religious Identity: Unforgotten Gods*. Maryknoll, NY: Orbis, 1998.

———. *That the People Might Live*. Oxford: Oxford University Press, 1997.

8

American Indian Theology

GEORGE (TINK) TINKER
(WAZHAZHE UDSETHE, OSAGE NATION)

Historical Backdrop

American Indian peoples became Christian at moments of utter despair and in the face of huge trauma that devastated them.[1] With the ever-present pressures of European colonialism on this continent, they turned to the very religion of their conqueror to find some sort of solace. As European mass murder and terrorism combined with European-generated epidemics took their toll on the aboriginal populations, suddenly the people found themselves with not enough knowledgeable participants to continue the old ceremonies.[2] One can add to these difficulties U.S. government political pressure on Indian communities to comply with demands for land cessions and reckless resource development, all of which contributed to the degradation of Indian communities.

Children were kidnapped from Indian families and incarcerated in facilities called boarding schools, kept at a distance from loving families for a dozen years each, finally returning home at eighteen with skewed perspectives on life itself, having been absent of familial love and the healthy personality development such love would have nurtured.[3] At the same time, the U.S. government, in collusion with the White Christian religious establishment, took legal action to outlaw the practice of many of the traditional ceremonials of Indian communities, making it even more difficult to find spiritual help in traditional ways.[4] Many of these ceremonies were practiced, however, but in hidden and secret locations and only by those brave enough to risk arrest and imprisonment. At the same time, many communities simply gave up trying to continue their ceremonies as the incursion of White culture decimated clan structures and made it much more difficult to find key participants to fulfill roles assigned to different clans.[5]

Throughout these beginnings, however, the missionaries never did learn to trust those Indians who converted. As a result, there were never many

Indian clergy serving Indian communities (i.e., congregations—but congregations do tend to be communities among Indian peoples). Two further points might be offered here. First, the generalization can be made that no Indian person ever made a perfectly free and informed choice for Christian conversion without the heavy-handed presence of colonial realities.[6] Second, in every tribal context the first missionary to proclaim the Christian gospel always functioned to divide the community. That is, a community where ceremony was always communal and involving the whole of a town or village was no longer whole when the first member of the community made the choice to become a Christian.

There were, of course, some well-known and celebrated Indian ministers through the colonization period. Yet these early Indian Christian ministers were not accommodationists to the same extent that their more modern Christian Indian descendents have become in recent times. Indeed, William Apess (Pequot, 1798–1839) was trained as a minister and living in Massachusetts early in the existence of the United States. He was a particularly incisive critic of American colonizer culture and its exercise of Christian preaching.[7] Samson Occom (Mohegan, 1723–1792) was an earlier Indian Christian minister in colonial New England, who made the attempt to serve Indian people while maintaining a genuine connection to the traditional culture.[8] Like Apess, he was clear in his criticism of White racism, noticing his bad treatment under Eliezer Wheelock, the Puritan founder of Dartmouth College, during a fund-raising trip to England and bitterly criticizing Wheelock's betrayal of Indian people with respect to the use of the monies that Occom had helped raise.

Peter Jones (Mississauga Ojibwe, 1802–1856) continued to serve as the chief of his community even as he became their pastor. As such, he also continued the communitarian values of their traditional Ojibwe culture as he worked to replace their old ceremonial traditions with the mission traditions he had adopted. Ultimately, his Christian mission discipline was challenged by traditionalists in the community, leading to a splintering of the band.

At the same time, there were persistent and consistent attempts in many Indian national communities to maintain traditional communal structures in spite of pressures to convert. People like Sitting Bull (Hunkpapa Lakota, d. 1890) engaged in active resistance against all of colonizer culture and its constant pressure to convert to Christianity. Sitting Bull's policy of "just say no" resulted in the sacrifice of his life, as the "Indian" agent on his reservation (that is, the appointed federal agent in charge of the Standing Rock Reservation, a white man named James McLaughlin) determined to punish the old chief for his refusal to learn European-style farming. Reservation police sent by the agent to move him from his American-style log cabin home murdered Sitting Bull.

After the death of Sitting Bull, Frank Fools Crow (Oglala Lakota) reports that many Lakota groups made self-conscious decisions to join different churches merely to satisfy the colonizer at a superficial level. The decisions were made not according to conviction but according to *tiospaye* (or clan) membership. Meanwhile, they continued their own religious and cultural traditions even while claiming to be Episcopalian or Roman Catholic, which is how Mr. Fools Crow, the great Oglala medicine man, had become a Catholic early in his youth.[9] Fools Crow goes on to say that the self-conscious tribal decision to split up their community by clans into different denominations had a result unexpected by the missionaries and inexplicable to them. Namely, inter-*tiospaie* marriage laws resulted in the unusual result that an Episcopalian always seemed to marry a Catholic, the very opposite of the sort of denominational loyalty the missionaries had hoped for.

In this same time period, Philip Deloria (Yankton/Hunkpapa, 1853–1931) became one of the most celebrated converts to Christianity. He gained churchwide fame as an Episcopal priest among his own peoples, and his is one of only three statues enshrined in the National Episcopal Cathedral in Washington, D.C. As his grandson, Vine Deloria Jr., relates the story, Philip Deloria both served the Episcopal Church faithfully and yet continued to hold on to aspects of the traditional culture and spirituality of his medicine man father.[10] Philip Deloria's embracing of Christianity was genuine, according to the younger Deloria, and provided Indian people with a "bridge" of transition from a life of freedom to their new postconquest life. Yet, the people in this story found ways to reshape the missionary gospel in order to embrace their own culture and traditions. Philip Deloria, it seems, was equally fluent in "talking" Episcopalian with the Episcopalians and in negotiating Yankton cultural and religious traditions. In the final analysis, according to his grandson, as Philip Deloria entered old age it was the traditional stories, culture, and lifeways of his people that captured his imagination and not the doctrines of his adopted church.

It is this context of contact between Christianity and traditional cultural practices and beliefs that provides the backdrop for Native American debate over the nature and meaning of liberation theology. It is in light of this often-violent contact with Christianity as a component of colonization that Native Americans wrestled with the possibility of doing theology in a way that promotes healthy life options, community, and wholeness.

Description

Very little scholarship has been written in terms of Native American theology; at least not much has been categorized as theology, per se.[11] Of course, one needs to begin by distinguishing between Native American "Christian" theologies and theologies that are more focused on the traditional religious traditions of Indian communities and their ceremonies. "Theology" is not a natural category of analysis for Indian people at all.[12] It is a European category that has been imposed on Indians like so many other categories, words, and definitions. Even the key root word in theology, the word "god" (Greek, *theos*), has no analogous meaning in any Indian language.[13] To use the word "god" as a casual translation for key terms in Indian languages ultimately makes it impossible to understand what the word might actually mean in its Native context.[14]

Indeed, for a White American to ask any Indian, "What is your word for God?" immediately forces a near-fatal compromise in the Indian worldview from which it is difficult to recover. It presumes that whatever is the case in the tribal worldview, it must necessarily have an easy analogy in the colonizer English language. This move on the part of the colonizer's Christianity disallows difference and forecloses any real negotiation of cultural or religious difference. By the early 1970s, Indian scholars seriously questioned whether Indian tribes actually had conceptions of dieties or of religion.

In another context I have argued that the ideal of cosmic balance is central to all Indian thinking rather than any notion of liberation—that is, everything from personal balance, to balance in the community, to the balance of the whole of the world.[15] Indian people only became cognizant of a need for "liberation" after the brutal tragedy of the European invasion and conquest generated the radical imbalance of the subjugation and genocide of the aboriginal owners of the land.

There are a number of contemporary Indian folk who have pressed theological issues from the perspective of traditional cultures. Robert Warrior (Osage) and William Baldridge (Cherokee) engaged in a useful dialogue some years ago that caught the attention of Indians who have been more inclined toward some sort of Christian-Indian thinking. Essentially (as discussed in chapter 7), Warrior began by demonstrating that the Judeo-Christian biblical "Exodus" tradition can only speak negatively to American Indians.[16] Because of the particularities of the history of colonial invasion, mass murders, and terrorism, along with the theft of land, Indian people, argues Warrior, must see themselves in the biblical story as the Canaanites. Black and Latin American liberation theologists use the Exodus story to highlight their understanding of god as a god of deliverance. Indians cannot even begin to see liberation here, simply because the Exodus story functions as a paradigmatic conquest narrative legitimating the European invasion and conquest of our lands and peoples. Baldridge, who was persistently critical of his own Baptist denomination for its entrenched missionary attitudes toward Indians, attempted to rescue some place in biblical interpretation for an Indian Christian presence.[17] He suggests instead that Indian Christians might play a significant role in the transformation of White Christianity in North America. To achieve this, argues Baldridge, Indian Christians must maintain their own religious values and bring those traditional values into their Christianity.

Phil Duran (Pueblo), a physicist by training, has written a deeply touching and personal reflection on the inherent tensions of being a scientist and honoring his own rich Native American cultural heritage at the same time. Along the way, he offers finely honed insights into the actualities of Indian cultures and the deluded misinterpretations that pass for White American descriptions of Indian deficiencies. He moves seamlessly from the utter complexities of our modern existence to affirming his own Pueblo Indian identity, providing us with a relentless and incisive analysis of Amer-European science and its religion, Christianity, and their effects on native peoples. Duran struggles to hold his commitments to the Christian gospel together with his Indian cultural identity, but he finally finds himself in a posture of resistance to the colonial religion by affirming his indigenous cultural values whenever the two conflict.[18]

Writing in a more straightforward liberationist and resistance modality is Andrea Smith (Cherokee), whose dialogue with Christian theology always challenges colonizer thinking. Her theological writings confront the colonizer with the harsh realities of their history of conquest.[19] More interesting in many respects have been those Indian writers who have spoken from their traditional cultural context. Perhaps the best example of this sort of writing is Barbara Mann's (Wendat/Seneca) book on *Iroquoian Women: The Gantowisas*.[20] With impeccable research, Mann demonstrates the power of Native matriarchy in Iroquois religious and cultural traditions.

Sources

What can be said here at the outset is that all Indian peoples did have ancient spiritual connections that were and often still are regularly nurtured in ceremonies and in their daily lives, and one might argue that these elements of culture frame and inform what could be thought of as Indian theology.

To understand Indian theology requires an understanding of the details of these ceremonial structures in their great variety across hundreds of distinct and disparate aboriginal communities that peopled the lands of North America in 1491 and the three hundred or so that have survived the European invasion. At the same time, there are some common theological universals among all Indian peoples to which we can point even when the particularities of one community's practice may differ widely from that of another. I have argued more thoroughly elsewhere that there is a set of four cultural differences that can begin to distinguish the American Indian worldview from the worldview imported by our European conquerors and imposed on Native peoples.[21] This list of four cultural factors that distinguish between Amer-European Whites and American Indians is, of course, not exhaustive. Nor does it attempt to rank these factors hierarchically. Rather, they must be taken together to give a more holistic picture of Indian cultures.

First, Indian people are communal in their worldview and social structuring, nearly a polar opposite to the radical individualism that emerged out of European "modernity." Thus our cultural and religious values are structured in ways that negate inclinations toward the sort of individualism so deeply valued in the modern or postmodern European worldview. The sun dance ceremony is famously danced "that the people might live," rather than for the individualized purpose of gaining personal spiritual power or status.[22] Even converted Indian Christians tend to experience their Christianity today in far more communitarian terms than the radical individualism of White Euro-Christian folk.

Second, Indian peoples are spatially oriented in their worldview rather than temporal, a characteristic feature of American Indian religious traditions clearly identified and described early on by Deloria.[23] While American European religious traditions generally build around temporal categories like the seven-day week, Indian ceremonial life and all of Indian existence is rooted in a profound notion of space and place. Where a ceremony is held and the spatial layout of the ceremony is far more important than the question of when it will happen. The circle that forms the sun dance altar among so many Plains Indian nations always opens to the east. Like our North American indigenous communities, Indian peoples of the south, such as the Mayans in Mesoamerica, say prayers to the four directions, or, rather, to the ancestors that live in those four directions.

Indian peoples tend to locate power and the sacred spatially. This is in stark distinction to European and American European religious traditions that tend to express spirituality in terms of time: a regular hour on Sundays and a seasonal liturgical calendar that is more and more distanced from any sense of the spatial. Of course, it is precisely this sense of temporality that gives the Euro-Western and American European worldview its equally powerful and destructive notions of progress and development.[24] This European myth of progress and ideologies of development have always failed to capture the imagination of Indian folk until their minds have been successfully bent toward the time-based cultural values of the colonizer.

There is no notion of a seven-day week with one of those days set aside for religious practice. Rather, the spatial relationship of moon and sun marks the Indian year and divides time into spatial segments. Even Indian architecture tends to follow spiritual spatial guidelines. In an Osage town, for instance, a road running east to west divided the town into its constituent moiety divisions[25] of *hunka* and *tzisho,* earth and sky divisions, with each clan specific to one division or the other. Like the structure of the Osage village, most Osage ceremonials are also structured around a north-south, Sky-Earth division, with openings to the east and west. In similar manner, the structure for a Green Corn Ceremony (Muskogee, Uchi, etc.), the subterranean location of a Pueblo/Hopi kiva,[26] the design of a sweat lodge, or the direction one turns in a pipe ceremony all have tribally specific cosmic representational value that reflect the spiritual relationship of a particular people with the spatial world around them.

This understanding of the importance of spatiality emerges in another critical aspect—namely, in the long-standing identification of places that are known to a tribe to be particularly powerful spiritually. For most Indian communities, there are several such places that have been long identified as powerful: the Black Hills and Bear Butte for the Sioux Nation; Blue Lake for Taos Pueblo; Mt. Graham for the San Carlos Apaches; the mountains that mark territorial boundaries in the four directions for the Navahos or any Pueblo community. These are just a few examples. It should be said here that this ideal of spatiality is what gives territoriality (the land) its particular prominence in Indian thinking.

Third, out of this foundational idea of spatiality also comes the ideal of harmony and balance. All ceremonies and every social and political act of the community and persons in the community are oriented toward establishing or reestablishing harmony. The balance of the community is predicated on the balance of persons and family units within the community, on the one hand. And it is equally predicated on the balance of the whole of the world (ecosystem) around the people, on the other. The sun dance, then, is most clearly articulated as an annual ceremony to bring healing and balance back into the community and even to the whole of the world around us. Rather than dancing to gather some personal power, their sacrifice is vicarious; they dance for the people, often voicing the prayer we have already noted above "that the people might live." The dancers do not traditionally dance to collect some sort of personal power or to enhance their personal standing in a community. Rather, their sacrifice is vicarious; they dance for the people.

Fourth, the particularity of the American Indian notion of harmony and balance can only make sense when we add the Indian understanding of interrelationship. American Indians have long experienced the interrelationship between the self and all other life on the planet. Thus, the Lakota prayer, *mitakuye ouyasin* (for all my relations) understands all life to be a relative. When Indian people pray this prayer, it must be understood that they are praying for more than immediate family, their national Indian community, or even for all human beings. Rather, relatives include the four nations of people symbolized in the medicine wheel or circle: humans, animals (four leggeds), flying things, and all the other living moving things, including trees, lakes, mountains, and fish. This means that Indian cultures do not privilege human beings in the sort of anthropocentrism that dominates all Euro-Western thought. For American Indian peoples, all of life is sacred and has the same rights as human beings. Or as Kenneth Morrison puts it, we humans are in reciprocal relationships with other-than-human-beings that also have reason and sentience.[27] Thus, before a Plains Indian community can cut down a tree for their sun dance, there are detailed ceremonies involving conversations with the tree itself, prayers for the life of the tree, and persistent demonstrations of respect for the life of the tree. The tree will become the focus of the prayers of the dancers and all of the people for four days. The attitude of respect for the tree continues from the cutting of the tree and the careful carrying of it to the dance arbor and, in most traditions, even to the way the tree is finally brought down at the end of the dance and carried to its final resting place.

These, then, are four key cultural differences that set Native America apart from Euro-America.

Theoretical and Methodological Considerations

Over a long career spanning more than four decades, Vine Deloria Jr. (Yankton/Hunkpapa), the most famous of the Indian literati, argued persistently for the coherence and rational logic of the Indian worldview and its attendant epistemology, arguing in essence that this logic and epistemology serve as a proper theoretical and methodological framework.

Indeed, Deloria built his illustrious career from the beginning by demonstrating the greater plausibility of Indian traditions and historical memories against the usually dismissive explanations offered by colonial White academics, missionaries, and government officials. In his last published book, *The World We Used to Live In: Remembering the Powers of the Medicine Men*, published right after his death, Deloria presents a collection of stories about Indian men who had a demonstrable spiritual power from late 19th and early 20th century ethnographies.[28] These are stories of the wonderful accomplishments of Indian medicine men from a great variety of different tribes, from Kiowa and Comanche to Dakota and Omaha. There are early descriptions of Ojibwe tent-shaking ceremonies, Lakota *lowanpi* ceremonies, and all sorts of other occasions. These are stories of power used to change the weather, to bring success in battle, and to impress White observers, or they are stories that were simply a natural part of some tribal ceremony. They involve dramatic interactions between humans and other animals or the fantastic healing of someone badly wounded or deathly ill.

The White writers (anthropologists and amateurs working for the U.S. government) who recorded these stories included them not as useful illustrations of the religious traditions of tribes they were recording but as illustrations of the lack of sophistication of Indian cultures. Although these stories were persistently dismissed as "conjuring" by White observers, Deloria demonstrates quite to the contrary that they be taken more seriously than the dominant White society has dared. By grouping them in coherent sets, he presents a convincing argument that these stories are not merely the trickery and deception of "witch doctoring." The experiences of these Indian ancestors follow a regular pattern that suddenly forces the reader to hear them as quite plausible narratives rather than as incredible fantasies. The exploits of these old men of great spiritual power are lined up next to one another in such a way as to make their stories compellingly credible.

Indeed, Deloria's collection of these written traditions demonstrates a consistent display of power in American Indian ceremonial and healing traditions. To paraphrase the Australian magistrate in *Where the Green Ants*

Dream, in his comment on aboriginal stories, these American Indian stories occur with such frequency and consistency that they cohere into a palpable truth.[29] Increasingly today across Indian Country in the United States, the healthier Indian self-understanding presents itself in radical religious and cultural resistance to the Imperial Other.

Ongoing Issues

A significant and ongoing issue involves the effect on theological formulation and life strategies of fundamentalist and evangelical Indians who have, relatively speaking, simply capitulated to Euro-White norms of religious discourse. They have, for instance, wholly bought into the Euro-individualism of the personal salvation experience that has come to dominate Euro-Christian theology since Luther. That is, American Indian Christianity has become, like American religion in general, wholly based on personal and individualized emotion (and ultimately achievement, the temporal progress toward a utopian goal—in this case, salvation) rather than any continuing sense of a particular tribal community as a whole and its historical and contemporary experiences of the sacred. Thus the historic communalism of Indian peoples has slowly given way to European radical individualism. To this extent, Christianity continues to play a significant part in the genocide of Indian peoples.

NOTES

1. For the missionizing context, see George Tinker, *Missionary Conquest: The Gospel and American Indian Genocide* (Minneapolis: Fortress, 1993).

2. For instance, it took specific elder functionaries from each of the twenty-four Osage clans, each trained for performing their roles, to conduct the traditional hunting or war ceremonies. When the structures of the clans had been thoroughly disrupted by the advance of colonial settlers to the point that not all the roles could be fulfilled in any performance of the ceremony, the ceremonies began to fall into disuse. Then, Osages began to look for other possibilities for engaging their religious attention, including both the colonizer religions brought by the missionaries and the peyote ceremonies of the Native American Church. Willard Hughes Rollings, *Unaffected by the Gospel: Osage Resistance to the Christian Invasion, 1673–1906—A Cultural Victory* (Albuquerque: University of New Mexico Press, 2004).

3. Ward Churchill, *Kill the Indian, Save the Man: The Genocidal Impact of American Indian Residential Schools* (San Francisco: City Lights, 2004).

4. Henry M. Teller, Secretary of Interior, "Courts of Indian Offenses: Extract from the *Annual Report of the Secretary of the Interior,* November 1, 1883" [*House Executive Document,* no. 1, 48th Congress, 1st Session, Serial 2190, x–xiii.], in *Documents of United*

States Indian Policy, ed. Francis Paul Prucha (Lincoln: University of Nebraska Press, 1975), 160–162. These laws were revised and strongly affirmed ten years later by Thomas J. Morgan, then the Commissioner of Indian Affairs: "Punishment of Crimes and Misdemeanors Committed by Indians," taken from Report of August 27, 1892, in *House Executive Document,* no. 1, part 5, volume 2, 52nd Congress, Second Session, Serial 3088, 28–31; excerpted in Francis Paul Prucha, *Americanizing the American Indian: Writings by the Friends of the Indian, 1880–1900* (Lincoln: University of Nebraska Press, 1978), 300–305.

5. See the description of the Osage ceremonial decline in Garrick A. Bailey, intro. and ed., *The Osage and the Invisible World: From the Works of Francis La Flesche* (Norman: University of Oklahoma Press, 1995). But note also Rollings, *Unaffected by the Gospel.*

6. See my general argument in Tinker, *Missionary Conquest.*

7. William Apess, *The Experiences of Five Christian Indians of the Pequod Tribe* (1833); *A Son of the Forest* (1829); *Indian Nullification of the Unconstitutional Laws of Massachusetts, Relative to the Marshpee [sic] Tribe* (1835); and *Eulogy on King Philip* (1836). For a recent edition, see Barry O'Connell, ed., *On Our Own Ground: The Complete Writings of William Apess, a Pequot* (Amherst: University of Massachusetts, 1992). Note also Robert Warrior, "Canaanites, Cowboys and Indians: Deliverance, Conquest, and Liberation Theology Today," *Christianity and Crisis* 49 (1989): 261–265.

8. Samson Occom Papers (1727–1808) (Hartford: Connecticut Historical Society, 1998), available at http://www.chs.org/library/ead/htm_faids/occos1792.htm (accessed August 2007).

9. Thomas E. Mails, *Fools Crow* (Lincoln: University of Nebraska Press, 1990).

10. Vine Deloria Jr., *Singing for a Spirit: A Portrait of the Dakota Sioux* (Santa Fe, NM: Clear Light, 1999).

11. George Tinker, "American Indian Traditions," in *The Handbook of U.S. Liberation Theologies,* ed. Miguel De La Torre (St. Louis, MO: Chalice, 2004), 330–346. In the same volume, see also Andrea Smith's chapter, "Anthropology," 70–84. An initial attempt at a Native American theology was written by Clara Sue Kidwell, Homer Noley, and George Tinker, *Native American Theology* (Maryknoll, NY: Orbis, 2001).

12. Native "theologians" from Vine Deloria Jr. to Andrea Smith and William Baldridge have consistently argued that theology is a category that does not fit American Indian realities. Vine Deloria Jr., "On Liberation," in *For This Land: Writings on Religion in America* (New York: Routledge, 1999), 100–107; Andrea Smith, "Dismantling the Master's Tools with the Master's House: Native Feminist liberation Theologies," *Journal of Feminist Studies in Religion* 22, no. 2 (2006): 88–89; and William Baldridge, "Towards a Native American Theology," *American Baptist Quarterly* 8 (1989): 228;

13. Viola F. Cordova, "The European Concept of *Usen*: An American Aboriginal Text," in *Native American Religious Identity: Unforgotten Gods,* ed. Jace Weaver (Maryknoll, NY: Orbis, 1998).

14. Vine Deloria Jr., *God Is Red: A Native View of Religion* (Golden, CO: Fulcrum, 2002); and Cordova, "European Concept of *Usen*," 26.

15. For a longer discussion of traditional American Indian notions with respect to liberation, see George Tinker, "American Indians and Liberation: Harmony and Balance," in *Liberation in World Traditions,* ed. Miguel De La Torre (Waco, TX: Baylor University Press, 2008).

16. Warrior, "Canaanites, Cowboys and Indians," 261–265; and the response to Warrior by William E. Baldridge, "Native American Theology: A Biblical Basis," *Christianity and Crisis* 50 (1990): 180–181.

17. William Baldridge, "Reclaiming Our Histories," in David Batstone, ed., *New Visions for the Americas: Religious Engagement and Social Transformation* (Minneapolis: Fortress, 1993), 23–32.

18. Philip H. Duran, *Bringing Back the Spirit: Indian Ways of Wholeness for Church and Society in Crisis* (Scotland, PA: Healing the Land, 2005).

19. For instance, Andrea Smith, *Conquest: Sexual Violence and American Indian Genocide* (Cambridge, MA: South End, 2005); and Smith, "Dismantling the Master's Tools with the Master's House: Native Feminist Liberation Theologies," *Journal of Feminist Studies in Religion* 22, no. 2 (2006): 87–99.

20. Barbara Alice Mann, *Iroquoian Women: The Gantowisas* (New York: Peter Lang, 2000).

21. For the boarding school phenomenon as a contribution to Indian genocide, see especially Churchill, *Kill the Indian, Save the Man,* and my preface to that volume: Tinker, "Tracing a Contour of Colonialism: American Indians and the Trajectory of Educational Imperialism," xiii–xli. See also Andrea Smith, "Boarding School Abuses, Human Rights and Reparations," *Social Justice* 31 (2004): 89–102 (accessed at Questia.com), reprinted in Smith, *Conquest*, 35–54. Francis Paul Prucha, *Americanizing the American Indian: Writings of the "Friends of the Indian," 1880–1900* (Lincoln: University of Nebraska Press, 1978), has collected excerpts of writings by missionaries and government officials on their attempt to radically modify Indian cultures and beliefs in the late 1880s.

22. T. Tinker, "Sun Dance, Further Considerations," in *The Encyclopedia of Religion,* 2nd ed., ed. Lindsey Jones (Farmington Hills, MI: Thomas Gale, 2005), 13:8848–8849.

23. Deloria, *God Is Red*: for example, chap. 4, "Thinking in Time and Space"; chap. 6, "The Concept of History"; chap. 7, "The Spatial Problem of History"; chap. 16, "Sacred Places and Moral Responsibility."

24. This is true also for the striving toward a utopia on a temporal-linear progression marked by idealized abstractions of achievement and success (with attendant material accumulations). See Rostow's early argument in favor of mass consumption society as an advanced stage of civilization: Walt Whitman Rostow, *The Stages of Economic Growth: A Non-Communist Manifesto* (Cambridge: Cambridge University Press, 1960).

25. The English usage of the word "moiety" means "half." The technical anthropology usage of the word indicates the division of a tribal community into two halves or divisions. The divisions are called moieties or halves.

26. "Kiva" is a Hopi word for an underground or partly underground chamber in a Pueblo village, used by the men especially for religious ceremonies or councils.

27. Kenneth Morrison, "Cosmos as Intersubjective: Native American Other-Than-Human Persons," in *Indigenous Religions: A Companion,* ed. Graham Harvey (London: Cassell, 2000), 23–36.

28. Vine Deloria Jr., *The World We Used to Live In: Remembering the Powers of the Medicine Men* (Golden, CO: Fulcrum, 2006).

29. This was the judge's conclusion before he nevertheless decided against the indigenous aboriginals before his court. *Where the Green Ants Dream* is a 1984 film by German director Werner Herzog, set in Australia. The film pits a modern corporation mining ura-

nium against the activist resistance of the indigenous aborigine community. After hearing the aboriginal complainants discuss their cultural perspectives that destroying the place where the green ants dream will result in the destruction of humanity, the judge rules finally against them and for the corporation. The law, "however regrettably," he concludes, "is the law of the land."

FURTHER STUDY

Deloria, Vine, Jr. *God Is Red: A Native View of Religion.* Golden, CO: Fulcrum, 2002.
———. *Singing for a Spirit: A Portrait of the Dakota Sioux.* Santa Fe, NM: Clear Light, 1999.
———. *The World We Used to Live In: Remembering the Powers of the Medicine Men.* Golden, CO: Fulcrum, 2006.
Duran, Philip H. *Bringing Back the Spirit: Indian Ways of Wholeness for Church and Society in Crisis.* Scotland, PA: Healing the Land, 2005.
Harvey, Graham, ed. *Indigenous Religions: A Companion.* London: Cassell, 2000.
Kidwell, Clara Sue, Homer Noley, and George Tinker. *Native American Theology.* Maryknoll, NY: Orbis, 2001.
O'Connell, Barry, ed. *On Our Own Ground: The Complete Writings of William Apess, a Pequot.* Amherst: University of Massachusetts Press, 1992.
Rollings, Willard Hughes. *Unaffected by the Gospel: Osage Resistance to the Christian Invasion, 1673–1906—A Cultural Victory.* Albuquerque: University of New Mexico Press, 2004.
Tinker, George. *Missionary Conquest: The Gospel and American Indian Genocide.* Minneapolis: Fortress, 1993.
Warrior, Robert. "Canaanites, Cowboys and Indians: Deliverance, Conquest, and Liberation Theology Today," *Christianity and Crisis* 49 (1989): 261–265.
Weaver, Jace, ed. *Native American Religious Identity: Unforgotten Gods.* Maryknoll, NY: Orbis, 1998.

9

Gay and Lesbian Theologies

ROBERT E. SHORE-GOSS

Historical Backdrop

Early gay activism[1] targeted the American Psychiatric Association and the American Psychological Association—resulting in removal of the diagnosis of homosexuality as a "sociopathic personality disturbance, sexual deviation" in the *Diagnosis and Statistical Manual II*.[2] In addition, the Metropolitan Community Church (MCC), the largest LGBT (lesbian, gay, bisexual, transgender) organization in the world, and denominational church groups such as Dignity (Catholic) and Integrity (Episcopalian) were born to support gay and lesbian Christians in accepting their sexual orientation, integrating their sexual orientation with their faith practice, and attempting to humanize ecclesial opposition to homosexuality. Just as the "Black is Beautiful" slogan emerged in the 1960s, the 1970s produced the "Gay is Good" slogan.

The period that followed (commonly referred to as the "Reagan years") was not so "good" for the LGBT community. The optimism of 1970s gay/lesbian theologies receded with the ravages of the AIDS pandemic and the escalating social hatred of the churches. As HIV/AIDS was in the national spotlight on nearly a daily basis, the Religious Right agenda drew an inextricable link with homosexuality and gays and lesbians. Many infected with HIV and those affected by HIV found themselves defensive in affirming that sexuality is a gift of God, despite the condemnation of churches.

The various groups of the Religious Right were focused on a wide variety of political issues from abortion to anticommunism. With the end of the cold war, the Religious Right turned its attention to the gay/lesbian movement, opportunistically using it as mechanism for fundraising and galvanizing its membership against the threat of an internal homosexual menace.[3] In the 1980s, translesbisexuals had responded to the AIDS pandemic as it affected gays, beginning a broad coalition based on HIV health issues and voluntarism in creating AIDS response organizations in every major city.

Coalitions of gays/lesbians expanded their concerns from a single-focused issue to face the challenges of multiple, intersecting forms of oppression. Gay men became concerned with women's issues such as reproductive freedom, sexism, and health issues, recognizing that lesbians had been there for their HIV gay brothers during the early ravages of the AIDS pandemic. AIDS activism and queer activism developed in response to social violence, apathy, negligence, and inactivity from the Reagan administration, discrimination, and the growing backlash from the Religious Right. In 1987, the AIDS Coalition to Unleash Power (ACT UP) formed as a political activist movement of those infected with HIV, gays/lesbians, and their friends; they were united in their anger, in direct action, and in wearing black T-shirts bearing inverted pink triangles with the slogan "Silence = Death." They staged nonviolent actions of civil disobedience, picketed legislators, and made confrontational challenges in public meetings and forums, including dramatic public actions at Wall Street, pharmaceutical companies, and the FDA: "The gay HIV-positive population fought the gross silence and inactivity of the Reagan administration; the bureaucracy of the Food and Drug Administration, the National Institutes of Health, the Centers for Disease Control, and the medical establishment; the profiteering of the pharmaceutical companies; the discrimination of the insurance companies, the unenlightened policies of state governments, educational institutions, and churches."[4] Not since Stonewall and the early 1970s was there such a burst of activism within the gay/lesbian community.

This activism was met with hate crimes. Queer Nation New York was formed in 1990 to protest the bombing of a gay bar, Uncle Charlie's; it drew over a thousand protesters. Queer Nation chapters arose in many United States cities to fight against homophobic violence and compulsory heterosexuality. They attempted to raise queer visibility, disrupting ex-gay organizations, staging kiss-ins in shopping malls, invading heterosexual spaces with leaflets and queer manifestos, and holding sit-ins and protests targeting the homophobic Cracker Barrel Restaurant chain, the Boy Scouts of America, and other heterosexist institutions. They shouted their mantra in heterosexual cultural spaces: "We're queer; we're here; get used to it." They were determined to make all public spaces safe for sexual- and gender-variant people.

ACT UP mixed sex with AIDS politics, mobilizing activists around issues of race, gender, and sexual orientation and then linking these issues with poverty, health care, the distribution of clean needles to drug users, prostitution, immigration law and reform, medical policies and research, drug accessibility, media hysteria, religious discrimination, and state and federal AIDS policies. They inserted sex orientation and gender into a whole economy of culture politics. No longer was the single issue of gay analysis sufficient: multiple "isms" were confronted; ACT UP gay men followed lesbian feminists into the complexities of social and political analyses that linked issues of race, ethnicity, age, and economics with homophobia and blatant AIDS-phobia. This new paradigm required sophisticated economic, cultural, and political analyses that earlier identity politics could no longer manage very well. It required an epistemological cultural and intellectual shift that could handle the messiness of queer grass roots activism and cultural analyses inclusive of fluid sexual orientation and gender diversity.

Since the early 2000s, two essays and one book have attempted to discuss the evolution of gay and lesbian theologies to queer theologies.[5] The challenge has been to examine the evolution from a different trajectory of theological development from my own earlier writings and those of Elizabeth Stuart. It is possible to follow the trajectories of gay/lesbian theologies along several evolutionary routes—apologetics, pastoral, liberation, feminist, and contextual theologies—to the development of queer contextual theologies. These routes were never linear or "straight" developments, for they crossed evolutionary routes and mingled with traditional theological disciplines in a very queer fashion. Moreover, they were deeply embedded in ecclesial and cultural developments within the gay/lesbian communities to such an extent that queer contextual theologies emerged not only in the United States but also in South America, the United Kingdom, and other countries.[6]

This explosion of resources was delineated by queer theologian Mark Jordan, pointing out that the bibliography of a 1966 Consultation on Theology and the Homosexual listed eighteen works—from Thomas Aquinas's and Karl Barth's negative positions on homosexuality to a few attempts to characterize homosexuality in somewhat more positive perspective.[7] In that same talk, Jordan pointed to the exponential growth of monographs on religion and homosexuality, from 37 in the 1960s to 1,829 by the 2000s.[8] There has been an explosion of religious discourse, both positive and negative, as the gay/lesbian communities have become more organized within American culture and churches.

Description

Gay Christians began their theological reflections about homosexuality with the intention to change the churches' position on the issue. Sally Gearhart (United Methodist Church) and William Johnson (United Church of Christ) produced the first book of the 1970s, *Loving Women, Loving Men:*

Gay Liberation of the Church.[9] Johnson and other contributors argued for the full inclusion of gay men and lesbians into the church, grounding their arguments in the validity and naturalness of loving the same gender. They picked up the reasoning of the 1960s sexual liberation movement and the advent of the birth control pill that widened the purpose of sexuality beyond procreation. It is noteworthy that Johnson attempted to liberate the church, while Gearhart reflected feminist and lesbian challenges to heteropatriarchy, urging an embodied theology over abstract theological systems. This difference between lesbian-feminist and gay theologies continued in more sophisticated theological enterprises from the 1980s into the next century. Few gay theologians, even today, speak of heteropatriarchy.

John McNeill's *The Church and the Homosexual* (1976) was not addressed merely to gay men and lesbians but also to institutional Catholicism.[10] McNeill mustered cogent arguments from the biblical tradition, Roman Catholic natural law and moral theology, and pastoral experience of ministering to gays and lesbians. His book was ostensibly directed to Catholic priests, religious orders, church leaders, and educated Catholic gays and lesbians. McNeill's line of reasoning had all the precision of a Jesuit philosopher, undermining the traditional condemnations of homosexuality. What was revolutionary about *The Church and the Homosexual* is that McNeill gave careful attention to the biblical texts often erroneously applied to homosexuality. He followed in the earlier footsteps of Derrick Sherwin Bailey to understand the story of Sodom and Gomorrah as a condemnation of inhospitality rather than homosexuality.

McNeill's book (translated into numerous languages) was moderate from the perspective of contemporary queer theology, yet it was as revolutionary in its time as any queer theology in recent years. It turned Catholic moral arguments upon themselves from the findings of psychology and scripture. McNeill made a strong case for a new pastoral approach to the condition of homosexuality and the treatment of Catholic homosexuals. He did not accept the judgments of earlier Catholic moral theologians that those gays/lesbians unable to change their sexual orientation had to live a life of forced abstinence.

In 1978, McNeill's book was followed by both Tom Horner's *Jonathan Loved David* and Virginia Ramey Mollenkott's and Letha Scanzoni's *Is the Homosexual My Neighbor?*[11] Horner expanded the biblical readings beyond the apologetic texts to find traces of homoeroticism in the stories of Jonathan and David and Ruth and Naomi; he was the first to give a systematic gay reading of the scriptures. Mollenkott, an evangelical Christian and professor of English literature, and Scanzoni, a sociologist, make a strong case for approaching homosexuals through the Golden Rule.

Although it was published in 1980, John Boswell's *Christianity, Homosexuality, and Social Tolerance* was written during the optimistic freedom of gay liberation in the late 1970s.[12] Boswell's work initiated a biblically based resistance, precipitating an apologetic battle against reading of biblical texts often (mis)applied to homosexuality by its ecclesial opponents while simultaneously engaging gay critics for optimistic readings of Christian texts and social history.[13] The Yale historian remained stubbornly a member of the Roman Catholic Church, and he became a zealous gay theological apologist, speaking both to gay/lesbian denominational conventions and to sympathetic, liberal churches. His evangelical missionary project of reclaiming a vision of a less-virulent and homophobic Christianity resulted in empowering the gay/lesbian Christian movement in the 1980s, but it also antagonized gay critics alienated from a violent Christianity.[14] When a 20th-century history of queer Christianity in the United States is written, John Boswell will be one of the leading pillars that strengthened denominational groups such as Integrity and Dignity and the MCC.[15]

These pioneers in the 1970s strengthened the nascent formation of denominational groups and the MCC congregations, but perhaps more important, they empowered a future generation of queer Christian scholars who are committed to finding the liberating resources within Christianity to fight against hatred and intolerance of gays and lesbians.

Gay theology in the 1980s centered on two issues: biblical texts that were used to justify homosexuality as sin and psychological issues of sexual orientation to deconstruct moral theologies based on natural law. It found itself in an apologetic mode attempting to make cosmetic changes within the churches to justify acceptance of gay/lesbians while dealing with the onslaught and tragic numbers of deaths among gay men.

Gay theology did not address the issue of sexism; it was unable to make theoretical connections between misogyny and homophobia or to connect homophobia to other forms of oppression. The writings of Chris Glazer (1980), John McNeill (1988), and John Fortunato (1982), among others, hardly cited the lesbian theologies of Carter Heyward or Virginia Mollenkott.[16] Although Boswell's earlier work was important to the gay/lesbian Christian movement in the 1980s, it had a major shortcoming in that almost all the material that Boswell covered was male homoeroticism, while the history of female homoerotic relations and desires within Christianity was conspicuously absent. Only in the 1990s did Bernadette Brooten's *Love between Women: Early Christian Responses to Female Homoeroticism* provide a correction to the absence of female voices in Boswell's work in early Christianity.[17] This early gay theology focused on the expulsion of "out" gay male and sometimes lesbian clergy, the denial of ordination to gays/lesbians, and the refusal to bless same-sex unions. Theological anthologies—with gay/lesbian, closeted, and straight contributors—responded with an apologetic for or against church statements on the issue of homosexuality.[18] These writings remained reactive to church statements about homosexuality. Gay theology remained a negative apologetic, reacting to the backlash from the Religious Right and conservative forces within mainline Christian denominations.

On Halloween, 1986, Cardinal Joseph Ratzinger released his infamous letter on homosexuality: *Letter on the Pastoral Care of Homosexual Persons.* There was nothing pastoral about the letter, which described gays/lesbians as "intrinsically evil" and "objectively disordered." Ratzinger's letter ignored all scientific evidence on the biological and psychological basis of homosexuality and disregarded all contemporary biblical exegesis applied to homosexuality. It was a violent, mean-spirited, and aggressive letter, intending to curb Dignity, reduce pastoral sensitivity to gay and lesbian Catholics, and deny the scientific trend toward a more open and tolerant society in the United States.[19] John McNeill spoke out against Cardinal Ratzinger's letter to the U.S. bishops. This set in motion a process of McNeill's expulsion from the Society of Jesus. The noted Protestant biblical scholar John Wink wrote to McNeill: "John, when the Vatican imprudently slammed the door on you, the gust of wind it set off blew open hundreds of doors. In the craftiness of God, I swear your impact will be increased exponentially."[20]

Immediately, McNeill then wrote *Taking a Chance on God,* one of the first positive books on gay Christian spirituality, brokering topics on hospitality, compassion, and discernment of spirits for gays living with homophobic institutional Christianity that promoted fear, shame, guilt, and self-hatred. He brought his experience as a gay psychotherapist to his philosophical training in the writings of Maurice Blondel to validate the revelatory experience of gays and lesbians. Both *Freedom, Glorious Freedom* and his autobiography, *Both Feet Firmly Planted in Midair,* elaborate on the painful process of expulsion from the Jesuits and his finding joy in his discernment process to obey and follow Christ over the Vatican and his Jesuit superiors.[21] McNeill provides a personal example to gay and lesbian Christians of how to discern the spiritual value of their erotic love and their experiences over the destructive authority of the Catholic Church.

Gay theology inevitably became problematic in its singular focus on gay male issues, excluding lesbian voices. The theological split along gender lines between gays and lesbians started in the late 1970s with the feminist movement, the rise of gay liberation, and radical lesbians. This cultural split between gays and lesbians slowed in the early years of the AIDS pandemic, as lesbians stepped forward to respond to the escalating HIV infection and death rates of gay men with their involvement in AIDS service organizations.

Carter Heyward, a lesbian Episcopal priest and theologian, developed a lesbian feminist liberation theology. Her book—*Our Passion for Justice* (1984)—began to critique patriarchal Christianity, articulating a relationship between homophobia and misogyny. Four years later, Heyward's book—*Touching Our Strength*—continued her critique of heterosexist Christian theology, offering an alternative constructive theology embodied in the erotic.[22] Carter Heyward expanded the black lesbian poet Audre Lorde's notion of the erotic by describing the erotic as our power in relation or mutuality.

Mutuality is a vision of justice by which the power of God calls us to reconcile ourselves, one to another, in an effort to usher forth our most liberating, creative possibilities and futures. Mutuality, unlike equality, signals relational growth and change, and it constitutes an invitation into shaping the future together.[23] Heyward's erotic theology highlights a cocreative language of grace, and she focused on mutual relationships that questioned the dualistic bifurcations of heterosexist constructions of gender and sexuality. Her stress on relationality brought Heyward into a social constructionist approach to sexual identity as queer theory was beginning to take shape. Heyward's theology was the most significant and sophisticated lesbian theological work of the 1980s, and it would influence the development of the gay theologies of J. Michael Clark, Daniel Spencer, Gary Comstock, and Marvin Ellison; the lesbian theologies of Mary Hunt and Kathy Rudy; and the queer theologies of Robert Williams and Robert Shore-Goss [formerly Goss].[24]

The theological significance of Carter Heyward was that she not only provided a theological bridge for dialogue between gays and lesbians but also prepared for the evolution of queer theologies and the later inclusion of bisexual and transgendered voices. The push for inclusion of lesbian voices influenced gay theology, expanding beyond its white, middle-class male parameters and addressing issues of gender, patriarchy, class, and race. For example, Clark's post-Christian theology developed insights from

Heyward's erotic theology into his ecotheology, influencing the development of Spencer's *Gay and Gaia*. Ellison's *Erotic Justice,* deeply influenced by Heyward, is one of the finest theological attempts to analyze the intersections of sexism, race, homophobia, and able-bodiedness. Finally, it took until the 1990s before gay/lesbian theology entered into dialogue with queer theorists, including the voices of bisexual and transgendered Christians. This explosion of scholarly activism transformed gay theology into queer theology and widened its dialogue partners.

A watershed year for gay theology was 1993, with the publication of Comstock's *Gay Theology without Apology,* Clark's *Beyond Our Ghettoes,* and [Shore-]Goss's *Jesus ACTED UP.*[25] Clark spoke with clarity and power as an openly HIV+ theologian to incorporate ecofeminism and Heyward's erotic justice-oriented theology into a gay environmental liberation theology. Comstock's book appealed to mainline Protestant denominations in the midst of divisive polarization over the inclusion of gays and lesbians. *Jesus ACTED UP* drew its audience from marginalized queer Christians within denominations, the MCC congregations, justice-oriented Christians, and queer Catholics.

The first theological works to use the word "queer" were Williams's *Just as I Am* (1992) and then *Jesus ACTED UP* (1993). Gay theology was attempting to fit politically into the American Academy of Religion, and "queer" was a term that made many gays and lesbians uncomfortable because it had been a derogatory epithet. However, both Williams and Shore-Goss trace gay/lesbian theological roots to the AIDS activism of ACT UP and Queer Nation in the late 1980s and early 1990s where LGBT activists and their heterosexual allies described themselves as queer. In *Jesus ACTED UP,* Shore-Goss described queer as "a term of political dissidence and sexual difference. It is part of the movement to reclaim derogatory words from oppressive culture."[26] In later writings, Shore-Goss wrote, "according to *Webster's Third New International Dictionary,* 'queer' as a verb means 'to spoil the effect of, interfere with, to disrupt, harm, or put in a bad light.' Queering an already spoiled and exclusive Christianity is to make it more inclusive for translesbigays."[27] For his theological enterprise, Shore-Goss found his dialogue partners with the French gay cultural critic and philosopher Michel Foucault, the beginnings of queer theorists in the early 1990s, and queer activism. At the gay and lesbian academic conference at Harvard University in 1990—"The Politics of Pleasure"—gay and lesbian academics in all disciplines engaged in conversations with queer and AIDS activists.[28] Elizabeth Stuart notes that *Jesus ACTED UP* marked a transition from gay and lesbian theology to queer theology:

Jesus ACTED UP remains a watershed in gay and lesbian theology for even though he did not follow Foucault's theory all the way through his book, [Shore-]Goss nevertheless flagged up the issues of discourse and identity. [Shore-]Goss also demonstrated a commitment to radical political action and a feminist and sex-positive theology did not have to involve a sweeping dismissal of the tradition. . . . [Shore-]Goss proved that it was possible to still do theology and be committed to gay and lesbian liberation.[29]

Queer theology is, in many ways, a branch of liberation theology, deriving from the roots of the Latin American, African American, and feminist liberation theologies. It shares much of the same methodologies as other liberation theologies, perhaps in closest resemblance to feminist liberation theologies because of the fact that heterosexism is embedded in cultural sexism.

In the 1990s, other theologians began to self-identify as queer in their theologies: Nancy Wilson, Kathy Rudy, Ibrahim Farajaje-Jones, Mark Jordan, Justin Tanis, Lisa Isherwood, Elizabeth Stuart, and Marcella Althaus-Reid.[30] Queer theologies look at the separation of sexuality from spirituality and its destructive effects, and in the spirit of Christian ethicist James Nelson, queer (as well gay and lesbian) theologies tried to reconnect.[31] Queer theory destabilizes essentialist notions of sexuality, identity, and gender; it renders fluid these cultural concepts and practices once considered stable. British scholar Jeremy Carette notes that queer theory destabilizes the essential self and the truth of Christian theology; he notes, "To queer religion is to queer the foundations of theology, its monotheism, its monosexuality, and its monopoly of truth. In the queer space of theology, we find 'ambiguity' and 'not knowing,' a performative self, which can . . . imaginatively recreate the symbolic." Later Carette asserts, "If Christianity is entwined with the discourse of sexuality, then to queer sexuality is simultaneously to queer the symbolic of theology."[32] Queer theology is a "transgressive reinscription" of Christian symbols, practices, and theological truths that have excluded LGBT folks.[33]

The theology of same-sex marriage and queer marriage follows the grassroots practice of LGBT religious groups. There is debate on which church— Unitarian Universalist Association of Congregations, United Church of Christ, or Metropolitan Community Church—was the first to initiate the practice of blessing same-sex unions. Nevertheless, the Metropolitan Community Church has blessed over 100,000 same-sex unions from its beginnings in 1968. It has been joined by some Episcopal churches and the United Church of Christ; clergy in other denominations have blessed same-sex unions "sub rosa" or as acts of public protest. The marriage equality movement from the 1990s to the present—especially with the recognition of same-sex civil unions in several U.S. states and same-sex marriage in Massachusetts—has propelled the development of queer theologies of marriage.

Theological reflection has resulted from two cultural factors. The horrific tallies of HIV among gay and bisexual men led to the development of queer families and the LGBT baby boom. Extended families of care were created around folks dying of HIV. Queer people and their friends became adept at the skill of creating new families of choice. The second factor was the reactionary movement of the Religious Right to promote "traditional family values" and the cultural hysteria that led to numerous state initiatives to define marriage as between one man and one woman. With missionary zeal, historian John Boswell lectured about the discovery of Christian liturgical texts that celebrated same-sex unions. His book—*Same-Sex Unions in Premodern Europe*—fueled the cultural debate on same-sex marriage. His work provoked a storm of criticism to debunk the possibility that the uncovered rites were same-sex marriages. Much criticism has been leveled at his scholarship for its interpretative excesses of studying more than sixty manuscripts from the 8th to the 16th centuries. Boswell concluded that the brotherhood rites (*adelphopoiesis*) "most likely signified a marriage in the eyes of most ordinary Christians."[34] There was no evidence that ordinary Christians viewed these brotherhood rites as marriages. Boswell hoped his retrieval of these rites could be used by LGBT Christians to justify a liturgical theology for blessing same-sex unions. Alan Bray's posthumously published book *The Friend* demonstrates how Christian same-sex couples celebrated their friendship with church rites.[35] Bray is less extravagant in his claims than Boswell, and he is enough of a historian to make the disclaimer that modern homoerotic relationships and friendship differed from premodern notions of same-sex friendships. Both works resulted from the cultural and religious wars over marriage; both highlighted that same-sex friendship rituals occurred. These brother and friendship rituals provided the cultural antecedents for LGBT ritualizations of their relationships.

In the early 1990s, Robert Williams wrote one of the first theological texts, claiming that queer marriages are sacramental and that they form a school of love.[36] He roots this argument within a Protestant theology of marriage derived from the notion of companionship. Williams notes that the values present in same-sex marriages are mutuality, an ability to make and keep intentional agreements, and sexual involvement. He notes that queer marriages, like heterosexual marriages, can be a school of love for queer Christians.

From his earliest work, Robert Shore-Goss argued for the sacramental quality of same-sex marriages. He develops Catholic moral theologian Andre Guindon's application of sexual fecundity to same-sex unions,[37] and he argues for the sacramentality of same-sex marriages that reflect more closely the egalitarian power relations, mutuality, and love of God's reign. In later writings, Shore-Goss takes the notion of procreativity, a theological strategy that is used to justify the purpose for heterosexual marriage, and queers it by deconstructing its monolithic application to heterosexual couples and by demonstrating that same-sex couples have adopted a number of procreative strategies.[38] Shore-Goss thus argues for a position of equal rites, and that churches extend the blessing of marriage to same-sex couples as well as opposite sex. Procreativity can no longer be the theological justification for heterosexual marriage alone.

In 1997, Shore-Goss and Amy Strongheart presented a collection of essays on the construction of families.[39] A number of the essays directly address the theological aspects of marriage. The strength of the volume encompasses the diversities of translesbigay relationships by expanding the traditional definitions of friendship, marriage, families, and community. Within that volume, Mary Hunt challenges patriarchal constructions of marriage and the danger of applying them to same-sex unions. She understands same-sex unions within a framework of friendship, for such a friendship model allows for partner equality and mutuality rather than gender hierarchies with heterosexist marriages.[40]

As the 2004 presidential election centered on the definition of and protection of marriage, Marvin Ellison provided a timely progressive Christian ethical analysis of same-sex marriage. His book *Same-Sex Marriage* underscores how patriarchal Christian notions of marriage have had little to no concern over justice for women. He argues for a justice ethic that same-sex couples should have equal access to the legal status and benefits of civil marriage that heterosexuals have. Ellison calls for a Christian rethinking of marriage and family to include LGBT marriage, and he ends with a prevailing image of God as "both unmarried and promiscuous lover, the divine lover whose love is not limited to only a certain people or groups, but rather expansively takes in all creation."[41]

Queer theologian Mark Jordan jumps into the fray of the same-sex marriage debate by revealing how Christians have for centuries quarreled over the theological elements of marriage. In fact, Christian marriage theologies have no unchanging core teachings; often, they resulted from the cultural improvisations from theological controversies on the legitimacy of sexuality and cultural shifts on notions of family.[42] Jordan explores out of the bounds

same-sex relationships, noting that the betrothal often has greater significance than the blessing in same-sex relationships. His discussion of same-
sex marital theology unmasks the inconsistencies of marital theologies that
attempt to prevent its recognition. What is really subversive about Jordan's
Blessing Same-Sex Unions is that he names Christian fears:

> The most urgent challenge for Christian marital theology has been to pre-
> vent the universality of the agapic feast from reaching erotic relationships—
> how to prevent the agapic community from enactment as erotic commu-
> nity, Christianity as latent polyamory. . . . When sex unions are imagined
> as suspiciously unbounded erotic relationships, they call up theological
> scripts developed to rebut the challenge of polygamy and (more urgently)
> to delimit unbounded Christian love, agape itself.[43]

For many Christians opposed to same-sex marriage, queer relationships
are perceived as a threat to marriage because the churches have forged "incoherent accommodations" between ascetic imperatives of denying sex and
allowing erotic desire for procreation within marriage. Jordan notes at the
heart of the Eucharist, "The indiscriminate feast is the joining of many, body
to body, regardless of sex, with the one and the many body of Jesus, from
whose sex Christology has been a long and terrified flight. Joining bodies
promiscuously is the great Christian mystery."[44] Jordan names the fear surrounding same-sex marriage: fear of unbridled erotic desire and the promiscuous joining of bodies. Along with Jordan, there have been several Christian theological explorations of polyamory, including Shore-Goss's article
titled "Proleptic Sexual Love."[45] Queer theological reflections on marriage,
erotic desire and new configurations, and nonheterocentric (and patriarchal)
models of families provide a liberating edge and challenge to Christian "family values" and its incoherent theologies of marriage.

Transgendered theologies have emerged as part of the queer paradigm for
theologizing around gender, destabilizing fundamentalist and rigid notions
of gender, and proposing a wide and queer range of fluid masculinities, femi-
ninities, and hybrid mixtures. Male-to-female transsexual Victoria Kolakowski and female-to-male Justin Tanis have pioneered transgendered theological reflection with contextual transgendered readings of scripture.[46] Tanis
expanded his D. Min. dissertation into *Transgendered Theology, Ministry, and
Communities of Faith.* He documented from surveys of transgendered folks
how they understood gender as a calling and how God was intimately part of
their process of the revelatory experience of transitioning:

Through trans and intersexed bodies, God reveals Godself to be a Creator who loves diversity and variation, a Creator who improvises and varies the melodies that call each person into being. Through such bodies, we see the intricate differences that make an individual a unique creation and a fluid transition from one being to another. Trans bodies show us that dichotomous ways in which we have viewed bodies are not God's ways because our bodies make it difficult to divide humans into two ways. We are the in-between, created in the image and likeness of God.[47]

Tanis's theology is totally body-centered, where Trans (his capitalization) bodies manifest the cocreation between God and humanity of what bodies are and what they become. Transsexuals are not only exercising their freedom to cocreate their bodies but also, in turn, manifesting the process of God's self-revelation within transitioning bodies. Tanis's body theology becomes a means of preparing faith communities to become more welcoming and hospitable to transgendered folks.

In *Omnigender: A Trans-Religious Approach*, lesbian feminist Virginia Mollenkott came out as male-identified.[48] She systematically deconstructs the validity of a binary gender system, exploring the biological middle group of intersexuality and cultural constructions of gender diversity. Mollenkott proposes an omnigender paradigm for comprehending gender diversity and understanding such diversity within a Christian theological framework. Omnigender includes a wide range of gender expressiveness, from masculine males on one side of the spectrum to feminine females on the other, and between those two poles, including transsexuals, intersexed folks, cross-dressers, drag queens and kings, gays, lesbians, and bisexuals who are infinitely expressive of the divine. She argues that males perpetrate the most physical violence against gender women and gender-variant folks. Mollenkott returns to the rich traditions of Christianity to mine gender-bending saints, queer texts such as Ephesians 5:25–27 that point out the gender *aporias* of the nuptial imagery of Christ and the Body of Christ, and the poet John Milton's notion of angels switching genders at will and reveling in their nuptials. Mollenkott thus undermines Christian gender fundamentalism and erotophobic symbols for a queer Christianity that is far more humane and more affirming of God's queer diverse gender creation.

In contrast, Vanessa Sheridan wrote first as a self-identified cross-dresser with her book *Cross Purposes,* and later she identified as a transgender woman.[49] Sheridan based her transgender theology on the principles and tenets of liberation theologies. She calls for gender-variant people to make a place for themselves within Christian churches and join the struggle for justice and acceptance with the churches. The number of transgender theologies has blossomed in recent years, while bisexual theologies are almost nonexistent.[50]

Sources

Scripture

Since the 1970s, a critical mass of gay/lesbian scholarship on same-sex affectional preferences countered oppressive biblical readings supported by interpretative communities that were heteropatriachal and often misogynist. Thus, many LGBT Christians, who journeyed into exile communities, found that they had to recover from the years of religious and homophobic biblical abuse from their previous churches. They found comfort in the LGBT scholars and their interpretative deflection of textual violence and abuse. As queer denominational groups, churches and synagogues formed in the late 1960s, and in the 1970s they created new interpretative communities engaging the scriptures not as enemy but as "friend." The pastoral practices of those churches, synagogues, and denominational groups have used these texts as liturgical readings in the blessings of same-sex unions and providing legitimacy to their unions.[51] LGBT Christians found themselves reflected in stories of Ruth and Naomi, Jonathan and David, and Jesus and the Beloved Disciple. These worship practices initially out-ed the homoerotic within the biblical text through communal imaginative readings. For example, John McNeill speaks of the gay centurion and his beloved boy: "Here we have the most direct encounter of Jesus Christ with someone who today would be pronounced 'gay' and Christ's reaction is acceptance of the person without judgment and even eagerness to be of assistance to restore the *pais* (boy) to health."[52]

Ministers, such as Rev. Elder Nancy Wilson, moderator of the MCC, counters pervasive biblical heterosexism by outing "eunuchs" and "barren women," Ruth and Naomi, Jonathan and David, the gay centurion, Lydia in Acts, and Jesus as bisexual. In other words, she is reclaiming the text for the queer community when she writes, "The Bible must be a holy text for gays and lesbians because we are truly human, created by the God who created heaven and earth." Queer folks are made in the image of God and thus have the right to be included within the text. Wilson articulates a tribal hermeneutic for gays and lesbians, reading eunuchs and barren women as gay, lesbian, and bisexual antecedents.[53]

Outing the biblical text has had two methodological limitations: falling into an essentialist understanding of sexual identities, and giving over too much legitimation to the text for their contemporary erotic lives. Validation of queer erotic lives must come from within themselves, realizing the goodness and God's original blessings of their sexualities. Such a priori validation means that queer folks need to come out and recognize the blessing of their sexualities and their gender variations before they engage the biblical text. Theologian Gary Comstock writes: "Instead of making the Bible into a parental authority, I have begun to engage with it as I would a friend—as one to whom I have made a commitment and in whom I have invested dearly, but with whom I insist on a mutual exchange of critique, encouragement, support, and challenge."[54]

Queer reading requires not surrendering to biblical authority as a parent but engaging the text as an equal, and in the encounter as friend, readers bring their own queer social context to the text. The authority of the text is located in the back and forth encounter of equals. For several decades, multicultural and contextual readings of the biblical texts were emerging. It was natural after African American, feminist, Hispanic, and contextual readings from Africa and Asia that LGBT contextual readings emerged. Stephen Moore has described queer engagements of biblical texts such as those typified by *Jesus ACTED UP, Take Back the Word,* and *Our Tribe* as "exegetical activism."[55] Exegetical activism really describes queer contextual readings of the biblical texts; it becomes a reading strategy of LGBT Christians to reappropriate the biblical texts for themselves. In *Take Back the Word: A Queer Reading of the Bible,* the editors Mona West and Robert Shore-Goss wrote:

> With the rise of postmodernism we have seen a shift in biblical hermeneutics that considers the role of the reader in assigning meaning to the biblical text. Not only have we come to realize that readers make meaning of texts, but readers also bring a particular "self" to the text which is shaped by a variety of factors such as race, ethnicity, gender, class, religious affiliations, socioeconomic standing, education, and, we would add, sexual orientation.[56]

Take Back the Word is a positive reading of the Hebrew and Christian scriptures. The coeditors chose "take back the word" after playing around with a number of titles. "Taking back the word" indicated not only our queer reclamation of the biblical text for ourselves but also our Christian activist inclinations. In the preface, biblical scholar Mary Ann Tolbert writes:

In the case of queers . . . the fact that all texts, including the biblical texts, are generally ambiguous and indeterminate, thus requiring readers to refine and complete their meaning, is something of a two-edged sword. Since reading is always and inevitably a process in which the commitments, views, and cultural and social location of each reader profoundly influences the way those ambiguities and indeterminacies are decided, readers of texts become the co-creators of their meanings.[57]

Tolbert recognizes that authoritative readings come not from the biblical text itself but from the assumptions that LGBT readers bring to it. Queer contributors foreground themselves as real flesh and blood readers, variously situated as they transgress heterosexist boundaries and even the sexual orthodoxies of gay and lesbian to include bisexual and transgendered contributors. Transgressing boundaries of dominant interpretative communities is a rebellious act that breaks the conceptual heterosexist interpretative lens and categories to biblical texts.

Take Back the Word was certainly not inclusive enough of all queer social locations, but it was a beginning, followed by Ken Stone's *Queer Commentary and the Hebrew Bible* and, in the United Kingdom, Thomas Bohache et al., *The Queer Bible Commentary,* in which queer scripture scholars, theologians, and pastors provide contextual readings.[58] The contributors used feminist, queer, and postmodern approaches to the Hebrew and Christian scriptures to transgress the cultural imperialism of heteropatriarchy that has justified sexist, racist, heterosexist, and colonial readings. They bring their own contextually queer experiences to the reading of individual books of the Bible, suspicious of readings that have been traditionally oppressive to themselves and to other groups. In his review of the commentary, religion sociologist Andrew Yip wrote:

What I find more satisfying is the contributors' creative attempts to uncover queer sensibilities and subjectivities in each text. This involves lifting the veil on hitherto silenced voices of homoeroticism and same-sex intimacy and care (for example, the devotion between Ruth and Naomi in Ruth; and David and Jonathan in 1 Samuel), as well as casting queer-friendly light on passages that are on the surface not relevant to LGBT experiences. It is hard not to be moved by the thought of an LGBT Christian declaring with pride, confidence and honesty that, "God, you fashioned me in my mother's womb . . . For I am awesomely and wondrously made."[59]

The queer contributors freed themselves from the decades of oppressive heterosexist interpretations of the scriptural texts and offered empowered and liberating interpretations compatible with LGBT lives.

Seminal Reports and Publications

Gay historians have pointed out that the early homophile organizations developed after World War II when gay and lesbian veterans settled in urban areas where they could support one another and organize as a movement. The popularization of psychoanalytic theories on homosexuality and its treatment dominated cultural discourse and supported the ecclesial language of the sin of homosexuality. Despite cultural and theological obstacles, there were two groundbreaking events. Published in 1948, the Kinsey study of male sexuality and homosexuality opened a door for understanding. Also groundbreaking for development of gay theology was Derek Sherwin Bailey's *Homosexuality and the Western Christian Tradition* in 1955.[60] Bailey, a British scholar and clergy, traced the development of homo-hatred from the biblical texts through the formation of Christian practice and theology in the early and late medieval ages. Bailey's work paved the way for the British *Wolfenden Report* (1957), leading to the legalization of homosexuality, and Bailey's work had deep influence on the nascent homophile movements and spurred the first explicit homosexual theology with Robert Wood's *Christ and the Homosexual* (1959).[61] There were several attempts at the formation of homophile churches such as the Church of One Brotherhood, but these were short-lived experiments.[62]

Protest Movements

Germinating in the 1960s was a series of cultural developments that would significantly affect the development of gay/lesbian theologies. The African American civil rights movement under Martin Luther King Jr. and other leaders gained impetus in the 1960s. This led to Black theology and the beginnings of its liberation theology. The advent of the birth control pill, women's greater independence, and the rise of the feminist movement provided the matrix for feminist liberation theology with Mary Daly and others in the 1970s. Within Catholicism, Vatican II provided a reform of the archaic structures and theologies. In the Latin American sector, Gustavo Gutierrez's *The Crucified Christ* launched liberation theology.

Theoretical and Methodological Considerations

The French cultural critic and postmodern philosopher Michel Foucault, who died of AIDS in 1984, became popular among feminists, gay/lesbian academic scholars, and gender/sex theorists. Foucault's three-volume work, *The History of Sexuality*, provided the intellectual, theoretical, and activist impulse for reflection on activists' appropriation of the term "queer," and queer became the paradigm that appropriated intellectual disruptive and transgressive potentialities of ACT UP and queer activism.[63] Queer theory became a reality in universities—especially, in departments of English literature and cultural studies. Eve Kosofsky Sedgwick, Michael Warner, David Halperin, Judith Butler, and others pioneered constructionist models of sexuality and gender; these constructionist models were very much indebted to Foucault's deconstructive methods, rendering concepts fluid and instable.[64]

Queer studies represented a paradigm or discursive shift in the way that scholars view sexual identity and gender. Queer theorists like Judith Butler comprehend gender as inscribed on the body through a performative repetition with subversive and critical potential. Butler argues for gender as taking the form of drag performance, thus rendering it as fluid. Queer theorists thus problematize gender and sexual diversities by unmasking the hegemonic social constructions of the sex/gender system:

> Queer Theory is suggesting that the study of homosexuality should not be a study of a minority—the making of the lesbian/gay/bisexual subject—but a study of those knowledges and social practices that organize "society" as a whole by sexualizing—heterosexualizing or homosexualizing—bodies, desires, acts, identities, social relations, knowledges, culture, and social institutions.[65]

Queer literary scholar Michael Warner defines "queer" as a transgressive paradigm, representing "a more resistance to the regimes of the normal."[66] In *Saint Foucault*, classicist David Halperin defines queer:

> Queer is by definition *whatever* is at odds with the normal, the legitimate, the dominant. *There is nothing in particular to which it necessarily refers* [Halperin's italics]. It is an identity without an essence. "Queer," then demarcates not a positivity but a positionality vis-à-vis the normative—a positionality that is not restricted to lesbians and gay men but is in fact available to anyone who is or feels marginalized because of her or his sexual practices.[67]

Queer theorists applied "queer" as a strategic method to deconstruct and expand the textual possibilities of cultural metanarratives—examining textual meshes, dissonances, absences, resistances, and disruptive potentialities.

The implications of queer theory for the reenvisioning of gay/lesbian Christian theologies of sexuality and gender became profound, opening single-issue analysis on sexual orientation to more complex social and cultural analyses of the sex/gender system. Gay/lesbian Christian theologies opened themselves to postmodern cultural studies and queer theory in academia and to queer activism, and the challenge of queerness became more inclusion. It questioned the dominant cultural use and political assumptions of the unity and the stability of sexual and gender identities. The previous border skirmishes of gay/lesbian theologies with Christian churches would be replaced by poststructuralist assault of queer theologies on Christianity and its theologies. It would be nothing less than storming the gates of the churches, disrupting the binary concepts of gender and sexuality on which many theological doctrines and scriptural readings were grounded.

Ongoing Issues
Marginalization of Queer Theology

There are two obstacles to queer theologies. First, gay/lesbian theologies and queer theologies tend to create anxiety in heterocentric Christian theologians, and they seldom read the works of queer theologians or review them.[68] It raises a subversive, albeit inclusive, theology that tears down the walls of ecclesial and theological exclusion. Second is the emergence of liberal gay/lesbian-affirming churches—mixed congregations sometimes affirming sanitized "gays" and "lesbians," those folks who most resemble the majority of the congregation. The inclusion of diverse LGBT would make these churches shudder in terror. These are congregations that will not easily accept queer theologies but only gay and lesbian theologies that most likely resemble their own denominational theology.

Queer theologies will continue to be cutting edge, pushing radical inclusion and reenvisioning inclusive, queer theologies. Such theologies will find a home in denominations such as the MCC congregations or pluralistic, Christian justice communities, and courses in seminaries. The Center for Lesbian and Gay Studies in Religion and Ministry at the Pacific School of Religion, Chicago Theological Seminary with its LGBT Religious Archives, and Emory University with its online bibliography of queer religious works are locations where queer theologies will prosper in the United States.[69]

Ineffectiveness for Social Transformation

Criticism, in contrast, has been leveled at queer theory for its cultural ineffectiveness in providing a discourse and praxis for social transformation. Gay anthropologist Max Kirsch writes:

> Queer theory has developed along a path that questions the basic tenets of past resistance movements while championing the right of inclusion. But despite the calls for recognition of diversity, it has done little to further a true inclusiveness that would have the ability to form communities of resistance. Again, this is primarily due to the insistence on the uniqueness of the individual and the relativity of experience. . . . But instead of focusing on the creation of a society that guarantees freedom and expression for all, it has focused on the individual as the site of change.[70]

Kirsch's criticism of queer theory is well grounded, for queer theory as a form of cultural and literary criticism has, at times, been elitist, individualist, a self-expression of desire, a "white" dilettante exercise in deconstruction, and an academic imaginative counterdiscourse. What queer theory lacks is a vision to create a movement for social change that is gender variant and sexually pluralistic from multiple social locations of race, class, ethnicity, age, and differently ablebodied. There is disjuncture (although not in all cases) between academic queer theory and the praxis of queer social change. Another weakness is queer theory's inability to generate a political discourse of challenge.

Translesbigay theologies as they engage queer theory, however, have a different trajectory than just mere academic deconstruction. Queer theology brings queer theory into dialogue with an established theological rhetoric that has focused on personal liberation and social transformation. Liberation theologies are communal praxes, intimately connected to utopian visions of equality, justice, and compassionate care; they are grounded in prophetic traditions of personal and social transformation. Queer theologies involve not only the querying of Christian texts and symbols but the queering of them as well. MCC clergy and author Thomas Bohache argues that "a queer hermeneutic . . . will not only *queer* but it will *query*: It must be a questioning and turning over of layers of heteropatriarchal tradition to reveal what lies beneath."[71] Queering represents a method of dislocation or transgression of fixed theological categories. For example, biblical scholar Halvor Moxnes uses "queer" as the best term to characterize Jesus: "To use the term 'queer' of Jesus describes the unsettling quality about him."[72] Bisexual-identified

Latina theologian Marcella Althaus-Reid envisions the indecent Jesus among the poor LGBT in Argentina. The queer Jesus is prevalent in gay, lesbian, bisexual, and transgendered Christologies and theologies.[73] Finally, lesbian theologian Carter Heyward elegantly sums up the connection of queer theology with Christian practice for justice and social change:

> The term "queer" as I am using it, let me be clear, is not simply a codeword for gay, lesbian, bisexual, transgender, and other ways of being at odds with dominant gender culture. "Queer" is not simply a reversal of a negative epithet so often hurled against GLBT folks in homophobic culture. "Queer" is not simply a synonym for being "odd," "unusual," or "out-there." Queerness is bigger than GLBT lives; queerness is more than a linguistic reversal; and queerness is way deeper than merely "odd." Queerness is public solidarity in the struggle for sexual and gender justice and of irrepressibly making connections to other struggles for justice, compassion, and reconciliation.[74]

Heyward thus places queer theologies within the Christian mission for "justice, compassion, and reconciliation." This transforms queer theory with an explicit rhetorical tradition and praxis of social transformation.

In light of recent international queer theology summits, it is critical to end this chapter with a couple of observations about the further development of queer theologies.[75] First, the future of theological studies will see greater networking and collaboration of self-identified queer theologians and biblical scholars across disciplinary, ethnic, and racial boundaries, between academic theologians and church leaders, setting up centers for archival work, mentoring a future generation of queer scholars and activists and queer clergy. Second, queer theologies will multiply and hybridize as they develop queer folks from different cultural, social, and international contexts. Third, queer theologies will continue to envision, foster, and nurture a countertheological (albeit "perverse," "indecent," or "queer") imagination that challenges churches and societies with the vision of radical inclusion. Even with this publication, several queer theologians are embarking on a venture to produce a text of queer theologies, comparable to *The Queer Bible Commentary*, as an attempt to prepare for the challenges of the next generation of queer scholars who will develop a queer *Summa Theologica* that will reenvision sexuality diversity and gender variance and thoroughly reenvision liberating theologies and praxes grounded in economic justice, compassion, peacemaking, and love.

1. In the United States, Reverend Troy Perry, thrown out of his church for being gay, founded the Metropolitan Community Church in 1968, now the largest LGBT organization in the world. The following year, the Stonewall Rebellion marked the birth of the gay/lesbian liberation movement in the United States, and it became the catalyst for the rise of a public gay/lesbian subculture.

2. Ronald Bayer, *Homosexuality and American Psychiatry: The Politics of Diagnosis* (Princeton, N.J.: Princeton University Press, 1987).

3. For a history of the Christian Right's construction of the gay and lesbian menace, see Didi Herman, *The Antigay Agenda: Orthodox Vision and the Christian Right* (Chicago: University of Chicago Press, 1997), 25–136. For a somewhat insider, now outsider, perspective, see Mel White, *Religion Gone Bad: The Hidden Dangers of the Christian Right* (New York: Penguin, 2006).

4. Robert [Shore-]Goss, *Jesus ACTED UP: A Gay and Lesbian Manifesto* (San Francisco: HarperSanFrancisco, 1993), 51.

5. Robert [Shore-]Goss, "From Gay Theologies to Queer Sexual Theologies," in *Queering Christ: Beyond Jesus ACTED UP* (Cleveland: Pilgrim, 2002), 239–258; Daniel T. Spencer, "Lesbian and Gay Theologies," in *Handbook of U.S. Theologies of Liberation*, ed. Miguel A. De La Torre (St. Louis, MO: Chalice, 2004), 264–273; and Elizabeth Stuart, *Gay and Lesbian Theologies: Repetition with a Critical Difference* (Surrey, U.K.: Ashgate, 2003).

6. For example: (Argentina) Marcella Althaus-Reid, *Indecent Theology: Theological Perversions in Sex, Gender, and Politics* (New York: Routledge, 2001); (Argentina) Althaus-Reid, *The Queer God* (New York: Routledge, 2003); (Brazil) Andre Muskopf, *Uma brecha no armário: Propostas para uma teologia gay* (São Paulo: CEBI [Center for Biblical Studies], 2005), available at http://www.cebi.org.br/pub_detalhes.php?produto_cod=317http://www.cebi.org.br; (Brazil) Talar Rosa, *Homossexuais e o Ministérico na Igreja São Leopoldo* (Rio Grande do Sul: Oikos, 2005), available at http://www.oikoseditora.com.br/precos.html - # 26; (United Kingdom) Elizabeth Stuart, *Just Good Friends: Towards a Theology of Lesbian and Gay Relationships* (London: Mowbray, 1995); and (Australia) Michael Carden, *Sodomy: A History of Christian Biblical Myth* (London, Equinox, 2005).

7. Handout from Mark D. Jordan: "Consultation on Theology and the Homosexual," prepared August 22–24, 1966, at the Queer Theology Summit, Emory University, February 23–24, 2007, available at http://web.library.emory.edu/r_guides/studies/LGBT/Queer Religion.html.

8. Ibid.

9. Sally Gearhart and William R. Johnson, eds., *Loving Women/Loving Men: Gay Liberation and the Church* (San Francisco: Glide, 1974).

10. John J. McNeill, *The Church and the Homosexual* (Kansas City: Sheed, Andrews, and McMeel, 1976).

11. Tom Horner, *Jonathan Loved David: Homosexuality in Biblical Times* (Philadelphia: Westminster, 1978); Virginia Mollenkott and Letha Scanzoni, *Is the Homosexual My Neighbor?* (San Francisco: Harper and Row, 1978).

12. John Boswell, *Christianity, Homosexuality, and Social Tolerance* (Chicago: University of Chicago Press, 1980). On Boswell's thesis and reclamation of gay voices in history, see

Matthew Kuefler, ed., *The Boswell Thesis: Essays on Christianity, Homosexuality and Social Tolerance* (Chicago: University of Chicago Press, 2006).

13. For an assessment of Boswell's evangelical mission, see Mark D. Jordan, "'Both as a Christian and as a Historian': On Boswell's Ministry," in *The Boswell Thesis: Essays on Christianity, Homosexuality and Social Tolerance*, ed. Matthew Kuefler (Chicago: University of Chicago Press, 2006), 88–107.

14. Some of the harshest gay critics published work to undermine Boswell's thesis; their work arises from institutional Christianity's hostility to homosexuality. For example, Warren Johansson, Wayne R. Dynes, and John Lauritsen, *Homosexuality, Intolerance, and Christianity: A Critical Examination of Boswell's Work*, available at http://www.galha.org/ptt/lib/hic/index.html.

15. Bernard Schlager, "Reading *CSTH* as a Call to Action: Boswell and Gay Affirming Movements in American Christianity," in *The Boswell Thesis: Essays on Christianity, Homosexuality and Social Tolerance*, ed. Matthew Kuefler (Chicago: University of Chicago Press, 2006), 74–87.

16. Maury Johnson, *Gays under Grace* (Nashville, TN: Winston-Derek, 1983); Chris Glaser, *Come Home* (San Francisco: Harper and Row, 1990); John McNeill, *Taking a Chance on God* (Boston: Beacon, 1988); and John Fortunato, *Embracing the Exile* (San Francisco: Harper and Row, 1982).

17. Bernadette Brooten, *Love between Women: Female Homoeroticism in Early Christianity* (Chicago: University of Chicago Press, 1996).

18. For example, Robert Nugent, ed., *A Challenge to Love: Gay and Lesbian Catholics in the Church* (New York: Crossroad, 1984); and Jeannine Grammick and Pat Furey, eds., *The Vatican and Homosexuality* (New York: Crossroad, 1988).

19. For understanding Roman Catholic rhetorical statements on homosexuality and its closeted priesthood and hierarchy, see Mark D. Jordan, *The Silence of Sodom: Homosexuality in Modern Catholicism* (Chicago: University of Chicago Press, 2000), 31–40. Jordan has understood the doublespeak of institutional Catholicism on the issue of homosexuality in Jordan, *Telling the Truth in Church: Scandal, Flesh, and Christian Speech* (Boston: Beacon, 2004). These two books are derived from his earlier project: *The Invention of Sodom* (Chicago: University of Chicago Press, 1997). See also Donald Boisvert and Robert E. [Shore-] Goss, eds., *Gay Catholic Clergy and Clerical Sexual Misconduct* (New York: Haworth, 2005).

20. Quoted in John R. McNeill, *The Church and the Homosexual* (Boston: Beacon, 1993), 241.

21. John R. McNeill, *Freedom, Glorious Freedom* (Boston: Beacon, 1995); and McNeill, *Both Feet Firmly Planted in Midair* (Louisville, KY: Westminster John Knox, 1998).

22. Carter Heyward, *Our Passion for Justice* (New York: Pilgrim, 1988); and Heyward, *Touching Our Strength: The Erotic as Power and the Love of God* (San Francisco: Harper and Row, 1989).

23. Heyward, *Touching Our Strength*, 34.

24. For gay theologies, see J. Michael Clark, *A Defiant Celebration: Theological Ethics and Gay Sexuality* (Garland, TX: Tangelwild, 1990); Daniel T. Spencer, *God and Gaia: Ethics, Ecology, and the Erotic* (Cleveland: Pilgrim, 1996); Gary David Comstock, *Gay Theology without Apology* (Cleveland: Pilgrim, 1993); and Marvin Ellison, *Erotic Justice* (Louisville, KY: Westminster John Knox, 1996). For lesbian theologies, see Mary Hunt, *Fierce Tender-*

ness: A Feminist Theology of Friendship (New York: Crossroad, 1991); and Kathy Rudy, *Sex and the Church* (Boston: Beacon, 1997). For queer theologies, see Robert Williams, *Just as I Am: A Practical Guide to Being Out, Proud, and Christian* (Crown, 1992); and Robert [Shore-]Goss, *Jesus ACTED UP: A Gay and Lesbian Manifesto* (San Francisco: HarperSan-Francisco, 1993).

25. J. Michael Clark, *Beyond Our Ghettoes: Gay Theology in an Ecological Perspective* (Cleveland: Pilgrim, 1993); Comstock, *Gay Theology without Apology*; [Shore-]Goss, *Jesus ACTED UP*.

26. [Shore-]Goss, *Jesus ACTED UP*, xix, 38–40.

27. Robert E. [Shore-]Goss, *Queering Christ: Beyond Jesus ACTED UP* (Cleveland: Pilgrim, 2002), 250.

28. David Halperin surveyed ACT UP activists on what book they carried with them. The number one answer was Michel Foucault's *The History of Sexuality: An Introduction* (New York: Vintage, 1990), vol. 1. David M. Halperin, *Saint Foucault: Towards a Gay Hagiography* (New York: Oxford University Press, 1995), 16. This illustrates what I experienced firsthand at the conference on the politics of pleasure, held at Harvard University, November 1990. There ACT UPers, queer street activists, and LGBT academics all quoted Foucault. No author at the time captured the queer imaginations of such diverse LGBT folks.

29. Elizabeth Stuart, *Gay and Lesbian Theologies: Repetitions with Critical Differences* (Burlington, VT: Ashgate), 86.

30. Nancy Wilson, *Our Tribe: Queer Folks, God, Jesus, and the Bible* (New York: HarperCollins, 1995); Rudy, *Sex and the Church*; Ibrahim (Elias) Farajaje-Jones, "Breaking Silence: Towards an In-the-Life Theology," in *Black Theology*, ed. James H. Cone and Gayraud S. Wilmore (Maryknoll, NY: Orbis, 1993), 2:139–159; Mark Jordan, *The Silence of Sodom* (Chicago: University of Chicago Press, 2000); Justin Tanis, *Trans-Gendered Theology, Ministry and Communities of Faith* (Cleveland: Pilgrim, 2003); Lisa Isherwood, *Liberating Christ: Exploring the Christologies of Contemporary Movements* (Cleveland: Pilgrim, 1999); Elizabeth Stuart, *Religion Is a Queer Thing* (Cleveland: Pilgrim, 1997); and Marcella Althaus-Reid, *The Queer God* (New York: Routledge, 2003).

31. James B. Nelson, *Embodiment: An Approach to Sexuality and Christian Theology* (Minneapolis: Fortress, 1979); Nelson, *The Intimate Garden: Male Sexuality, Masculine Spirituality* (Philadelphia: Fortress, 1988); and Nelson *Body Theology* (Louisville, KY: Westminster John Knox, 1992).

32. Jeremy Carette, "Beyond Theology and Sexuality: Foucault, the Self, and Que(e) rying of Monotheistic Truth," in *Michel Foucault and Theology: The Politics of Religious Experience*, ed. James Bernauer and Jeremy Carette (Burlington, VT: Ashgate, 2004), 225, 228.

33. Jonathan Dollimore, *Sexual Dissidence* (Oxford: Clarendon, 1991), 323–324.

34. John Boswell, *Same-Sex Unions in Premodern Europe* (New York: Vintage, 1995), 191.

35. Alan Bray, *The Friend* (Chicago: University of Chicago Press, 2003). See also Bray, "Friendship, the Family, and Liturgy: A Rite for Blessing Friendship in Traditional Christianity," *Theology and Sexuality* 13 (2000): 15–33.

36. Williams, *Just as I Am*, 206–216. See also Williams, "Toward a Theology for Gay and Lesbian Marriage," in *Christian Perspective on Sexuality and Gender*, ed. Adrian Thatcher and Elizabeth Stuart (Grand Rapids, MI: Eerdmans, 1996), 279–300.

37. [Shore-]Goss, *Jesus ACTED UP,* 136–138.

38. [Shore-]Goss, *Queering Christ,* 113–139.

39. Robert [Shore-]Goss and Amy Adams Squires Strongheart, eds., *Our Families, Our Values: Snapshots of Queer Kinship* (New York: Haworth, 1997).

40. Mary Hunt, "Variety Is the Spice of Life: Doing It Our Ways," in *Our Families, Our Values: Snapshots of Queer Kinship,* ed. Robert [Shore-]Goss and Amy Adams Squires Strongheart (New York: Haworth, 1997), 97–106.

41. Marvin Ellison, *Same-Sex Marriage? A Christian Ethical Analysis* (Cleveland: Pilgrim, 2004), 166.

42. Mark D. Jordan, *Blessing Same-Sex Unions: The Perils of Queer Romance and the Confusions of Christian Marriage* (Chicago: University Chicago Press, 2005), 100–110. He bases some of his work on earlier insights in Jordan, *The Ethics of Sex* (Malden, MA: Blackwell, 2002).

43. Jordan, *Blessing Same-Sex Unions,* 165.

44. Ibid, 166.

45. Robert [Shore-]Goss, "Proleptic Sexual Love: God's Promiscuity in Christian Polyamory," *Theology and Sexuality* 11, no. 1 (2004): 52–63.

46. Victoria Kolakowski, "Toward a Christian Ethical Response to Transsexual Persons," *Theology and Sexuality* 6 (1997): 10–31; and Tanis, *Trans-Gendered Theology.*

47. Tanis, *Trans-Gendered Theology,* 166.

48. Virginia Ramey Mollenkott, *Omnigender: A Trans-Religious Approach* (Cleveland: Pilgrim, 2001).

49. Vanessa S. (Sheridan), *Cross Purposes: On Being Christian and Crossgendered,* (Decatur, IL: Sullivan, 1996); and Sheridan, *Crossing Over: Liberating the Transgendered Christian* (Cleveland: Pilgrim, 2003).

50. Virginia Mollenkott and Vanessa Sheridan, *Transgender Journeys* (Cleveland: Pilgrim, 2003); Leann McCall Tigert and Maren C. Tribassi, *Transgendering Faith: Identity, Sexuality, and Spirituality* (Cleveland: Pilgrim, 2004); and Pat Conover, *Transgender Good News* (Silver Spring, MD: New Wineskins, 2002). Bisexual theology is at its very beginnings; for example, Debra R. Kolodny, *Blessed BiSpirit* (New York: Continuum, 2000). From Argentina, Marcella Althaus-Reid writes as a bisexual theologian.

51. Gay/lesbian liturgical practice in same-sex unions frequently used the scriptural texts of Ruth 1:16–17, 1 Samuel 18:3, and 2 Samuel 1:26. See Elizabeth Stuart, *Daring to Speak Love's Name* (London: Hamish, Hamilton, 1992), 54, and Kittredge Cherry and Zalmon Sherwood, eds., *Equal Rites* (Louisville, KY: Westminster John Knox, 1995), 100.

52. McNeill, *Freedom, Glorious Freedom,* 132.

53. Wilson, *Our Tribe,* 112, 120–131.

54. Comstock, *Gay Theology without Apology,* 11.

55. Stephen D. Moore, *God's Beauty Parlor: And Other Queer Spaces in and around the Bible* (Stanford, CA: Stanford University Press, 2001), 209.

56. Mona West and Robert E. [Shore-]Goss, Introduction to *Take Back the Word: A Queer Reading of the Bible,* ed. Mona West and Robert E. [Shore-]Goss (Cleveland: Pilgrim, 2000), 4.

57. Mary Ann Tolbert, Foreword to *Take Back the Word: A Queer Reading of the Bible,* ed. Mona West and Robert E. [Shore-]Goss (Cleveland: Pilgrim, 2000), x.

58. Ken Stone, ed., *Queer Commentary and the Hebrew Bible* (Cleveland: Pilgrim, 2001); and Thomas Bohache, Deryn Guest, Robert [Shore-]Goss, and Mona Wests, eds., *The Queer Bible Commentary* (London: SCM, 2006). See also Ken Stone, *Practicing Safer Texts: Food and Sex, and Bible in Queer Perspective* (New York: T and T Clark, 2005); Tom Hanks, *The Subversive Gospel* (Cleveland: Pilgrim, 2000); and Deryn Guest, *When Deborah Met Jael* (London: SCM, 2005).

59. Andrew Yip, "The Gay Guide to God's Word" (A Review of *The Queer Bible Commentary*), *London Times*, April 6, 2007, available at http://www.timeshighereducation. co.uk/story.asp?storycode=208541&sectioncode=40.

60. Derek Sherwin Bailey, *Homosexuality and the Western Christian Tradition* (New York: Longmanns Green, 1955).

61. *The Report of the Departmental Committee on Homosexual Offenses and Prostitution* ("Wolfenden Report") (London: Her Majesty's Stationary Office, 1957); and Robert Wood, *Christ and the Homosexual* (New York: Vantage, 1959).

62. Mark D. Jordan, "Theater of the Soul," paper delivered at the Queering the Church Conference at the Boston University School of Theology, April 19, 2007. It will be forthcoming in a volume on Queering the Church to be published by SCM.

63. Foucault, *History of Sexuality*; and [Shore-]Goss, *Jesus ACTED UP*, 181–190.

64. Here are some classics: Eve Kosofsky Sedgwick, *Epistemology of the Closet* (Berkeley: University of California Press, 1990); Sedgwick, *Tendencies* (Durham, NC: Duke University Press, 1993); Michael Warner, *Fear of a Queer Planet: Queer Politics and Social Theory* (Minneapolis: University of Minnesota Press, 1993); Warner, *The Trouble with Normal: Sex, Politics, and Ethics of Queer Life* (New York: Free Press, 1999); David Halperin, *One Hundred Years of Homosexuality* (New York: Routledge, 1990); Halperin, *Saint Foucault*; Judith Butler, *Gender Trouble: Feminism and the Subversion of Identity* (New York: Routledge, 1990); and Butler, *Bodies Matter: On the Discursive Limits of Sex* (New York: Routledge, 1993). For surveys of queer theory, see Annamarie Jagose, *Queer Theory: An Introduction* (New York: New York University Press, 1996); William Turner, *A Genealogy of Queer Theory* (Philadelphia: Temple University Press, 2000); and Donald Hall, *Queer Theories* (New York: Palgrave Macmillan, 2003).

65. Steve Seideman, ed., Introduction to *Queer Theory/Sociology* (Oxford: Blackwell, 1996), 13.

66. Warner, introduction to *Fear of a Queer Planet*, xxvi.

67. Halperin, *Saint Foucault*, 62.

68. Bjorn Krondorfer presents clusters of anxieties in heterosexual theologians over queer works: indifference, boundary violations, the gay-of religion, autobiographical insertions, and erotic confessions. Bjorn Krondorfer, "Who's Afraid of Gay Theology?" *Theology and Sexuality* 13, no. 3 (2007): 257–274. In *Sexual Diversity and Catholicism,* all the contributors, except for Mary Hunt, never mention former Jesuit John McNeill. Patricia Beattie Jung and Joseph Andrew Corey, eds., *Sexuality Diversity and Catholicism: Towards the Development of Moral Theology* (Collegeville, MN: Liturgical, 2001).

69. Center for Lesbian and Gay Studies in Religion and Ministry, Pacific School of Religion, available at http://www.clgs.org/; LGBT Religious Archive Network at Chicago Theological Seminary, available at http://www.lgbtran.org/; and Emory University, available at http://web.library.emory.edu/r_guides/studies/LGBT/Queer Religion.html.

70. Max H. Kirsch, *Queer Theory and Social Change* (New York: Routledge, 2000), 131.

71. Thomas Bohache, "Embodiment as Incarnation: An Incipient Queer Christology," *Theology and Sexuality* 10 (2003): 25.

72. Halvor Moxnes, *Putting Jesus in His Place: A Radical Vision of Household and Kingdom* (Louisville, KY: Westminster John Knox, 2003), 6.

73. [Shore-Goss], *Jesus ACTED UP*, 61–86; [Shore-]Goss, *Queering Christ*, 170–184; and Althaus-Reid, *Indecent Theology*, 94–124.

74. Carter Heyward, available at http://www.episdivschool.edu/worship/Sermon%20 CH%202%2019%2004.htm.

75. The Queer Theologians Summit at Emory University on February 22–24 was cosponsored by Mark D. Jordan at Emory, the Human Rights Campaign, and the Center for Lesbian and Gay Studies in Religion and Ministry at the Pacific School of Religion.

FURTHER STUDY

Althaus-Reid, Marcella. *Indecent Theology: Theological Perversions in Sex, Gender, and Politics*. New York, Routledge, 2001.

———. *The Queer God*. New York, Routledge, 2003.

Boswell, John. *Christianity, Homosexuality, and Social Tolerance*. Chicago: University of Chicago Press, 1980.

Brooten, Bernadette. *Love between Women: Female Homoeroticism in Early Christianity*. Chicago: University of Chicago Press, 1996.

Clark, J. Michael. *Beyond Our Ghettoes: Gay Theology in an Ecological Perspective*. Cleveland: Pilgrim, 1993.

Comstock, Gary David. *Gay Theology without Apology*. Cleveland: Pilgrim, 1993.

Gearhart, Sally, and William R. Johnson, eds. *Loving Women/Loving Men: Gay Liberation and the Church*. San Francisco: Glide, 1974.

Goss. See Shore-Goss.

Grammick, Jeannine, and Pat Furey, eds. *The Vatican and Homosexuality*. New York, Crossroad, 1988.

Heyward, Carter. *Our Passion for Justice*. New York: Pilgrim, 1988.

———. *Touching Our Strength: The Erotic as Power and the Love of God*. San Francisco: Harper and Row, 1989.

Horner, Tom. *Jonathan Loved David: Homosexuality in Biblical Times*. Philadelphia: Westminster, 1978.

Hunt, Mary. *Fierce Tenderness: A Feminist Theology of Friendship*. New York, Crossroad, 1991.

Jordan, Mark D. *The Silence of Sodom: Homosexuality in Modern Catholicism*. Chicago: University of Chicago Press, 2000.

———. *Telling the Truth in Church: Scandal, Flesh, and Christian Speech*. Boston: Beacon, 2004.

McNeill, John R. *The Church and the Homosexual*. Boston: Beacon, 1993.

Mollenkott, Virginia, and Vanessa Sheridan, *Transgender Journeys*. Cleveland: Pilgrim, 2003.

Rudy, Kathy. *Sex and the Church*. Boston: Beacon, 1997.

[Shore-]Goss, Robert. *Jesus ACTED UP: A Gay and Lesbian Manifesto*. San Francisco: HarperSanFrancisco, 1993.

Stuart, Elizabeth. *Gay and Lesbian Theologies: Repetition with a Critical Difference*. London: Ashgate, 2003.

———. *Just Good Friends: Towards a Theology of Lesbian and Gay Relationships*. London: Mowbray, 1995.

———. *Religion Is a Queer Thing*. Cleveland: Pilgrim, 1997.

West, Mona, and Robert E. [Shore-]Goss, eds. *Take Back the Word: A Queer Reading of the Bible*. Cleveland: Pilgrim, 2000.

10

Feminist Theology

MARY MCCLINTOCK FULKERSON

Historical Backdrop

It was not until 1913 that "feminism" became a frequently used term in the United States. Originating in a French activist group in the 1880s, the label "feminist" migrated to the Americas through Britain. Until then, the activism of North American women had been identified as the "woman movement." Frequently associated with 19th-century organizing for women's suffrage, the "woman movement" included a host of other forms of activism, such as the public challenges of the 1848 Seneca Falls Declaration of Sentiments, which demanded access to all vocations for women and equity in politics and religion.[1] With the term "feminist" in the 1920s, a new set of convictions emerged. Those called "feminists" continued to combine convictions about equal treatment with men with commitments to the special gifts of women. However, once these were linked with pushes for women's sexual pleasure and freedom, the term "feminist" became a marker of a more radical agenda and named a much narrower population in the early decades of the 20th century.[2]

The 1960s saw an explosion of concern for women's public agency, antidiscrimination in hiring laws, the wider rights of equal access, protection from sexual exploitation, and the problematic legacies of "separate spheres,"[3] and the "feminist" label gained a larger referent group and public audience. Along with the legacy of the 19th-century woman movement, 20th-century influences ranged from the varieties of feminist activism in the 1920s, repercussions of white women's access to the paid work force in World War II, and the so-called sexual freedom of the 1960s, to the civil rights and antiwar movements of those decades. The convergence of these energies helped spawn what has come to be called the "second wave" feminist movement of the 1960s and 1970s. Betty Freidan's famous *Feminine Mystique* of 1963 is considered a founding text of the movement. In that same year, the Presidential Commission on the Status of Women chaired by Eleanor Roosevelt signaled groundbreaking public acknowledgment of women's problems.[4] Along with these and other secular forces in the advancement of "women's liberation," as it was sometimes called, there were important religious influences. Listed in a chronology of events constituting the women's liberation movement, for example, is the 1974 illegal ordination of eleven women as Episcopal priests.[5]

While the second wave is not typically narrated in relation to religion, the symbolic resources that fueled its activism and the hope for change inevitably had roots in faith traditions, as well as liberal democratic discourse. Religion had certainly been crucial to 19th-century activism. Historian Nancy Cott points out that, despite its restrictive gender conventions, Protestantism was an important force in the expansion of women's sense of their "moral and social role" in the movement as women "apprehended Protestant teachings at a different angle from that intended by most ministers."[6] Women had long contested the patriarchal traditions within the Bible. Some even studied the original languages of scripture in order to correct some of the anti-woman interpretations.[7] Convinced that Christianity had better things to offer than biblical prohibitions on women's agency, Elizabeth Cady Stanton brought together a group of scholars to produce The Women's Bible (1895), a monumental scholarly commentary on the passages in Christian scripture that denigrated women. More widespread sources of support from religion surfaced in the 20th century. The consciousness of many women, black and white, was significantly expanded by the civil rights movement, which was grounded in religious vision.[8] Historian James J. Farrell tells of the religious convictions that shaped what he calls the "political personalism" that dominated the 1960s movements for change. An activism based on convictions of the value of all human beings, not all of political personalism was religious, but a significant part of it was generated by respect for God-sourced dignity thought to be owed all human beings.[9] While it is difficult to say with precision which of these social forces in the wider culture directly affected the emergence of feminist theology, the religious imagination did matter for feminism. A different kind of challenge, however, emerges with the naming of significant agents in the movement.

The narrative of second wave feminist activities has typically been told as a story of white women's activism, with occasional invocations of African Americans such as Michelle Wallace, Audre Lorde, or Shirley Chisholm.[10] This primarily white women-defined liberation movement took place through women's consciousness-raising groups, public protests, the work of National Organization of Women (NOW) for broader legislation assuring women of equal protection by the law, and the creation of radical feminist separatist women's cultures. While new research goes on, it must be said that the story of this chapter in feminist history has not yet been completely retold in light of the work for change that was occurring in various communities of women of color.[11] Sometimes this "whiteness" is due to the explicit racism and classism of competing agendas. Collaborations of abolitionist white women with African Americans in the 19th century, for example, typically broke apart when the white women saw their class and racial privileges threatened by the needs of the African American communities.[12]

At another level, the whiteness of historical narratives has to do with lack of access and is the effect of such marginalizations. Grassroots (that is, "on-the-ground") activism is not directly correlated to access to public recognition. There were and always have been women of faith of every class, ethnicity, and race who have lived out values consonant with those of "feminism"—for the well-being of women, for example.[13] They did not always have the respect of the public eye, however, nor did they have access to knowledge-producing institutions. As one book puts it, much of the activism of those the dominant group designates as "Other"—particularly women "living in poverty, immigrant women, and women of color"—will be invisible, their accomplishments akin to *A Tradition That Has No Name.*[14]

Description

In an effort to name the activism and wisdom of countless women of faith over the ages, feminist theology emerged as scholarship that deems the use of religious and cultural traditions to enhance women's flourishing and to contest those traditions that diminish their status. This is to acknowledge that the category "feminist theology" has been primarily identified with the literature on women's issues and religions produced within the official publishing world of the North American community of scholars. As the historical backdrop has indicated, in its more narrow sense the scholarship about women's activism and wisdom has been associated primarily with Western white women in the United States. Thus, the so-called founding feminist theologies associated with second wave feminism are dominated by white women—those who have had the privilege of higher education.

And while this limitation has to do with both the incapacity of a dominant group to "see" those who are outside of their group and with the question of access to production of accounts of women's accomplishments, the racial and class marking of feminist theology has had constructive outcomes as well.[15] The "whiteness" of feminist theology has to do with the important development of alternatively named theologies, such as womanist, Latina, mujerista, and Asian American, by women "of color."[16] Although it has not always acknowledged this, feminist theology is a "marked" literature; it is about the discernments and insights of particular communities and traditions of interpretation. As such, feminist theology is a rich and vital contribution to theology; it does not and cannot claim to speak for all women, however. Given this portrait's primary focus on the relation of feminism to Christianity, it should be said that the literature by feminists of other major religious traditions has been crucial to the conversation, including such founding Jewish feminists as Judith Plaskow and Naomi Goldenberg and (more recently) Miriam Peskowitz. The work of Islamic feminist thinkers such as Leila Ahmed, Fatima Mernissi, and Saba Mahmood is becoming increasingly fundamental to a global feminism.

What contemporary feminist theology does offer is a wealth of critical, constructive, and located imagination for rethinking dominant Christian theological and other religious discourses. Two founding 20th-century feminist authors illustrate this point. Valerie Saiving, a graduate student at the University of Chicago, and Mary Daly, a Roman Catholic philosophical theologian who taught at Boston College, generated new levels of feminist theological criticism. Saiving's now classic essay, "The Human Situation: A Feminine View" (1960) made two crucial points.[17] First, the essay basically amounts to an argument that experience matters when constructing theology: Saiving insisted that male experience skewed theological constructs, but theology required attention to *women's* experience as well. Second, she showed the significance of this claim in her analysis of concepts of sin and love in the theologies of Reinhold Niebuhr and Anders Nygren. Pride was a sin more fitting for males, she argued. In contrast to self-aggrandizement, women's sin is more likely to be loss of or lack of self. Given this difference, the selflessness of agape-love commended by Nygren, she continued, would not address women's sin but only further diminish them.[18] Despite later judgments that her accounts of male and female experience were inadequate, Saiving's category criticism was fundamental to the generative character of feminist theology.

Another pivotal feminist theologian was Mary Daly. Daly's first book, *The Church and the Second Sex* (1968), critiqued the patriarchal structures and practices of the church, holding out the possibility for women's liberation within Christianity. In contrast, *Beyond God the Father* (1973), her second book, read the basic doctrines of Christianity as patriarchal to the core. A consummately artful book, sometimes seen as a parody, this Daly text argued that such doctrines as the Trinity, dominated by male symbols for God, basically reproduced the hierarchical sexism of patriarchy. Simply put, "if God is male, then male is God." Daly's uniquely creative skill with language carried such insights as Saiving's (that theological concepts are marked by the worldview of their authors) to a new level of analysis as she disclosed the gendered character of classic doctrines. Given the traditional blaming of Eve for the fall, feminist theology must "exorcise evil from Eve" and thereby "fall into freedom," as her chapter on sin put it.[19] Daly's work also moved beyond Christianity to develop new gynocentric language worlds that honor and celebrate women.

Saiving's and Daly's were not the only feminist theological writings of that first decade of the 1960s, but they helped fuel a broader feminist consciousness that, combined with the equal rights discourse of the time, shaped women's activism in faith communities. Much of that activism was directed at the exclusionary practices of Christian churches. As mentioned earlier, eleven women defied Episcopal Church law at the height of second wave feminism and were ordained in 1974. This "irregular" ordination helped inspire a 1975 gathering of the Roman Catholic Women's Ordination Conference (WOC). The conference was wildly successful, and WOC developed as a permanent organization, widening its projects and linking with the world organization Roman Catholic Women that performs what are, in the Roman Catholic Church, illegal ordinations of women. The formation of "women-church" communities of spirituality and worship, was another outgrowth of this activism, a theological practice made famous by the writings of feminist theologian, Rosemary Radford Ruether.[20] Worship in traditional churches became a focus as well, with the demand for inclusive language and the production of feminist liturgies.[21]

Feminist theology as activism and academic discourse alike was and continues to be about resisting existent patriarchal hierarchies. In the time since these founding writings and organizations, feminist theology has continued to develop more complex approaches to naming the problems and forms of resistance and transformation. Race, class, ethnicity, and sexual orientation have become key to its reading of gender and proliferation of constructive visions. Recognition of the forces of globalization and its precursors in the forms of Western colonialism and imperialism is increasingly affecting the feminist theological conversation as well. As unfinished as it is, this brief gesture at a history of feminist theology makes an important point. The story of feminist theology is not an account of all historical agency for women's flourishing. Just as it called into question the primarily male-dominated categories for defining which agency matters, its emergence as a challenge to the reigning discourse is a continual reminder that the very categories defining theology, history, biblical, and other areas of study will always need rethinking.[22]

Sources

Women's experience with sexism has served as the primary source from which feminist theologians have drawn the perimeters of their discourse. Feminist theology in the United States assumes that sexism—the view that women are inferior to men—is a problem demanding redress by religious as well as secular traditions and practices. Women are and have been excluded and rendered second-class citizens throughout the history of the nation and the church. Feminist theology also assumes that naming women, making them visible, is key to imagining a world without sexism; it draws on a wide range of resources to counter the effects of sexism and its collaborative oppressive social structures. Not all feminist theologians agree with Mary Daly that Christianity *is* incurably patriarchal. More than one account of the problem and its resolution have developed, for central to the creativity of feminist theologies are the many ways that the Christian faith can be appropriated to address the sin of sexism.

At the opposite end of the spectrum from a Daly critique comes a feminist theological approach called "evangelical" or "biblical" feminism. While not the only kind of feminist theology that appropriates the Christian Bible, evangelical feminism is distinctive for its insistence that all Christian practice and thinking, feminist or otherwise, be authorized by scripture. Historically, many U.S. denominations were "evangelical," in the sense of participating in revivalism and focusing on personal piety.[23] Evangelical feminism, however, emerged from the modern evangelical movement of the 1950s and 1960s. This form of evangelical is made up of mostly nondenominational groups that insist on the "literal" meaning of scripture. For such groups, contemporary culture and modern knowledge such as psychology or social analysis, if allowed at all, cannot be determinative, in the final analysis, for women's struggle for equality. Thus tied to the biblical text, the creativity of evangelical feminism is found in its exploration of the many possibilities that text offers for rejecting sexism and affirming women.

Evangelical feminists are convinced that the Bible, *properly interpreted*, supports the equality of men and women. Such thinkers as Virginia Mollenkott, Letha Scanzoni, and Patricia Gundry have been prolific students of the ancient languages and the vast complexities of the biblical text. One of the

creative contributions of the biblical focus has been recovery of biblical feminine images of God and, more generally, stories of women in scripture.[24] The
most explicitly evangelical feminist task, however, is the work to "redeem"
antiwomen texts.[25] To defend the Pauline writings and the pastoral epistles,
evangelical feminists have spilled much ink on producing accurate translations and discovering the original contexts of the "prohibition" passages and
the real meaning of such terms as "kephale" in Ephesians 5 (is the husband
the "head," as in, the *ruler* of the wife?).

While they share the same primary focus—the biblical text—these evangelical feminists have different methodological assumptions. The more conservative scholars refused to acknowledge the full humanity of the texts,
including the possibility that Paul and other authors were fallible and in
error. More "liberal" evangelical feminists such as Scanzoni and Mollenkott
assume that the basic message of scripture is love and justice but that some
of scripture is culturally conditioned; thus biblical themes such as Galatians
3:28 and Jesus' treatment of women have more authority for the church than
the prohibitions. Furthermore, they argue that the latter were addressed
only to a particular cultural situation and do not have continued claim on
the contemporary church. Current options include both egalitarian notions
of women's leadership and complementarian, where leadership is defined by
the "gifts" peculiar to maleness and femaleness.[26]

Another theological map for sexism is found in the work of such feminist
theologians as Rosemary Radford Ruether, Sallie McFague, Letty Russell, and
Elizabeth Schussler Fiorenza, among others. In distinction from evangelical
biblical feminists, the trajectory shared by these thinkers is social liberationist; women's problems are not simply exclusion but the social, political, and
economic structures of power that define and constrain human life. This map
assumes not only that the biblical and other normative traditional texts are
human and fallible, marked by the cultural worldviews of the ancient times,
but also that, like any other human product, sacred texts bear the imprint
of the power-laden, self-interests of the dominant populations that produce
them. And as men are the dominant populations in much of church history, the normative texts and decisions of the church are inflected with male
biases. Scripture and doctrine alike are shaped by "patriarchy," social structures defined by male dominance.

In contrast to evangelical feminism, this approach is more complex than
a permission project focused on getting the Bible to say that women are
equal in worth to men. What is basically a liberation model of feminist theology sees the problem as the power structures of a society—for example, its

cultural views and its economic and political arrangements—and, thus, as requiring radical social change. Liberation feminist theology demands that scholarship attend to social constructions of masculinity and femininity—gender—in the history of church and society and their effects.[27] Its theological mapping thus requires that women's experience have traction in theological judgments and the use of a much broader set of resources, such as tools for social analysis, and its goal is to advance practices that liberate women (and men) in the church and the wider society.

The creative trajectories of a liberation model of feminist theology range considerably, and early on, most of its adherents acknowledged other marginalizing social forces of oppression in addition to patriarchy. Ruether appropriated the prophetic, justice-oriented traditions of scripture, as she famously called into question the adequacy of male language for God and a male savior for women, charting the role of Jesus' masculinity in denying women full agency in Christianity. Russell also wrote on the justice patterns of Christian community that transcend the flaws of authoritative texts and constructed liberative visions from traditional feminine images of "good housekeeping," such as tables of hospitality, a "household of freedom," and "partnerships."[28] McFague offers radical reimagining of the way in which theology thinks of God in relation to the world, a reimagining that counters sexist constructions of women's sexualized bodies. Her work on rethinking the gendered language for God—God as Mother, Lover, and Friend—is powerfully extended through the proposal that the world is God's body.[29] Such concern with the feminist critiques of mind-body dualism and the anthropocentrism of much Christian theology contributed to the emergence of ecological feminism by feminist ethicists and theologians.[30] While the founding liberation feminist theologians made gender central and did not explore their own markers of whiteness and privilege, most invoked the oppressive power of racism and classism, as well as heterosexism. Elizabeth Schussler Fiorenza proposed the category of "kyriarchy" to replace patriarchy in order to indicate the multiple intersections of oppressive power structures.[31]

Another trajectory of feminist theological thinking opens up the conversation outside of Christianity and by definition has an open-ended range of sources. Found in a variety of forms, this feminist thinking remains "religious" but refuses to be bound by the doctrinal or biblical traditions of Christianity, Judaism, or any existent religious tradition.[32] Recovering and displaying the divine feminine is as serious a search—or sometimes more so, given the constraints of established denominational traditions—for feminist spirituality as it is for explicitly Christian feminist theologians. There is no need to think within any kind of traditional boundaries; the Trinitarian conception of God is not at issue. Constructive alternatives to the restriction of "feminist theology" to institutional religious traditions are found, for example, in the recovery of ancient practices of Goddess worship.

Indeed, this trajectory of feminist theology has taken the maleness of symbols so seriously, that, like Mary Daly, it has despaired of Christianity (or Judaism) ever breaking free of the dominance of the idealized male. Repair of this consciousness requires a variety of woman-centered spiritualities and ritual practices. As the introduction to a classic book on feminist spirituality says, "religious symbols are both models *of* divine existence and models *for* human behavior."[33] Quite powerful, the dominant symbols of our cultures, especially those of religions, shape human psychological and social realities about what is valued and how. To communicate to women that they are not subordinate, second-class citizens to (divinely authorized) men, then, symbols must be recovered and created that challenge patriarchal value systems. To communicate to women that their bodies and the processes they undergo are not carnal or dirty in the ways that much religious tradition has assumed, symbols and rituals must be created that provide alternative imaginations. Spiritualities that divinize the female are judged to be absolutely essential in this process. Goddess worship, including historical retrievals of religious rituals and symbolisms that celebrate women's bodies, have funded these spiritualities. Religions from ancient pre-Christian times, to Hindu, to Native American and African traditions have provided rich resources.[34]

Theoretical and Methodological Considerations

There is no such thing as deployment of a single model of feminist theology in lived practice. Not only does academic work fail to correlate directly with the complexities of life strategies, but also no one should try to make it so. To suggest these three models as the sources from which feminist theology has based its scholarship is not to suggest that they alone serve as the theories and methods operative within the discourse. Overlaps abound. For example, biblical study is important for liberationists and evangelical feminists alike. A liberationist love affair with ideological criticism can surface new and life-giving ways to hear the stories of women in scripture. So any one account of the problem or its resolution inevitably borrows from other accounts. These "models" are useful because they suggest various accounts of the problem and methodological sources drawn on by feminist theologies.

Nor do these models suggest that feminist theology is confined to the issues that birthed them. They have continued to develop. For example, new insights have been generated by the liberationist model's focus on the social construction of human identities and the role of political structures of power in the oppressive forces in human lives, as well as the liberative possibilities.[35] Recognition that gender is a social construction has been extended by queer theories in order to refute the distinction between sex and gender assumed by much liberation-type feminist theology. Feminist theologians use the work of queer theorists such as Judith Butler to challenge the heteronormativity of the notion that there are simply two kinds of sexed people, men and women, and what needs to be challenged is the social definitions of masculinity and femininity. No, says queer theory; binary sex is a social construction, as well, a construction that normalizes heterosexuality. So liberationist feminist critiques of complementary notions of gender get extended by such theologians as Marcella Althaus-Reid to critiques of "binary" sex/gender.

Another example of developments in the suggested models is found in that of woman spirituality. Its trajectory outside of Christian sources for feminist theology continues to raise important questions about the continued dominance of Christian versions of feminist theology and to challenge the notion that "theology" is identical with "Christian." The appropriation of other sources expands to include attention to philosophical accounts of natality and desire, as well as the instability of language and its connection to the unconscious such as found in the work of Lacan and French feminism.[36]

Ongoing Issues

Conceptualization

One of the most often cited sets of ongoing issues in feminist theology has to do with how to conceptualize the subject. What has become a dilemma has to do with the feminist theological appeal to "women's experience" as a basis for the charges against the dominant discourse. While it is true that theological reflection is a result of human experience, and human experience is gendered, one of the primary challenges to this claim early on was its use to falsely universalize the category of "women."[37] Just as feminist theology had challenged the claim of male-authored theology to be about all humanity, so have a number of groups challenged the first generation of feminist theologians' blindness to other social markers. As noted earlier, one of the signal critiques has been the failure of feminist theology to acknowledge race. It is not simply that some theologians leave out the question of race in their appeal to "women's experience," although that does occur. The complaint is more likely to be directed at a kind of "add-on" approach, where gender is considered the primary form of oppression to which race, class, sexual orientation, or other marginalizing markers are added. As one author puts it, to simply add race (or any other marginalizing marker) to predetermined gender oppressions ignores "that 'race' does not simply make the experience of women's subordination greater. It qualitatively changes the nature of that subordination."[38]

If an appeal to "women's experience" is a false universal of sorts, an ongoing conversation concerns how to structure the interplay of marginalizing factors so as to take seriously the distinctiveness of difference. Theorist Denise Riley argues for the destabilizing of the binary male-female: "the arrangement of people under the banners of 'men' or 'women' are enmeshed with the histories of other concepts too, including those of 'the social' and 'the body.'"[39] Such destabilizations have drawn on poststructuralist and semiotic analyses that suggest how subjects, like meanings, never have a fixed identity. The interplay of differing discourses and dispersed forms of power socially locate women in a variety of ways, offering a variety of possibilities, as well as constraints peculiar to their social location; concepts such as "intersectionality" and "subject positions" help flesh out the ways such categories as gender, race, class, and sexuality interrelate.[40] An inevitable result of such accounts is the critique of binary theories of power: oppressive structures versus oppressed women. The master/subject model is inadequate to the complexities of subject positions.[41]

Along with this destabilizing of "woman," however, comes the worry over loss of a category fundamental to feminist thinking. The charge of essentialism against views of "woman" insufficiently respectful of difference is countered by concern over the loss of an agent. While formatted as debate, both concerns matter and will continue to be explored. A helpful distinction is suggested by women's studies scholar Mary Maynard: both the appeal to "women's experience" and the destabilized subject function as disclosive patterns with different but important purposes for feminist theology. An appeal to "woman" as a *unifying term* rather than a unified one is crucial to "locating possible common experiences around which a sense of commonality and community might be developed." This needs to be read as a kind of "strategic essentialism," not an appeal to a unitary or false universal category.[42] Attention to the material processes that construct women differently is just as necessary for the different goal of addressing formerly unseen or new configurations of oppression.

Tradition

A second ongoing issue for feminist theology is its relationship to "the tradition." Evangelical feminist theology is clearly committed to the normative status of Christian scripture. However, even that conservative approach must continue to struggle with the relativizing forces of critical disciplines on "the tradition." More widely, feminist theology has called into question the very notion of a uniform given called "the" tradition. Whether it is the negative judgment of what has counted as the Christian tradition, such as found in moves to other spiritual resources, or the recognition by liberationist approaches that social location and its blinding interests render "the tradition" problematically partial, feminist theology continues to struggle with the normative status of this fallible, human, sometimes pernicious source of authority.

Recognition of new ways to "do" or perform tradition continue to emerge. Since its beginnings, feminist theology has interpreted classic Christian doctrines through the lens of gender, from the reformulation of Trinitarian doctrine, a feminist appropriation of Reformed doctrines of justification by faith and sanctification, to recent feminist treatments of atonement theory.[43] A slightly different interest in classic tradition, however, stems from worry about the negative effects of "modernity" on the feminist theology of a Ruether or a Schussler Fiorenza.[44] Such effects include too much focus on efficacy and power, along with the worry that images such as victimhood and innocence have dominated feminist thinking about women. A recent call for feminist theology to appropriate traditional themes more fully has generated considerations of the relevance of patristic theologians such as Gregory of Nyssa, including dialogical appropriations of queer theorist Judith Butler and patristic theologians.[45]

Globalization

A third contemporary issue is globalization. A process typically associated with the global spread of capitalism, globalization is rooted in five centuries of colonial expansion by Western European countries. In many ways an extension of liberation feminist theology's recognition of the complexities of structural effects on human life, respect for globalization demands that feminist theology come to terms with the often more subtle but powerful forces that impinge on every "local." From the effect of multinational corporations and the blurring of national boundaries on the economic privileges of U.S. white women, to the effects of forced migration of (mostly) women from so-called third world countries on the latter's job opportunities, the "local" must now be read as "global." The impact of globalized markets and economy, as well as the globalized commodified culture, are of fundamental importance for women, especially women of color, and the diversity of such women challenges feminist theology to move beyond the binary of African American and white. Globalization requires feminist theology to recognize its Western bias along with its whiteness and privileged class as it learns from the wisdoms of a heretofore unseen majority, women of colonized worlds.

NOTES

1. Nancy F. Cott, *The Grounding of Modern Feminism* (New Haven, CT: Yale University Press, 1987); and Eleanor Flexner and Ellen Fitzpatrick, *Century of Struggle*, enl. ed. (Cambridge, MA: Belknap, 1959, 1975, 1996).

2. Cott (*Grounding of Modern Feminism,* 40–50) suggests this was a label that was taken by more highly educated women of privilege. Some of it also tended to disassociate from Christianity.

3. Rosalind Rosenberg, *Beyond Separate Spheres: Intellectual Roots of Modern Feminism* (New Haven, CT: Yale University Press, 1982).

4. Organized by President John F. Kennedy, the Commission documented discrimination against women in all areas of life. The Civil Rights Act of 1964 and the Equal Employment Opportunity Commission established in 1964 were also significant developments.

5. Rachel Blau DuPlessis and Ann Snitow, eds., *The Feminist Memoir Project: Voices from Women's Liberation* (New York: Three Rivers, 1998), 508.

6. Cott, *Grounding of Modern Feminism,* 17

7. Sarah Moore Grimke wrote *Letters on the Equality of the Sexes, and the Condition of Women,* in 1838.

8. For examples of the widespread force of religious faith in the civil rights movement, see Charles Marsh, *The Beloved Community: How Faith Shapes Social Justice, from the Civil Rights Movement to Today* (New York: Basic, 2005).

9. James J. Farrell, *The Spirit of the Sixties: The Making of Postwar Radicalism* (New York: Routledge, 1997)

10. Angela Davis points out that the Seneca Falls Declaration (1848) did not even mention black women's needs. Her account of two centuries of feminist activity is quite pointed about its racial divides. Davis, *Women, Race, and Class* (New York: Random House, 1981). Thanks to Delores Williams for reminding me of this. Williams, "The Color of Feminism," *Journal of Religious Thought* 43, no. 1 (1986): 44.

11. There are a number of books on the activism of women of color, and general accounts do refer to this. For example, Nancy Cott's history recognizes African American women's activism, pointing out that the decade of 1910 was the most class and racially diverse period of the early movement, in great contrast to the well-known racism of the 19th-century suffrage movement. Cott, *Grounding of Modern Feminism,* 30–32. However, the intersections of these histories attending to the "whiteness" of the "woman movement" have not been fully developed.

12. Davis, *Women, Race, and Class,* recounts a number of these stories of ill-fated collaborations revealing the racist and classist worldviews of many of the "heroines" of the woman movement and 20th-century feminism.

13. As noted, this research is ongoing. For example, Eugenia Delamotte, Natania Meeker, and Jean O'Barr, *Women Imagine Change: A Global Anthology of Women's Resistance from 600 b.c. to Present* (New York: Routledge, 1997).

14. Mary Field Belenky, Lynne A. Bond, and Jacqueline S. Weinstock, *A Tradition That Has No Name: Nurturing the Development of People, Families, and Communities* (New York: Basic, 1997), 3.

15. An example of racism in publishing is found in a 1959 response to a white feminist author. Author of one of the most significant histories of women's struggles, Flexnor was told that she would have to eliminate the material on African American women in her book for it to be published. Fortunately, she refused to comply. Flexnor and Fitzpatrick, *Century of Struggle,* xxiv. This phenomenon is also connected to the level of diversity hiring, which impedes the production and dissemination of scholarship that counters the mainstream narratives. As Randi Warne says, "We do not have a dominant discourse on economic elites encoded in our academies as articulated by the poor and homeless because they are excluded from those institutions." Randi R. Warne, "(En)gendering Religious Studies," in *Feminism in the Study of Religion: A Reader,* ed. Darlene M. Juschka (New York: Continuum, 2001), 151.

16. I put these phrases in quotes to indicate that they are social conventions.

17. Valerie Saiving, "The Human Situation: A Feminine View," in *Womanspirit Rising: A Feminist Reader in Religion,* ed. Carol P. Christ and Judith Plaskow (San Francisco: Harper and Row, 1979), 25–42. This chapter was originally written in 1960 for the *Journal of Religion.*

18. An important follow-up was Judith Plaskow's dissertation at Yale in 1975, later published as *Sex, Sin and Grace: Women's Experience and the Theologies of Reinhold Niebuhr and Paul Tillich* (Washington, DC: American University Press, 1980).

19. Mary Daly, *The Church and the Second Sex* (Boston: Beacon, 1968); and Daly, *Beyond God the Father* (Boston: Beacon, 1973).

20. Rosemary Radford Ruether, *Women-Church: Theology and Practice of Feminist Liturgical Communities* (San Francisco: Harper and Row, 1985). Ruether's prolific feminist writings began in the 1970s with *Religion and Sexism: Images of Women in the Jewish and Christian Traditions* (New York: Simon and Schuster, 1974).

21. Arlene Swidler's edited volume of feminist liturgies was the first published. Arlene Swidler, ed., *Sistercelebrations: Nine Worship Experiences* (Philadelphia: Fortress, 1974). Thanks to Teresa Berger, ed., *Dissident Daughters: Feminist Liturgies in Global Context* (Louisville, KY: Westminister John Knox, 2001), 232.

22. Andrea Smith recently asked what if "we *re-centered* Native women in an account of feminist history"? This would mean beginning "with 1492 when Native women collectively resisted colonization. In this new history, the importance of anti-colonial struggle would be central in our articulation of feminism." Unpublished essay. This argument is also available in "Indigenous Feminism without Apology," available at www.newsoialist. org/newsite/indexphp?id=1013 (accessed July 6, 2009).

23. Regarding the rise of evangelical feminist theology, see Pamela D. H. Cochran, *Evangelical Feminism: A History* (New York: New York University Press, 2005); and Betty

DeBerg, *Ungodly Women: Gender and the First Wave of American Fundamentalism* (Minneapolis: Fortress, 1990).

24. Virginia R. Mollenkott, *The Divine Feminine: The Biblical Images of God as Female* (New York: Crossroad, 1983).

25. Patricia Gundry, *Women Be Free!* (New York: Zondervan, 1977); Alvera Mickelson, ed., *Women, Authority and the* Bible (Downer's Grove, IL: Intervarsity, 1986); Virginia Mollenkott, *Women, Men, and the Bible* (Nashville, TN: Abingdon, 1977); and Letha Scanzoni and Nancy Hardesty, *All We're Meant to Be: A Biblical Approach to Women's Liberation* (Waco, TX: Word, 1974). Mollenkott's later work moves out of this model, when she comes out and explores what she calls "omnigender."

26. While the latter may not be "feminist theology," it is part of the evangelical feminist conversation and debates. For example, James R. Beck, ed., *Two Views on Women in Ministry* (Grand Rapids, MI: Zondervan, 2005).

27. By "liberation" I refer to the origins of theological criticism in Latin American thinking which recognized that Christian faith and theology are shaped by social power.

28. Letty M. Russell, *Household of Freedom: Authority in Feminist Theology* (Philadelphia: Westminster, 1987), 13; and Russell, *Church in the Round: Feminist Interpretation of the Church* (Louisville, KY: Westminster John Knox, 1993).

29. Sallie McFague, *Metaphorical Theology: Models of God in Religious Language* (Philadelphia: Fortress, 1982); and McFague, *The Body of God: An Ecological Theology* (Minneapolis: Fortress, 1993).

30. Carol J. Adams, *Ecofeminism and the* Sacred (New York: Continuum, 1993); Rosemary Radford Ruether, *Integrating Ecofeminism, Globalization, and World Religions* (Lanham, MD: Rowman and Littlefield, 2005); and Laurel Kearns and Catherine Keller, eds., *Ecospirituality, Religions, and Philosophies for the Earth* (New York: Fordham University Press, 2007).

31. Elizabeth Schussler Fiorenza, *But She Said: Feminist Practices of Biblical Interpretation* (Boston: Beacon, 1992), 7–8.

32. Carol Christ insists that religious traditions are appropriated through a modern feminist lens. There is no interest in the religions with goddess traditions that still subordinate them to male gods. Carol P. Christ, "Why Women Need the Goddess," in *Womanspirit Rising: A Feminist Reader in Religion,* ed. Carol P. Christ and Judith Plaskow (San Francisco: Harper and Row, 1979), 276.

33. Crist and Plaskow, Introduction to *Womanspirit Rising,* 2. Ten years later, Judith Plaskow and Carol Christ complicated the sources and communities of feminist spirituality in *Weaving the Visions: New Patterns in Feminist Spirituality* (San Francisco: Harper and Row, 1989).

34. Starhawk, *The Spiral Dance: A Rebirth of the Ancient Religion of the Great Goddess,* 10th anny ed. (San Francisco: Harper and Row, 1989). See also Mary Daly, *Websters' First New Intergalactic Wickedary of the English Language,* conjured by Mary Daly in cahoots with Jane Caputi (Boston: Beacon, 1987); and Charlene Spretnak, ed., *The Politics of Women's Spirituality* (New York: Anchor, 1994).

35. Sin as oppression, then, is not reducible to intentional acts of malice but includes the inherited socializations that create oblivious to the humanity of marginalized groups, as well as the harmful impact on economic and political structures of these socializations.

36. Grace Jantzen, *Becoming Divine: Toward a Feminist Philosophy of Religion* (Blooming-ton: Indiana University Press, 1999); and C. W. Maggie Kim, Susan St. Ville, and Susan M. Simonaitis, eds., *Transfigurations: Theology and the French Feminists* (Minneapolis: Fortress, 1993).

37. Sheila Greeve Davaney, "The Limits of the Appeal to Women's Experience," in *Shaping New Vision: Gender and Values in American Culture*, ed. Clarissa W. Atkinson, Constance H. Buchanan, and Margaret R. Miles (Ann Arbor, MI: UMI Research, 1987).

38. Mary Maynard, "'Race,' Gender, and the Concept of 'Difference,'" in *Feminism in the Study of Religion: A Reader*, ed. Darlene M. Juschka (New York: Continuum, 2001), 439.

39. Denise Riley, *"Am I That Name?" Feminism and the Category of "Women" in History* (Minneapolis: University of Minnesota Press, 1988), 7.

40. Kimberle Crenshaw develops "intersectionality" in "Intersectionality and Identity Politics: Learning from Violence against Women of Color," in *The Public Nature of Private Violence*, ed. Martha Albertson Fineman and Roxanne Mykitiuk (New York: Routledge, 1994), 178–193. A theological example of "subject positions" employing poststructuralism is found in Mary McClintock Fulkerson, *Changing the Subject: Women's Discourses and Feminist Theology* (Minneapolis: Fortress, 1994).

41. Margaret D. Kamitsuka, *Feminist Theology and the Challenge of Difference* (New York: Oxford University Press, 2007), 89–114.

42. Mary Maynard, "Beyond the 'Big Three': The Development of Feminist Theory into the 1990s," in *Feminism in the Study of Religion: A Reader*, ed. Darlene M. Juschka (New York: Continuum, 2001), 308.

43. Elizabeth Johnson, *She Who Is: The Mystery of God in Feminist Theological Discourse* (New York: Crossroad, 1992); and Serene Jones, *Feminist Theory and Christian Theology: Cartographies of Grace* (Minneapolis: Fortress, 2000).

44. Susan Frank Parsons, ed., *Challenging Women's Orthodoxies in the Context of Faith* (Aldershot, Eng.: Ashgate, 2000).

45. Sarah Coakley is a prominent feminist theologian of this sort.

FURTHER STUDY

Adams, Carol J. *Ecofeminism and the Sacred*. New York: Continuum, 1993.

Atkinson, Clarissa W., Constance H. Buchanan, and Margaret R. Miles, eds. *Shaping New Vision: Gender and Values in American Culture*. Ann Arbor, MI: UMI Research, 1987.

Daly Mary. *Beyond God the Father*. Boston: Beacon, 1993. Originally published 1973.

———. *The Church and the Second Sex*. Boston: Beacon, 1986. Originally published 1968.

DeBerg, Betty. *Ungodly Women: Gender and the First Wave of American Fundamentalism*. Minneapolis: Fortress, 1990.

Fulkerson, Mary McClintock. *Changing the Subject: Women's Discourses and Feminist Theology*. Minneapolis: Fortress, 1994.

Johnson, Elizabeth. *She Who Is: The Mystery of God in Feminist Theological Discourse*. New York: Crossroad, 1992.

Jones, Serene. *Feminist Theory and Christian Theology: Cartographies of Grace*. Minneapolis: Fortress, 2000.

Kamitsuka, Margaret D. *Feminist Theology and the Challenge of Difference*. New York: Oxford University Press, 2007.

Kearns, Laurel, and Catherine Keller, eds. *Ecospirituality, Religions, and Philosophies for the Earth*. New York: Fordham University Press, 2007.

McFague, Sallie. *The Body of God: An Ecological Theology*. Minneapolis: Fortress, 1993.

———. *Metaphorical Theology: Models of God in Religious Language*. Philadelphia: Fortress, 1982.

Mollenkott, Virginia R. *The Divine Feminine: The Biblical Images of God as Female*. New York: Crossroad, 1983.

Plaskow, Judith. *Sex, Sin and Grace: Women's Experience and the Theologies of Reinhold Niebuhr and Paul Tillich*. Washington, DC: American University Press, 1980.

Plaskow, Judith, and Carol Christ *Weaving the Visions: New Patterns in Feminist Spirituality*. San Francisco: Harper and Row, 1989.

Ruether, Rosemary Radford. *Integrating Ecofeminism, Globalization, and World Religions*. Lanham, MD: Rowman and Littlefield, 2005.

———. *Religion and Sexism: Images of Women in the Jewish and Christian Traditions*. New York: Simon and Schuster, 1974.

———. *Women-Church: Theology and Practice of Feminist Liturgical Communities*. San Francisco: Harper and Row, 1985.

Russell, Letty M. *Church in the Round: Feminist Interpretation of the Church*. Louisville, KY: Westminster John Knox, 1993.

———. *Household of Freedom: Authority in Feminist Theology*. Philadelphia: Westminster, 1987.

Schussler Fiorenza, Elizabeth. *But She Said: Feminist Practices of Biblical Interpretation*. Boston: Beacon, 1992.

Spretnak, Charlene, ed. *The Politics of Women's Spirituality*. New York: Anchor, 1994.

Welch, Sharon. *A Feminist Ethic of Risk*. Minneapolis: Fortress, 1990.

———. *Sweet Dreams in America: Making Ethics and Spirituality Work*. New York: Routledge, 1998.

Contributors

STACEY M. FLOYD-THOMAS is currently the Associate Professor of Ethics and Society at Vanderbilt University Divinity School and Graduate Department of Religion. A graduate of Vassar College (B.A.), Emory University's Candler School of Theology (M.T.S.), and Temple University (M.A. and Ph.D.), she is an ordained American Baptist and Progressive National Baptist pastoral counselor and cofounding executive director of the Black Religious Scholars Group (BRSG). Her research and teaching interests lie at the intersection of liberation theology and ethics, feminist/womanist studies, critical pedagogy, critical race theory, and postcolonial studies that engage broad questions of moral agency, cultural memory, ethical responsibility, and social justice. She has published three books—*Mining the Motherlode: Methods in Womanist Ethics* (2006), *Deeper Shades of Purple: Womanism in Religion and Society* (2006), and *Black Church Studies: An Introduction* (2007)—and is the editor of two series with New York University and Abingdon Presses. She has received numerous honors and awards, including the JPMorgan Chase/Texas Business Press Great Women of Texas Award and the American Academy of Religion Excellence in Teaching Award.

MARY MCCLINTOCK FULKERSON is currently Professor of Theology at Duke Divinity School. An ordained minister in the Presbyterian Church (USA), she received her Ph.D. from Vanderbilt University. Her primary teaching interests are feminist theologies, theology and culture theories, and authority in theology. Her work is published in journals such as the *Journal of the American Academy of Religion, Journal of Feminist Studies in Religion,* and *Modern Theology.* Her book *Changing the Subject: Women's Discourses and Feminist Theology* examines the liberating practices of feminist academics and nonfeminist churchwomen. She has written articles challenging theologies that identify normative Christianity with heterosexuality. Her recent book *Traces of Redemption: Theology for a Worldly Church* interprets the doctrine of the church in light of racial diversity and the differently-abled.

GRACE JI-SUN KIM is Associate Professor of Doctrinal Theology at Moravian Theological Seminary. She is passionate about theology as is evident from her research, publications, guest presentations, and teaching. She received her Ph.D. from the University of St. Michael's College, University of Toronto, in 2001 and her M.Div. from Knox College. She has published several articles and is the author of *The Grace of Sophia* (2002), which examines religious and cultural suffering in Korea and the current casualties of racism, classism, and sexism in North America, to offer an empowering women's Christology. Presently she is working on a volume on 1 and 2 Chronicles, Ezra, and Nehemiah, in *Theological Commentary on the Bible* (scheduled for publication in 2010).

ANDREW SUNG PARK is Professor of Theology at United Theological Seminary in Dayton, Ohio. He was born in a North Korean refugee family. His family moved a number of times in Korea and immigrated to the United States in 1973. For two years, he washed dishes, bused tables in a hotel, worked in a factory assembly line, and labored in a foundry. When he studied theology after these experiences, he was naturally interested in liberation theologies, particularly *minjung* theology. Park received his Ph.D. from Graduate Theological Union in 1985. He served churches for six years and taught at Claremont School of Theology in California (1987–1992). Andrew has been at United Theological Seminary in Ohio since 1992. Andrew's teaching and research interests include systematic theology, global theology, cross-cultural theology, Asian-American liberation theology, Christian mystics, the dialogue between theology and science, and Christian ethics. Park has published several books, including *The Wounded Heart of God: The Asian Concept of Han and the Christian Doctrine of Sin; Racial Conflict and Healing: An Asian-American Theological Perspective; From Hurt to Healing: A Theology of the Wounded;* and *Triune Atonement: Christ's Healing for Sinners, Victims, and the Whole Creation.*

NANCY PINEDA-MADRID is Assistant Professor of Theology and U.S. Latino/a Ministry at Boston College. She holds a Ph.D. in Systematic and Philosophical Theology from Graduate Theological Union (Berkeley, California) and an M.Div. from Seattle University. She works at the intersection of systematic and practical theology and has authored chapters in the fields of U.S. Latino/a theology and feminist theology. Currently, Pineda-Madrid is working on a book that examines the problematic intersection of suffering and the quest for salvation from a Latina feminist perspective.

ANTHONY B. PINN is currently the Agnes Cullen Arnold Professor of Humanities and Professor of Religious Studies at Rice University. He received a Ph.D. from Harvard University, and his other professional commitments include service as the executive director of the Society for the Study of Black Religion. Pinn has published more than twenty books, most of which address issues of theory and method for the study of Black religion, as well as providing a richer sense of the religious plurality that marks African American communities. Expanding the work done by William R. Jones, he is also deeply involved in the development of an African American humanist theology that draws on underappreciated areas of popular culture such as rap music and the nontheistic religious tradition of African Americans. His more recent work involves issues of aesthetics and embodiment within Black theological discourse.

ROBERT E. SHORE-GOSS is Senior Pastor of Metropolitan Community Church in the Valley. He received a Th.D. from Harvard University in Theology and Comparative Religion. He teaches at Claremont School of Theology and California State University, Northridge. His first book, *Jesus ACTED UP: A Gay and Lesbian Manifesto,* begins the emergence of queer theology from gay/lesbian theologies. He is author of *Queering Christ: Beyond Jesus ACTED UP* and coauthor of *Dead but Not Lost: Grief Narratives in Religious Traditions.* Shore-Goss is coeditor *of Take Back the Word: Queer Readings of the Bible; The Queer Bible Commentary;* and *Gay Catholic Priests and Clerical Sexual Misconduct: The Silence of Sodom.*

ANDREA SMITH is Assistant Professor of Media and Cultural Studies at the University of California—Riverside. She is the U.S. coordinator for the Ecumenical Association of Third World Theologians (EATWOT). Smith is also the cofounder of INCITE! Women of Color against Violence and the Boarding School Healing Project. She is the author of numerous works, including *Native Americans and the Christian Right: The Gendered Politics of Unlikely Alliances* (2008), *The Revolution Will Not Be Funded* (2007), and *Conquest: Sexual Violence and American Indian Genocide* (2005).

GEORGE (TINK) TINKER is Clifford Baldridge Professor of American Indian Cultures and Religious Traditions at Illif School of Theology (Denver). He holds a doctorate from Graduate Theological Union (Berkeley). He is a widely sought after speaker and a highly regarded scholar and activist. Tinker's writings, speeches, and activism bring attention to the liberation efforts of American Indians and critique the colonialism perpetuated against American Indians. In this way, his theology tends to be more committed to sociopolitical issues than to more abstract discussions of traditional theological themes such as the doctrine of God. He is the author of numerous books, including *Missionary Conquest: The Gospel and Native American Cultural Genocide* (1993) and *Native American Theology* (2001). Tinker has worked as director of the Four Winds American Indian Survival Project in Denver, served as president of the Native American Theological Association, and is a member of EATWOT. Committed to ecumenism, he also works with both the National Council of Churches and the World Council of Churches.

BENJAMÍN VALENTÍN is Professor of Theology and Culture at Andover Newton Theological School in Newton Centre, Massachusetts. His teaching and research interests are in contemporary theology and culture, constructive theology, liberation theology, and U.S. Hispanic/Latino(a) theology. In general, his focus is on leading people to explore the possibility of a theological outlook that can be responsive to new occasions, challenges, duties, and perceptions in our late modern era. Valentín received his Ph.D. from Drew University (in Madison, NJ). He is the author of the award-winning *Mapping Public Theology: Beyond Culture, Identity, and Difference;* editor of *New Horizons in Hispanic/Latino(a) Theology;* and coeditor of *The Ties That Bind: African-American and Hispanic-American/Latino(a) Theologies in Dialogue* and *Creating Ourselves: African Americans and Latino/as, Popular Culture, and Religious Expression.*

Index

AAR (American Academy of Religion), 49
academia, 9, 14n18
Acosta-Belen, Edna, 91
ACT UP (AIDS Coalition to Unleash Power), 182–183, 188, 198, 204n28
adelphopoiesis (brotherhood rites), 190
AETH (Association for Hispanic Theological Education), 93
African Methodist Episcopal Church, 28
Agosto, Efrain, 96–97
Ahmed, Leila, 212
AIDS Coalition to Unleash Power (ACT UP), 182–183, 188, 198, 204n28
AIM (American Indian Movement), 4–5
Allen, Richard, 16–17
Althaus-Reid, Marcella, 189, 201, 218
Althusser, Louis, 158
American Academy of Religion (AAR), 49
American Indian Movement (AIM), 4–5
American Indian theology, 168–180; ceremonies in, 172–173; Christianity and Native traditions, 168–170, 172; Christianity of American Indians, 177; cosmic balance in, 171; description, 171–172; development of, 5; Exodus story in, 171–172; fundamentalist and evangelical Indians, 177; historical backdrop, 168–170; ongoing issues, 177; sources, 172–175; theology as inconsistent with Native worldviews, 171, 173–175, 178n12; theoretical and methodological considerations, 176–177; *tiospaye* (clan) membership and, 170. See also Native feminist theology
"American Indian Women" (Jaimes), 152–153
American Indians. See Native Americans
American Psychiatric Association, 181
American Psychological Association, 181

Anderson, Victor, 26
Andrews, Dale, 32
Anselm, Saint, 77
Apess, William, 169
apocalyptic theology, 116–117
Aponte, Edwin, 95
Apuntes (journal), 65, 93
Aquinas, Saint Thomas, 77, 183
Aquino, Jorge, 96
Aquino, María Pilar: as editor, 73; feminism and, 67; *Feminist Intercultural Theology* (with Rosado-Nunes), 71; Hispanic/Latino(a) theology and, 95, 96; Latina/o theology and, 65, 67–69; *Our Cry for Life*, 68; *Religion, Feminism and Justice* (with Rodríguez and Machado), 71; "The Veneration of Mary and 'Mary' of the Veneration," 67
Ar'n't I a Woman? (White), 39–40
"Asia" (the term), 145n14
"Asian" (the term), 135
"Asian American" (the term), 145n14
Asian American Christians, 119
Asian American feminist theology, 131–148; "betwixt and between" theme in, 143–144; Bible in, 139; Confucianism and, 136; description, 134–135; dialogical imagination in, 139; *han* in, 137–138; *han-pu-ri* in, 138; historical backdrop, 131–134; hybridity in, 139–140; immigration restrictions against Asians, 133–134; inductive nature, 137; interstitial integrity, 142–143; Latina theology and, 81; marginality, experience of, 143–144; *minjung* in, 138; multifaith hermeneutics in, 139; ongoing issues, 140–144; Orientalism and, 141–143; Otherness in, 142; *pneuma* in, 136; pneumatology in, 136–137;

Asian American feminist theology
(*continued*): racism, fight against, 143;
ruach in, 136–137; sexuality and, 140–141;
sources, 135–138; The Spirit/*chi* in,
136–137; theoretical and methodological considerations, 139–140; wisdom in,
135–137, 145n21; *won-han* in, 138. *See also*
Asian American theology
Asian-American Ministries Center, 115
Asian American political activism, 5–6
Asian American theology, 115–130; apocalyptic theology in, 116–117; Asian cultural
values in, 117; "betwixt and between"
theme in, 118, 122–124, 127; Bible, biculturalism in the, 117; Black theology and, 5,
116; description, 115–116; Fernandez and,
Eleazar S., 126–128; Filipino American
theology, 127–128; *hahn* in, 126; *han* in,
125, 126; hermeneutics, 118, 119; historical
backdrop, 115; imagination and memory
in, 118; intracommunal oppression
and repression, focus on, 116; Jesus as
immigrant, 119; Jesus as paradigmatic
marginal man, 124; *jung* in, 126; Korean
American theology, 120–122, 125–126;
Latin American liberation theology and,
116; Lee and, Jung Young, 123–124; Lee
and, Sang, 122–123; liminality in, 123;
marginality in, experiences of, 122–124;
Matsuoka and, Fumitaka, 119–120; Min
and, Anselm, 120–122; *mut* in, 126; ongoing issues, 126–128; Park and, Andrew
Sung, 124–126; Phan and, Peter, 118–119;
pilgrim theology in, 122–123; racism and,
8; scripture in, Hebrew and Christian,
116–117; sin as desiring to be white,
127; "solidarity of others," 121; sources,
116–122; stages, 116; theoretical and
methodological considerations, 122–126;
transmutation theology in, 124–126; *triet
Ly tam tai* (heaven, Earth, and humanity),
119; unfinished dreams in, 126–127; Vietnamese American theology, 118–119. *See
also* Asian American feminist theology
Asian immigration, 90, 132–134, 142
Association for Hispanic Theological Education (AETH), 93
Augustine, Saint, 28, 77, 104

Bailey, Derrick Sherwin, 184, 197
Baker, Ella, 40
Baldridge, William, 171–172, 178n12
Bañuelas, Arturo, 95
Barbara, Saint, 102
Barth, Karl, 9, 23, 183
Batista, Fulgencio, 64
Bedford, Nancy Elizabeth, 73
"betwixt and between" situation: in Asian
American feminist theology, 143–144; in
Asian American theology, 118, 122–124,
127
Beyond God the Father (Daly), 45, 212–213
Beyond Our Ghettoes (Clark), 188
Bible: in Asian American feminist theology,
139; biculturalism in, 117; in Black theol-
ogy, 28–29; in Black women's literature,
51; dialogical/corelational model of
biblical interpretation, 101; in Hispanic/
Latino(a) theology, 100–101; homo-hatred
in, 197; outing of, 194–196; patriarchal
traditions in, 210; translations of, 159;
wisdom in, 136
The Black Christ (Douglas), 50
Black churches: anti-intellectualism in,
37; Black theology and, 30–31, 32; Black
women and, 51; sexism of, 37, 51; woman-
ist theology and, 48, 56–57
Black Economic Development Conference
(Detroit, 1969), 19
Black feminism, 41–43
Black Feminist Thought (Collins), 42–43
*Black Macho and the Myth of the Super-
woman* (Wallace), 41
Black Manifesto, 19
Black men, Black women and, 38
Black Panther Party, 3
Black power, 3, 18, 40
Black religion, deradicalization of, 17
Black studies, Black women and, 38
Black theology, 15–36; African American
experience in, 27–28; African American
popular culture in, 29–30, 33–34; African
practices in, traditional, 23; agenda, 8;
Asian American theology and, 5, 116;
Bible in, 28–29; Black churches and,
30–31, 32; black liberation and, 20; Black
power and, 18; Black women and, 38;

Blackness in, 20–21, 24, 25–26; Catholicism and, 24–25; Christian traditions in, 28; Christianity, deradicalization of, 17; as a church theology, 28; civil rights movement and, 18, 20; Cone and, Cecil, 22, 23; Cone and, James H., 20–21, 24; description, 19–27; European theologians in, 23; Evans and, James, 24; Exodus story in, 172; generations of theologians, 24, 35n9; God's identification with the oppressed, 20–21; heaven in, 22, 24; hermeneutics of suspicion in, 31; historical backdrop, 15–18; Hopkins and, Dwight, 24; humanity in, 21–22, 24; Jesus as the Black Messiah, 21; Jesus's ministry, 29; Jones and, William R., 22, 23–24, 34; justice in, 22, 24–25; King, Martin Luther, Jr. and, 18; King and, Martin Luther, Jr., 20; Latina theology and, 32–33, 77, 81; LGBT people and, 25; Malcolm X and, 18, 20; male orientation, 26; Mariology in, 25; middle-class blacks and, 25; moral evil in, 24, 34; ongoing issues, 32–35; ontological Blackness, 20–21, 24, 25–26; oral traditions in, 154; political power and, 19; postcolonial studies and, 31; Protestantism and, 24; race and racism, focus on, 19–20; racism as dominant mode of oppression, 26, 34–35; redemptive suffering argument and, 34; religious pluralism and, 25; Roberts and, J. Deotis, 22–23; sacred texts of, 28–29; salvation in, 17, 22, 24; scripture in, Hebrew and Christian, 29; sexism of, 26; sociopolitical transformation in the name of religion, 17–18; sources, 27–30; theoretical and methodological considerations, 30–31; Wilmore and, Gayraud, 22–23, 23; womanism and, 26–27, 53
Black Theology (journal), 33
Black Theology and Black Power (Cone), 1, 20, 45
A Black Theology of Liberation (Cone), 1, 20–21
Black Womanist Ethics (Cannon), 47–48, 49
Black women: Black churches and, 51; Black feminists and, 41–43; Black men and, 38; Black studies and, 38; Black theology and, 38; in civil rights movement, 41; feminism and, 38–39; feminist theology and, 38–39;

historical presence of, 43; literature by, 51–52, 154; political activism of, 221n11; sin from mistreatment of, 50; stereotypes of, 40; white women and, 40–41; womanism and, 45; womanist theology and, 37, 46, 48–49, 50–53; women studies and, 38; women's movement and, 38
Blackness: ontological, 20–21, 24, 25–26; oppression and, 25; womanist theology and, 48
Blessing Same-Sex Unions (Jordan), 192
Blondel, Maurice, 186
body theology, 192–193
Bohache, Thomas, 196, 200, 201
Bonhoeffer, Dietrich, 45
Boswell, John, 185, 190
Both Feet Firmly Planted in Midair (McNeill), 186
Bourdieu, Pierre, 158
Boy Scouts of America, 182
Bray, Alan, 190
Brite Divinity School, 115
Brooten, Bernadette, 185–186
brotherhood rites *(adelphopoiesis),* 190
Brown Berets, 3
Budda (Enlightened One), 134
Burlein, Ann, 164
Burroughs, Nannie Helen, 37
Butler, Judith, 160, 198, 218, 220
Butler, Lee, 32

Caminemos con Jesus (Goizueta), 94
Canaan, 15
Canaanites, 150, 171
"Canaanites, Cowboys, and Indians" (Warrior), 150
Cannon, Katie Geneva: Black theology, critique of, 26; *Black Womanist Ethics,* 47–48, 49; on Black women's literature, 154; "The Emergence of Black Feminist Consciousness," 47; womanist theology and, 26, 47, 49, 50
Cardoza-Orlandi, Carlos, 95
Carette, Jeremy, 189
Catholic Church: Black theology and, 24–25; El Movimiento (Chicana/o movement) and, 65; "Los Doce," 61–62; Mariology in, 25; in New Mexico, 63–64

Eve, 213
evolutionary theory and liberal theology, 10
exegetical activism, 195
Exodus, 29, 77, 150, 171–172

The Faith of the People (Espín), 95
the Fall, 124
Farajaje-Jones, Ibrahim, 189
Farnham, Christie, 43
Farrell, James J., 210
FDA (Food and Drug Administration), 182
FEM (journal), 67
Feminine Mystique (Friedan), 209
feminism: Aquino and, María Pilar, 67;
    Black feminists, 41–43; Black women
    and, 38–39; Christianity, relation to, 212;
    ecological feminism, 216; Euro-American
    feminists, prejudice among, 66; grass-
    roots activism in, 211; intellectualism of,
    43; Isasi-Díaz and, Ada Maria, 67; Latina
    theology and, 67–69, 78–79, 82; marginal-
    ization of Latinas in, 66; Native American
    women and, 152–153, 160–162; religious
    imagination in, 210; white feminists,
    43–44; womanism compared to, 45
"feminist" (the term), 209
Feminist Intercultural Theology (Aquino and
    Rosado-Nunes), 71
feminist movement: abolition movement, 6;
    Black racial equality, 6; civil rights move-
    ment and, 6–7; racism and, 8; "second
    wave," 209–211, 213; waves of, 6–7
feminist theology, 209–225; 1950s, 214;
    1960s, 212–213, 214; 1970s, 213; agenda,
    8; biblical study in, 217; Black women
    and, 38–39; Daly and, Mary, 212–213;
    description, 211–214; destabilization of
    the binary male-female in, 219; ecological
    feminism and, 216; evangelical feminist
    theology, 214–215, 217, 220; focus, 211–212,
    213–214; founding theologies, 211–212;
    gender in, 219; globalization, effects of,
    220–221; historical backdrop, 209–211;
    Latina theology and, 77; liberation
    model of, 215–216, 217, 218; as a "marked"
    literature, 212; modernity, effects of, 220;
    ongoing issues, 218–221; queer theorists
    and, 218; race and, 218–219; Saiving and,

Valerie, 212–213; scripture in, Hebrew
    and Christian, 214–215; sources, 214–217;
    theoretical and methodological consid-
    erations, 217–218; tradition, relationship
    to, 220; Western bias of, 221; "whiteness"
    of, 211–212; woman-centered spiritualities
    in, 216–217, 218; womanist theology and,
    53; women's experience in, appeal to, 214,
    218–219. *See also* Asian American feminist
    theology; Native feminist theology
Feminist Theory (hooks), 42
Ferdinand II of Aragon, 61
Fernandez, Eleazar S., 126–128
Figueroa-Deck, Allan, 95
Filipino American theology, 127–128
Filipino Americans, political activism of, 5
Flores, Juan, 90
Floyd-Thomas, Stacey, 26, 53–55, 56
Food and Drug Administration (FDA), 182
Fools Crow, Frank, 170
Foote, Julia, 46
Forman, James, 19
Fortunato, John, 185
Foucault, Michel, 188, 198, 204n28
freedom, 17, 21
Freedom, Glorious Freedom (McNeill), 186
Friedan, Betty, 38, 209
The Friend (Bray), 190
From the Hearts of Our People (Espín and
    Díaz), 106
Fulkerson, Mary McClintock, 160
The Future Is Mestizo (Elizondo), 104

Galilean Journey (Elizondo), 92, 107
Gallardo, Gloria Graciela, 65
García, Ismael, 96
García, Sixto, 95
García-Rivera, Alex, 95
García-Treto, Francisco, 95
Gay, Ebenezer, 10
Gay and Gaia (Spencer), 188
gay and lesbian theologies, 181–208; 1970s,
    184–185; 1980s, 185–188; 1990s, 188–189;
    AIDS activism and, 182–183, 188; the
    Bible, outing of, 194–196; body theology,
    192–193; description, 183–194; exegetical
    activism of, 195; gay male issues, focus
    on, 185–187; gay theology, 185–186, 187;

Harvard conference (1990), 188; hate crimes against gays and lesbians, 182; heteropatriarchy and, 184; historical backdrop, 181–183; liberal gay/lesbian-affirming churches, emergence of, 199; mutuality in, 187; ongoing issues, 199–201; protest movements, influence of, 197; queer hermeneutics, 200; queer theology, 188–189, 199, 200–201; queer theory, ineffectiveness of, 200–201; Religious Right and, 181, 186, 190; same-sex marriage, theology of, 189–192; scripture in, Hebrew and Christian, 184–185, 194–197, 205n51; seminal reports and publications, 197; separation of sexuality from spirituality, effects of, 189; sources, 194–197; theoretical and methodological considerations, 198–199; transgendered theologies, 192–194

Gay Liberation Front, 7

Gay Theology with Apology (Comstock), 188

Gearhart, Sally, 183–184

Gender Trouble (Butler), 160

Genesis, 77

Glazer, Chris, 185

God: in American Indian languages, 171; of deliverance, 150; freedom and, 17; "kindom of," 105; male language for, 216; in marginality paradigm, 124; as Mother, Lover, and Friend, 216; ontological Blackness of, 20–21, 24, 25–26; the oppressed, identification with, 20–21, 46–47; oppressors, siding with, 23–24; sexuality as gift of, 181

God Is Red (Deloria), 171

Goizueta, Roberto, 94, 107

Goldenberg, Naomi, 212

González, Juan, 101

González, Justo, 93–94

González Maldonado, Michelle A., 72, 96, 97, 107

Grant, Jacquelyn, 26, 47–48, 50

Gregory of Nyssa, 220

Guadalupe-Hidalgo, Treaty of (1848), 61, 76

Guerrero, Andres, 94–95

Guindon, Andre, 191

Gundry, Patricia, 214–215

Gutierrez, Gustav, 197

Hagar, 49, 154

hahn, 126

Hall, Prathia, 46

Halperin, David, 198, 204n28

Ham, 15

Hamer, Fannie Lou, 37

han, 125, 126, 137–138

han-pu-ri, 138

Harden, Lakota, 160–162

Harrison, Bev, 46

"Has the Lord Spoken to Moses Only?" (Murray), 37

Hawaii, 132

Hear the Cry (Recinos), 96

heaven, 22, 24

hermeneutics, biblical, 97

hermeneutics, multifaith, 139

hermeneutics, queer, 200

hermeneutics of suspicion, 31, 118

Herrera, Marina, 65, 69

heteropatriarchy, 184

Heyward, Carter: gay theologians and, 185; lesbian feminist liberation theology, 187–188; *Our Passion for Justice,* 187; on queer theology, 201; *Teaching Our Strength,* 187

Hill, Renee, 56

"Hispanic" (the term), 82n1, 109n1

Hispanic activism, Black power and, 3

Hispanic/Latino(a) theology, 86–114; 1975-1990, 92–95; 1991-2000, 95–96; 2001 and after, 96–97; Bible in, 100–101; biblical hermeneutics in, 97; borderlands in, 92; common persons, focus on religious understanding of, 101–102; communal images, enhancement of, 98; critical denunciation, use of, 105; cultural imperialism, concern with, 99–100, 108; culture in, 93, 102–103; description, 98–100; dialogical/corelational model of biblical interpretation, 101; *dignidad* in, 106; diversity in Hispanic/Latino(a) culture, 89–91; ecclesiology and, 109; Elizondo and, Virgilio, 91–93; exilic sensibility in Hispanic/Latino(a) culture, 91; festivities in, 102; González and, Justo, 93–94; historical backdrop, 86–97; human experience in, meaning of, 102–103; incorporation of concrete voices of people in theology, 104;

the oppressed: economic and political justice for, 24–25; God's identification with, 20–21, 46–47; Jesus's commitment to, 9; in Latina theology, 78

oppression: Blackness and, 25; Christianity in justifying, 31; gendered, 37; intracommunal, 116; participation in one's, 22; patriarchy, 38, 51; racialized, 37; racism as dominant mode, 26, 34–35; sin as, 223n35; via cultural imperialism, 99–100, 108

oppressors, God's siding with, 23–24

Orbis Books, 11

ordination of women as Episcopal priests (1974), 210

Orientalism, 141–143

Orientalism (Said), 141

Ortega, Gregoria, 65

Our Cry for Life (Aquino), 68

Our Lady of Charity (La Virgen de la Caridad), 102

Our Lady of Guadalupe (La Virgen de Guadalupe), 69, 102

Our Lady of Guadalupe (Rodríguez), 69, 95

Our Passion for Justice (Heyward), 187

Our Tribe (Wilson), 195

Out of Every Tribe and Nation (González), 93

Out of Silence (Matsuoka), 119

Pacific and Asian American Center for Theology and Strategies (PACTS), 115

Pacific School of Religion, 199

Palmer, Aaron, 132

Palo, 102

pan-Latino identity within United States, 90–91

PANA Institute (Institute for Leadership Development and Study of Pacific and Asian North American Religion), 115

Park, Andrew Sung, 124–126, 129n28

Parks, Rosa, 37

pastoral theology in Latina theology, 69–70, 74, 79

patriarchy: Asian American women's context, 134; Asian culture, 131; Biblical traditions, 210; Christianity, 38, 51, 135, 212–213, 214; heteropatriarchy, 184; Latina theology, analysis of in, 82; in scripture, 215; Yi dynasty (Korea), 132

patron saint celebrations (Las Fiestas Patronales), 102

Paul, 16, 215

Paz, Octavio, 72

Pedraja, Luis, 95, 107

Peña, Milagros, 70

performativity in Native feminist theology, 155–156

Perry, Troy, 202n1

Personal Politics (Evans), 40

Pesantubbee, Michelene, 153

Peskowitz, Miriam, 212

Pew Hispanic Center, 80

Phan, Peter, 118–119

pilgrim theology, 122–123

Pineda, Ana María, 69–70

Pineda-Madrid, Nancy, 74, 96

Pinn, Anthony, 25, 30–31, 32

Plaskow, Judith, 212

Plenty Good Room (Riggs), 57

pluralism. *See* religious pluralism

pneumatology in Asian American feminist theology, 136–137

political activism: of African American women, 221n11; AIDS activism, 182–183, 188; of Asian Americans, 5–6; of Chinese Americans, 5–6; of Filipino Americans, 5; of Japanese Americans, 5; of Korean Americans, 6; of LGBT, 7–8; liberation theology and, 8; of Mexican Americans, 3; of Native women, 153, 154–155, 163–165; queer activism, 182; of white women, 210–211

political power, Black theology and, 19

polyamory, 192

"Popular Religion, Political Identity, and Life-Story Testimony in an Hispanic Community" (Recinos), 104

popular religions, non-Christian, 102

postcolonial studies, 31, 79, 97

postmodernism, 31, 79

Povinelli, Elizabeth, 157

pragmatism, 79

Presidential Commission on the Status of Women (1969), 209–210

Princeton Theological Seminary, 115

Progressive Baptist Convention, 28

"Proleptic Sexual Love" (Shore-Goss), 192

Prosser, Gabriel, 17
Protestantism: Black theology and, 24; colonization of Puerto Rico, 63; in Latina theology, 63, 70, 71–72; manifest destiny and, 63; women's sense of themselves, 210
proyecto histórico, 76
Puerto Rican migration to United States, 90
Puerto Rican political activism, 3–4
Puerto Rico, colonization of, 63

Queen Nation, 182
"queer" (the term), 198–199, 200–201
queer activism, 182
The Queer Bible Commentary (Bohache et. al.), 196, 201
Queer Commentary and the Hebrew Bible (Stone), 196
queer hermeneutics, 200
queer marriage, 189–192
queer studies, 198–199
queer theology, 188–189, 199, 200–201
queer theory, 200–201, 218
Quinceañeras ceremonies, 102

race, feminist theology and, 218–219
racial pluralism, 120
racism: Asian American theology and, 8; against Asian American women, 143; Black theology and, 19–20; feminist movement and, 8; LGBT political activism and, 8; in publishing, 222n15; race-based discrimination, 16–17; sin as surrender to, 22; surrender to, 22; white women and, 40; in Womanchurch movement, 66
Ranke, Leopold von, 118
Ratzinger, Joseph, 186
"Reading the Bible as Hispanic Americans" (Segovia), 95
Realizing the America of Our Hearts (Matsuoka and Fernandez), 120
Recinos, Harold, 96, 104, 107
Red power movement, 4
redemptive suffering, 34, 46–47
Reed, Ralph, 164
religion: non-Christian popular religions, 102; race-based discrimination and, 16–17; slavery and, 15–16; sociology of, 70;

sociopolitical transformation in the name of, 17–18
Religion, Feminism and Justice (Aquino, Rodríguez and Machado), 71
religious affiliation of Latina/os in United States, 80
religious pluralism, 25, 56
Religious Right, 181, 186, 190. *See also* Christian Right
representation, politics of, 156–158
Revelation, 117
Riebe-Estrella, Gary, 95
Riggs, Marcia, 57
Riley, Denise, 219
Rivera, Luis, 95
Rivera, Mayra Rivera, 72, 73, 97
Rivera Pagán, Luis N., 95
Roberts, J. Deotis, 2, 22–23, 27
Rodríguez, José David, 95
Rodríguez-Holguin, Jeanette, 69, 71, 73, 95
Roman Catholic Women's Ordination Conference (1975), 213
Roman Catholicism. *See* Catholic Church
Roosevelt, Eleanor, 209–210
rosary prayers (Los Rosarios), 102
ruach, 136–137
Rudy, Kathy, 187, 189
Ruether, Rosemary Radford, 213, 215, 216, 220
Ruiz, Jean-Pierre, 95
Russell, Letty, 215, 216
Ruth, 117, 184, 194, 196, 205n51

Said, Edward, 141
Saint Foucault (Halperin), 198
St. Martin de Porres (García-Rivera), 95
Saiving, Valerie, 212–213
salvation: in Black theology, 17, 22, 24; in liberal theology, 10–11; as liberation, 22; reenvisioning of, 9; as restoration of life options for Black women, 50; in womanist theology, 50
same-sex friendship rituals, 190
same-sex marriage, Navajo tribal ban on, 164
same-sex marriage, theology of, 189–192
Same-Sex Marriage (Ellison), 191
Same-Sex Unions in Premodern Europe (Boswell), 190

Williams, Robert, 187, 188, 190
Wilmore, Gayraud, 17, 22, 23
Wilson, Nancy, 189, 194
Wink, John, 186
wisdom, 135–137, 145n21, 146n38
Wittig, Monique, 160
Wolfenden Report (1957), 197
woman-centered spiritualities, 216–217, 218
Womanchurch movement, 65, 66
womanism: Black theology and, 26–27, 53;
    Black women and, 45; critical engage-
    ments in, 54=55; feminism compared to,
    45; radical subjectivity of, 53; redemptive
    self-love in, 54; tenets of, 53–55; tradi-
    tional communalism in, 53–54
Womanist Justice, Womanist Hope (Townes),
    50
womanist theology, 37–60; aim of, primary,
    56; Black churches and, 48, 56–57; Black
    women and, 37, 46, 48–49, 50–53; Black-
    ness and, 48; Cannon and, Katie Geneva,
    26, 47, 49, 50; Christ-event in, 49–50;
    definition, 8–9; description, 47–50; Doug-
    las and, Kelly Brown, 50; early phase,
    47, 49; feminist theology and, 53; focus
    of, 48–49; God's identification with the
    oppressed, 46–47; Grant and, Jacque-
    lyn, 26, 47–48, 50; historical backdrop,
    37–47; impact, 56; intent, types of, 52;
    interdisciplinary methods of, 55; issues of
    sexual orientation, 9; justice in, 46; Latina
    theology and, 66, 77, 81; as a liberation-
    ist discourse, 45–46; Lorde and, Audre,
    47–48; ongoing issues, 55–57; origins, 26;

race, sex and class, intersection of, 45, 52,
    53; redemptive suffering in, 46–47; reli-
    gious pluralism and, 56; salvation in, 50;
    scripture in, Hebrew and Christian, 49;
    sexuality and, 56; social transformation
    as a requirement of the gospel, 46–47;
    sources, 50–52; theological language, 52;
    theoretical and methodological consid-
    erations, 52–55; Townes and, Emilie M.,
    50; Union Theological Seminary and, 47;
    Williams and, Delores, 26, 47–48, 49–50,
    52; "womanist," Alice Walker's definition
    of, 44–45, 50, 52, 55–56
women. *See* Black women; white women
Women, Race, and Class (Davis), 40
"women-church" communities, 213
Women of All Red Nations (WARN), 152
women studies, Black women and, 38
The Women's Bible (Stanton et. al.), 210
women's movement, 38, 210, 213
Women's Ordination Conference (1970s), 65
won-han, 138
Wood, Robert, 197
World Liberation Theology Forum (2005),
    162
The World We Used to Live In (Deloria), 176

X, Malcolm, 18, 20

Yahweh the conqueror, 150
Yip, Andrew, 196
Young, Josiah, 25

Zinn, Howard, 7

Made in the USA
Lexington, KY
12 March 2018